Pra

"Wijnand Jongen shares a pro retailers must continue to adapt th _____ online and offline sales channels to a customer-centric view that embraces the role of technology, its impact on consumer behaviors, and the need for new disruptive business models. His book is an important read for all who play in the influential and ever-evolving global retail industry."

Matthew Shay, President and CEO of the National Retail Federation (US)

"Wijnand Jongen is one of the most authoritative leaders in e-commerce today. A must-read!"

Brian McBride, CEO of Asos.com (UK)

"Wijnand Jongen's book presents a unique and fascinating overview of what the future will bring to the exciting world of retailing. Highly recommended!"

Xavier Court, Associate Co-founder of Vente-Privee Group (FR)

"Wijnand Jongen has been around the shifts in e-commerce for a long time. His book is in fact a very positive and frank assessment of the exciting opportunities for cross border trade in the evolving consumer direct world. It is my pleasure to endorse this book as an essential read by participants in our dynamic ecosystem."

Paul Greenberg, Founder of NORA.org.au (AU)

"A great book for those who want an insight into the change that is happening in the e-commerce industry and the future ahead."

Yasui Yoshiki, Founder and CEO of Origami.com (JP)

"Wijnand Jongen has distilled all the core topics of retail, from mobile shopping to artificial intelligence to the sharing economy to Amazon and Alibaba, into one readable and engaging book that is a must-read for anyone in the world who is in the retail industry."

Sucharita Mulpuru, World-renowned retail industry analyst (US)

"This is an engaging and generously researched must-read for senior retailers who are looking to understand and anticipate the pressures and trends that are changing our industry – and take action to thrive in the new state of retail."

Ian Jindal, Co-founder and Editor in Chief of InternetRetailing (UK)

"Wijnand Jongen's book is of great help to establish a shared internet future in the context of the One Belt One Road Initiative, and a great reference for Chinese enterprises who want to strengthen cooperation and improve international trade and cross-border e-commerce."

Prof. Binyong Tang, Donghua University, Shanghai
Chairman of China Cross-Border Ecommerce Application Alliance
Member of the One Road One Belt Expert Advisory Group (CN)

THE END OF
ONLINE
SHOPPING

THE FUTURE OF
NEW RETAIL IN AN
ALWAYS CONNECTED
WORLD

Wijnand Jongen

Chairman of Ecommerce Europe, and
CEO of Thuiswinkel.org

WS Professional

NEW JERSEY · LONDON · SINGAPORE · BEIJING · SHANGHAI · HONG KONG · TAIPEI · CHENNAI

Published by

WS Professional, an imprint of
World Scientific Publishing Co. Pte. Ltd.
5 Toh Tuck Link, Singapore 596224
USA office: 27 Warren Street, Suite 401-402, Hackensack, NJ 07601
UK office: 57 Shelton Street, Covent Garden, London WC2H 9HE

National Library Board, Singapore Cataloguing in Publication Data
Name(s): Jongen, Wijnand.
Title: The end of online shopping : the future of new retail in an always connected world /
    Wijnand Jongen.
Description: First edition. | Singapore : World Scientific Publishing Co. Pte. Ltd. ;
    Hilversum, Netherlands : NUBIZ, [2018]
Identifier(s): OCN 1040026569 | ISBN 978-981-32-7454-9 (hardcover) |
    ISBN 978-981-3274-76-1 (paperback)
Subject(s): LCSH: Electronic commerce. | Teleshopping. | Consumer behavior. | Retail trade.
Classification: DDC 381.142--dc23

British Library Cataloguing-in-Publication Data
A catalogue record for this book is available from the British Library.

For any available supplementary material, please visit
https://www.worldscientific.com/worldscibooks/10.1142/11106#t=suppl

Desk Editor: Karimah Samsudin

Printed in Singapore

Contents

"If we know where to look, we can see the new emerging."

MARTIN LUTHER KING,
BAPTIST MINISTER AND ACTIVIST

Introduction

A new economic paradigm is beginning to dawn: *onlife retail,* where online and offline become one. Onlife retail is based on four new and mutually reinforcing developments, each whith its own dynamic: the smart economy, the sharing economy, the circular economy and the platform economy. It is the synergy of these different "movements", that will cause huge social and economic changes.

In the past decades, we have welcomed the World Wide Web, email, social media and big data into our lives, to name but a few. We have embraced mobile Internet, smartphones, the cloud *and* online shopping, the latter of which has become an everyday pastime for hundreds of millions of people around the world. The impact of technology on retail is unprecedented, the selling of consumer goods and services has forever changed.[1]

Virtually every single business realm in the Western world is beginning to transform from an old economic order into a new reality. The digitization of society and the economy has, of course, an impact on everything and everyone.

Since the mid-1990s I have watched online shopping as it unfolded, initially from an entrepreneur's perspective and later in my capacity as an ecommerce representative in the Netherlands, Europe and around the globe.

Since the early days I have witnessed the skepticism of traditional entrepreneurs and the hesitance of governments and other stakeholders. At the same time, there always were many — often young — entrepreneurs who simply exuded euphoria, bursting to share their ideas for new ventures and business models.

Policy makers and (political) decision makers have since been roused to the transformational process and impact on the retail business. All over the world, governments are bravely attempting to get a hold on the upheaval through all kinds of initiatives. After all, governments, retailers, travel organizations, banks and insurance companies ought to be able to adapt to consumer needs as they rapidly change: not next year or next week, but preferably today, this minute even.

In this book, I will describe how retail is being turned upside down, as part of society and the economy. Chapter 1 is the foundation for this description, where I outline the *onlification* of society. In Chapters 2 through 5, I will shed some light on the four new economies, discussing the various opportunities and threats as they occur. Next, we turn our attention to the new onlife customer and the new *customer journey* and its many characteristics, which are often beyond our imagination. It's up to retailers and service providers to reinvent themselves, using new business models and organizational structures. In the final chapter, I will sketch an outline of the network society where retailers can find endless opportunities in the emerging world of onlife retail.

Let's get to work!

"Pure e-commerce will be reduced to a traditional business and replaced by the concept of New Retail – the integration of online, offline, logistics and data across a single value chain."

**JACK MA,
FOUNDER AND CHAIRMAN OF ALIBABA**[1]

1

The onlification of society

I clearly remember the first email I ever sent and the sense of pride I felt every single time I bought the latest model Nokia. When Apple launched the first iPhone and iPad, I was at the front of the line to get one. Now, all you need to do is swipe open a newspaper to realize how many more profound changes are in store for us.

On the pages of this book, I will describe the changes that are coming to the retail sector — incidentally, these are part of a wider pattern of transformation, affecting all of society. The overwhelming adoption and use of the Internet has resulted in people's lives unfolding online more than ever.[2] Throughout this book, I will use the term "onlife" to refer to this phenomenon.

WHAT IS ONLIFE?

The term "onlife" was coined by the Italian philosopher Luciano Floridi. In 2012, the European Commission made him the chairman of a European think tank intended to delve into the effects of the digital revolution on our way of thinking.[3] In *The Onlife Manifesto*, Floridi and his team found that the distinction between online and life is becoming ever more blurred to the point where it will disappear altogether.[4] The *here* (analogue, offline) and *there* (digital, online) will merge to produce a single *onlife experience*.[5]

Onlification

In recent years, virtually everyone has exchanged their landlines and cell phones for a smartphone; we've adopted GPS navigation systems in our cars to find our way, and Wikipedia has smoothly taken the place of encyclopedias, just as Google Earth has made atlases obsolete. We use apps to do our banking and turn to Google Translate instead of a dictionary to translate massive swathes of text. E-readers and tablets have found a comfortable home in our laps, and we simply stream our music, films and TV shows *on demand* whenever we feel like it.

Really, this is just the beginning. Within the past decade, we have completely redefined our social lives, not to mention how we learn, solve problems, help each other or make decisions.[6] The simple fact that so many brands have been adopted as verbs is an indication of how much has changed.[7] There we go, Facebooking, Tweeting, Skyping, Snapchatting, WhatsApping, Instagramming and FaceTiming all over the place. Even my 90-year-old mother-in-law knows how to Google and use her tablet to communicate with her (grand)children and conduct online banking. Recent US research has found that people who are active online live longer.[8] Not only does an active social life correlate with better general health, but it turns out that people who send more friendship requests even live longer.[9]

Social networks apparently offer a way of communicating that satisfies that very human urge to present yourself and leave a mark.[10] Sociologist Barry Wellman refers to this as *networked individualism:* "Even though we are more independent than ever, more inclined to individualism, we still want to be part of a community.[11] People are not hooked on the Internet or gadgets; they are hooked on each other and their social needs being met, right here and right now."[12]

ONLINE GENERATIONS

To *millennials* – otherwise known as Gen-Y, referring to people born between 1980 and 1995 – the onlife experience is relatively commonplace. Having grown up with computers, cell phones, iPods and video games, they were the first to make online shopping a habit.

Generation Z – born after 1995, sometimes called iGeneration – takes this to the next level. As "tomorrow's consumers," they cannot even imagine a world without Internet. Social networks are what they grew up with, as were the games that they played from childhood, in which they connected with others all over the world. Millennials and Gen-Z-ers are the early adopters of new technologies and possibilities. They hardly use words like "online" or "Internet". To them, being connected 24/7 is a given.

Generation X (the 35 to 50 age bracket) and Baby Boomers (45- to 65-year-olds) are both spending more time online than ever, with even the Silent Generation (over 65) joining in. Despite growing up with type-writers, desktop computers, achingly slow dialup Internet and analogue cell phones, many of these people have adapted – and mind you, are adapting faster than ever – to the altered circumstances and options.

Technology waits for no man. Without a second thought, people start using new machines and devices in their everyday lives. Out-dated thermostats are replaced by "smart" ones that allow you to adjust your energy consumption remotely. Old-school washing machines make room for new ones that instinctively know when is the best – most economical – time to do a load. Old-fashioned TV's are being replaced by interactive smart TV's, offering online films and music, access to social networks and the ability to com-municate with each other.

All this technology is connected online, over the Internet, with people – with us, that is – but also with each other, with *other* tech-nology, other machines and new smart home devices. The com-mon denominator is that they help simplify people's lives, making life more comfortable and more budget-friendly. These are the first applications of the Internet of Things (IoT) in our homes. Gartner, the US research firm, has stated that by 2020 there will be some-where between 500 and 700 million *smart connected homes.*[13]

Virtual reality (VR) and *augmented reality (AR)* will become more important in years to come. The next generation of VR glasses will allow us to step into a 360-degree virtual world, indistinguishable from the real world. The distinction between real and virtual will start to blur.[14] AR will bring us extra (verbal or visual) information which is being added to what you see on your smartphone screen or tablet.

In the future, we might stop differentiating between personal conversations and digital interactions as we become able to share our experiences with that friendly robot assistant of ours. We can try on outfits in a virtual dressing room, our cars will drive themselves, and we use cryptocurrency for payments just as easily as regular currency.

THE VIRTUAL SHOPPING CITY OF MACROPOLIS

In 1997, Macropolis was launched in the famous Leidseplein Theatre in Amsterdam. A packed audience of retailers, business partners and media watched in awe when we presented our computerized shopping city Macropolis on the theatre's big screen. A young entrepreneur at the time, I launched Macropolis with partner Niek Vrielink. We called it *virtual shopping in a computer-shopping city,* and distributed it on CD-ROM through participating retail outlets.

In the Macropolis VR world, you could ride through virtual shopping streets in a Yellow Cab. Or choose to wander around the shopping streets – incidentally, these were empty otherwise – with your own *avatar.* Choosing to navigate according to product was another menu option. When you arrived at a store, the storefront was 'loaded' with the set product information from the CD-ROM. Over 50 Dutch stores and supermarkets were persuaded to join. There were just a few stores where you could click on the items displayed behind the storefront. The modem would splutter, crackle and pop when it started, only to grind to a halt upon discovering there wasn't much for sale online.

The very next year, realizing people and computers were not ready for shopping in a VR world, we decide to turn Macropolis into a website, and in the summer of 1999, the *smart shopping* feature on Macropolis goes live, with over 5,000 (web)stores taking part! The Internet bubble was yet to burst.

Onlification is being fueled by five paradigm shifts:[15]
1. The boundaries between online and offline are being erased in our everyday lives. There is no need to talk about online versus offline anymore. Online and offline are merging into onlife.
2. It is becoming more and more unclear what is real and what is virtual or augmented in our lives. How can we manage to continue to distinguish between what is real and what is not?
3. What's natural and what's artificial is becoming less defined. After enduring 20 years of paralysis, Cathy Hutchinson is now

able to operate a robotic arm by using her brain.[16] If we are able to replicate or improve organs and implant them in the body, are we still truly natural? Does it matter, anyway?

4. Formal dimensions are becoming less defined. In the future, 4D printers will be able to produce objects — without any human guidance or interference — that can change shape in particular circumstances, such as a rise or fall in temperature.

5. Time and space are becoming less defined. Virtual and augmented reality and new hologram technology can make us believe we are somewhere else than we actually are. Time and space seem to become one.

Impact on society

The Internet is also having a greater impact than ever on social and political issues and debates. Hundreds of millions of people turn to social media as a means of communicating, offering their opinions, responding to other people's posts, and sharing messages from others. They might encourage others to vote or take up an issue, toss some *likes* at politicians, or join forces with likeminded souls.[17] The influence of people's *onlife engagement* expands in times of global disaster, national crises or small-scale local events. The 2011 Arabic Spring is often referred to as the "Facebook Revolution." Social media play a significant role in refugee crises: the tweets, photos and videos shared online are an important emotional and factual touchstone for both refugees and citizens, as well as politicians and reporters. And United States president Donald Trump has adopted Twitter as his prime communication channel to respond to (fake) news.

Work-life balance

As we see online and offline converging, people are having more and more difficulty keeping strict boundaries between their work lives and their spare time. Employees' desire for flexible work hours is another change to the balance between work and private life. Quickly tying up loose ends for work in the evenings or weekends has become a fact of life. Similarly, we have fewer qualms in handling personal matters during office hours. Working from home, on the road or "wherever, whenever" are all aspects of our everyday lives blending with new ways of working.

THE NEW, INDUSTRIAL REVOLUTION

Economists Jeremy Rifkin and Klaus Schwab believe we are at the dawn of a new industrial revolution. In *The Third Industrial Revolution*[18], Rifkin – a best-selling author and frequent adviser to heads of state all over the world – has described the rise of the Internet and access to new sources of energy as key factors in the transformation. After all, previous industrial revolutions saw how new communication technologies (books, newspapers and the telegram, followed by the telephone, radio and television) *and* new sources of energy (steam engines, followed by electricity and oil) were catalysts for immense social change. Now, it's the rise of the Internet, paired with renewable and sustainable energy, such as the sun, water and wind. All of this will produce a "powerful new infrastructure that will change the world." [19]

Hundreds of millions of people will be able to produce their own energy over the next few decades with the help of Internet-based technology (energy Internet); they will, in fact, move beyond producing by using, reusing and sharing the energy. At the same time, the Internet will enable us to communicate through a wide range of media (communication Internet) and help us transport endless products and services (logistics Internet). Rifkin believes these three systems are what our future society will require to be effective. Besides, the three are inextricably joined together.

Schwab, the founder of the World Economic Forum (WEF), even believes that we should use the phrase "fourth industrial revolution" in the wake of the digital or technological revolution that took place from the 1970s through the 1990s.[20] He believes this fourth revolution is hurtling past, exhibiting unprecedented speed, depth and broadness of impact. Massive technological developments such as robotization, 3D printing, self-driving vehicles and nanotechnology are very real challenges for virtually every single industry in every conceivable country. What we need now are new economical structures and organizations, which, Schwab notes, means that suppliers and consumers need to reinvent themselves entirely.

The blurring of boundaries between online and life, between offline and online and between work and home all make everyday life an onlife experience. The way we work, learn, maintain our relationships, care for others, serve as politicians and even fight wars are all altered profoundly. Not to mention, the onlification of society impacts the way we shop. Slowly but surely, retail is being transformed. Analogue becomes digital, vertical becomes horizontal, centralized becomes local, top-down becomes bottom-up and bureaucracies are replaced by networks. These are all manifestations of how the structure of retail is changing profoundly, its balance of power being altered at the same time.

The end of online shopping

In the next decade, the retail and service sector will be swallowed up by what I like to call *onlife retail*, a new economic order. Consumers will see shopping turn into a full-blown onlife experience where it is no longer relevant that there are online and offline sales channels. For businesses, online and offline sales channels will merge as the boundaries between sectors and fields of business start to crack under pressure. All the participants within retail — producers, retailers and consumers alike — will be enticed into new roles.

The following five major developments are going to end online shopping as we know it today.

1. Online and offline become one

Over the next decade, millions of stores and service providers will change from traditional businesses into *connected stores*, serving as places for inspiration, experiences, showcases and service centers. New 24/7 store concepts and smart apps are going to provide the consumer with ways to scan and buy anything and everything they encounter in their everyday lives. The instant consumers are able to complete the online retail experience they started at home or on the road, in the shopping street or *online in-store* — that is when the end of online shopping is truly near.

We can expect a sharp uptick of the interactive technology that brings online and offline retail together, such as that found in so-called *all-in-one apps*, which are prime samples of onlife retail.

Take the Chinese super app WeChat, which already allows you to sort out practically anything you want: finding and booking a vacation, paying in online and physical stores, balancing your check book, splitting the check at a restaurant, setting up an appointment with your hair stylist, or writing online reviews. Apps such as WeChat are blending online and offline together. Now, around 1 billion Chinese cannot imagine life without it.[21]

FROM ONLINE TO OFFLINE IN CHINA

China has brought us the umpteenth e-commerce acronym: "O2O" ("O-two-O"), which means *online to offline.* The idea is to use the online channel to strengthen offline shopping.[22] An app, online store or platform is the place to purchase and pay for goods and services. Then you pick the actual product up at a local store or use the services of a local business. The essence of O2O is the synergy of online and offline consumer data that can be used to improve the overall customer experience.

In China, o2o became the ultimate buzzword in 2015 when e-commerce titan Alibaba struck a deal for 4.6 billion US dollars with the Suning Commerce Group, an electronics chain. The purchase of several discount stores in 2016 and a chain of department stores in 2017 has seen Alibaba continuing this trend.[23] The strategic cooperation with the BAILAN Group, a retailer with 4,700 stores in 200 cities, is another prime example. Acquisitions and strategic partnerships are swiftly helping the company expand its range of electronic and other goods while simultaneously boosting its service level in logistics.[24] The ability to deliver the goods within two hours – regardless of where within China's 2,800 districts the consumer is located – is what turns this into a win-win situation for everyone involved.[25] On the other hand, offline stores can expand to online on Tmall.com, where they can increase their reach online, and where Alibaba uses its successful platform to complete the transaction for them.[26]

It is the ultimate strategy of Jack Ma and Alibaba to transform retail based on an integration of online, offline, logistics and data. "We want to create a new economy where the online world is integrated with the physical world," Ma explains. "We're building an economic entity – a virtual economy on the Internet."[27]

The happy union of online and offline could hardly be made clearer than in the huge rise of so-called *pickup points*. This is where consumers can pick up their online orders, or return them if need be. Many consumers find these pickup points invaluable, as they eliminate having to pay for the delivery and waiting at home for the delivery person. Increasingly, the role of pickup points is being filled by small local stores in addition to larger malls and supermarkets. Sometimes, gas stations act as pickup points, where they might pair a drive-through concept (think: McDonald's) with a service desk.[28] This may well prove to be a viable business model in the future, when electronic cars have eliminated the need to pump gas at gas stations.

2. Moving from clicks to bricks

Why should large online retailers not open their own physical stores? Local government and real estate developers, in particular, are very interested in this. However, the business model of online stores cannot be transformed into a *bricks-and-clicks* proposition overnight. Certainly, we will see web stores opening up more physical stores of their own in the near future, though this is unlikely to become widespread enough to combat the empty storefronts with which many towns are struggling. Nor does it need to happen on such a scale; for some online retailers, having a physical store on a key national shopping street will suffice. Others will stay close to home and open a showroom store at their distribution center, in their hometown or open pop-up stores in carefully selected cities.

In the US, hip New York eyewear brand Warby Parker has been successful in their transition to physical stores. The brand had garnered an online following, leaving them room to experiment with small physical spaces, such as showrooms, shop-in-shops and pop-up stores. They even restyled an old school bus for customers to try out eyewear frames before purchasing them online.[29] Since then, the company has set up a flagship store in New York — albeit quite a small one — and several other branches along the US West Coast to create authentic relationships with customers.

Online retailer Amazon is due to open more (book)stores and convenience stores to provide a new shopping experience for its customers.[30] Key to these new revolutionary store concepts is to provide Amazon shoppers with a seamless personal customer journey. The takeover of American supermarket chain Whole Foods, numbering some 460 organic supermarkets in the US, UK and Canada, allows them to integrate Amazon's existing digital services in the physical world.[31]

Online apparel retailer Bonobos (acquired by Walmart) has been opening "guideshops", believing the ability to see, touch and try on are pivotal factors of purchasing. The real benefit for Bonobos: the information collected digitally, the relationships built in person, and the chance to reduce the high cost of returns.

In China, Alibaba has been working on an onlife retail strategy for years, creating New Retail propositions by bringing together physical stores and online shopping.[32] Moving from clicks to bricks, it was Alibaba who started New Retail driven Hema supermarket stores in 2015, planning to open another 2.000 new stores in China over the next five years.[33] Tencent/WeChat and Beijing based online retailer JD.com are following this trend.

In 2017, fashion platform Zalando tentatively began using brick stores in major European cities through their acquisition of German brand Kickz – a specialist in basketball goods with 15 stores.[34] It is even planning to open flagship stores in London, Paris and Berlin, in an effort for its fans to engage with the Zalando brand.[35] It all should help transforming Zalando into an Amazon-style retail platform.[36]

Opening flagship stores in a prime location in various key cities is a popular option for some online retailers, and this will only become more prevalent as time goes by. Branding is in fact the main focus for flagship or brand stores, together with marketing, service and hospitality. They provide businesses with a means of distinguishing themselves from their competitors, showcasing the web store as an actual brand and giving the consumer a more personal shopping experience. Web stores with physical flagship stores are still few and far between, though.

Other flexible types of retail, some of them temporary, are also gaining the interest of online retailers. Pop-up stores are mainly used for branding and marketing, whereas shop-in-shops are useful points of sale as well. Amazon is planning to roll out over a hundred pop-up stores in the next few years.[37] Zalando is experimenting with pop-up stores in various European stores. Another new and increasingly popular retail phenomenon is the on-wheels store, particularly for large-scale events. What these flexible formats have in common is an element of surprise, paired with a steady flow of store traffic.

WATCH OUT – HERE COMES AMAZON!

Amazon has adopted the Treasure Truck, which zips through the streets of big US and UK cities, and completely blends the worlds of online and offline shopping. The matching app sends extra-special offers that might be passing by any minute to loyal customers, ranging from a beautiful cut of meat to a video camera. Amazon's Treasure Truck started rolling up to Whole Foods stores as part of the integration between the now-combined companies.[38] This is how Amazon manages to seduce its customers with impulse purchases of every possible kind, using something that is little more than a mobile supermarket!

---

3. Ongoing retail diversification

It's been a topic of conversation for a while now: companies that no longer confine their sales of goods and services to the traditional areas of business. Retailers now offer services, too, and service providers no longer shy away from selling actual goods. Diversification is not new, by the way. For years, supermarkets have sold both foodstuffs and non-food products, a phenomenon sometimes referred to as "Aldification," named after German budget grocer Aldi. In fact, they have moved to the next level by giving German consumers unlimited access to US brand Napster's music library in their new service Aldi Life. There are scores of other examples: LIDL-Reisen is a well-known concept in Germany, where the discount supermarket has taken to selling package travel deals on its website. Bookseller Barnes & Noble has branched out into drugstore items, UK supermarket chain Morrisons started selling fashion online, LEGO now makes computer games and movies, electronics giant Media Markt provides its own music streaming service Juke, and insurance companies have started selling home safety products, Zalando is now selling beauty and cosmetic products and Amazon is planning to sell health care products and (insurance) services.[39]

Diversification has been happening online, too. In the mid-1990s, eBay set the stage by offering all conceivable goods and services. Alibaba has been selling all kinds of goods and services since the company began in 1997. Amazon was quick to morph from bookseller into an *everything store*, with an almost infinite array of goods.

When diversification becomes commonplace, it makes room for new market entrants to grab opportunities — often popping up in unexpected niches of the market, catching established businesses off guard, or because they are forced to do so. In China, the Industrial and Commercial Bank of China (ICBC, the country's second largest government bank) has set up a marketplace to sell goods to consumers directly. It was their only recourse, as the bank was losing out on millions of transactions every single day to Alibaba's Alipay.

4. Channels flowing together

The familiar distinction between business-to-consumer (B2C) and business-to-business (B2B) is likely to evaporate in years to come. Everyone will be selling to everyone else. The sharing economy has opened up new channels, including consumer-to-consumer (C2C) and consumer-to-business (C2B).

Retailers no longer focus solely on consumers. Web stores are now just as willing to sell to businesses, frequently setting up dedicated B2B online stores. Slowly but surely, businesses that preferred to sell exclusively to other businesses are testing the waters and shifting focus to the consumer market. This goes beyond large brands; even wholesalers are making this transition. After all, what reason is there to refrain from selling your goods or services to consumers directly?

Consumers selling to other consumers has been mainstream for years. Online market places such as eBay and Alibaba's Taobao have millions upon millions of transactions daily. Consumers have even been known to sell their goods to businesses, using online marketplaces, platforms or auctions. Web stores have discovered eBay and the likes, where they can offload large batches of outdated goods to consumers or other businesses. Even traditional stores have found this to be a profitable channel for getting rid of surplus goods and experimenting with new products or services.

The marketplaces of Chinese e-commerce superpower Alibaba have actually done away with the distinction between different channels and areas of business. If you really wanted to fit it into a model, it would be a B2B2C2C2B-model. In other words, the channels have all flowed together to become one. This is just a preview of what the retail world will look like in a few years' time.

5. Integrating other roles from the value chain

Having diversification is one thing; the fact is that many companies will have to adopt new roles — ones that were previously played by other participants in the retail value chain.

Giants like Amazon and Alibaba have a history of bringing retail, technology, logistics and services together. In the process, they have assumed all sorts of roles within the value chain by offering fulfillment services including storage, *order picking* and packaging goods for other retailers. They provide logistical support for third parties, enable webhosting in their cloud for businesses, and so on. Until recently, these were all roles that specialized companies filled and executed.

Producers are assigning themselves new tasks as well. Brands like Adidas, Miele, Nike, Philips and Sony have taken to selling their merchandise directly to consumers. This often happens with the handbrake on, fearful as they are of disrupting traditional distribution channels, though a no-qualms-approach is becoming more prevalent. Manufacturers such as Unilever have started to acquire successful online retailers such as the Dollar Shave Club — at a very high cost — simply to find a direct sales channel to the consumer.[40]

Air travel is going through an equally interesting change, with companies adopting new roles: the US company Delta Airlines acquired an oil refinery, not just for the purpose of securing adequate supplies of cheap kerosene, but also with the goal of actually trading oil. AirAsia now has its own branded credit card, which lets customers do more than just purchase AirAsia-related items. Norwegian airline Wideroe has branched out into the insurance business, and German Lufthansa Technik has become a well-respected software provider.

In 2015, I was in Tokyo and met with Yasui Yoshiki, the young founder and CEO of Origami, a Japanese portal for lifestyle products. I was expecting to have a conversation with a young and ambitious retailer. I could hardly have been further off the mark: Yoshiki quickly informed me that his main goal is to roll out an online platform for mobile payments. Consumers can use this to (already) do online payments and will be able to do offline one-click payments on their smartphones. When I asked him about his vision and goals for the long term, he told me his ultimate goal is to become an actual bank.[41]

In Kenya, the telecom provider Safaricom has added financial services to its portfolio in a country with no largescale banking infrastructure; consumers in over ten countries can use its M-PESA platform to transfer money, accrue savings or take out small loans. By now, more than 30 million people — most of them with no bank accounts — use M-PESA via their smartphone.[42] Traveling to Kenya in 2017 I was astonished to see how adopting a new role in the value chain led to one of the most successful payment systems in the world, helping consumers with (very) little to spare paying (very) small retailers for basic goods and services.

"You have to start with the customer and work backwards to the technology."

STEVE JOBS,
CO-FOUNDER AND FORMER CEO OF APPLE

2

Onlife retail in the smart economy

Traditional economy	Smart economy
Analogue	Digital
Automation	Robotization
"Beam me up, Scotty"	Hologram
Car	Self-driving vehicle
Catalogue	Virtual reality
City	Smart city
Data	Big data
Encyclopedia	Smart home speaking device
Home	Connected home
Human intelligence	Artificial Intelligence (AI)
Internet	Internet of Things (IoT)
Light switch	Domotics
Linear growth	Exponential growth
Mail man	Drone delivery
Mass production	Custom made
Printshop	3D printing shop
Reality	Augmented reality
Shoplifting	Cybertheft
Supply	Demand
Telephone	Smartphone
Two dimensional	Three dimensional
Writing code	Machine and deep learning

New technology has always been the catalyst for large social and economic transitions. During the first two industrial revolutions, new energy sources, technologies and means of communication brought true revolution to society, the economy and individuals. They also created profound changes in retail and consumer behavior. In the twentieth century, the rise of mass media, telephones, radios and TVs all helped bring retailers and consumers closer together.

Since the 1990s, Internet and digitization have created technological breakthroughs. The new economic paradigm of the "smart economy" provides the foundation for onlife retail.

Today, we are experiencing the dawn of a new wave of technology — let's call it a "new industrial revolution" or "age." The new smart economy is having an unprecedented impact. It is both exciting and daunting at the same time.

In this chapter, I will deal with seven new technologies. Together, they will cause a veritable landslide in retail. What do these technologies have to offer retail, and what do they mean for people and society in general? All these different technological developments have one thing in common: they are based on big data being universally available. Imperceptibly, they go about making people's lives easier, simpler and more pleasant. On the downside, we are becoming increasingly dependent on technology. Our privacy is one of the key areas of impact. For that very reason, I round off the chapter with the effects of a smart economy on the privacy of onlife consumers.

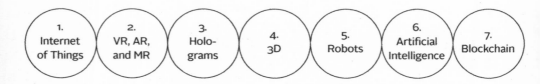

But first I will start with the foundation of all new technologies: big data.

Big data

Big data is not merely about the collection of huge amounts of data; the key is to collect massive amounts of valuable and relevant data. Scientist Viktor Mayer-Schönberger and journalist Kenneth Cukier — data expert for *The Economist* — say that big data "refers to our burgeoning ability to crunch vast collections of information, analyze it instantly, and draw sometimes profoundly surprising conclusions from it."[1] They compare it to taking a photograph. When you take a picture and focus on a single thing, that is similar to taking a sample of random information. On the other hand, a digital photo with everything in focus allows you to decide afterwards which part to bring forward or fade out; that is what big data is like.

There are gurus who believe that big data is an absolute blessing for humanity: it will help combat fraud, track down terrorists, eliminate the distribution of child pornography and even predict and prevent epidemics. The retail sector may also benefit greatly from big data. Producers could use it for analyzing their production methods, and retailers can take advantage of better ways to serve their customers.

Others believe that big data is a threat to our way of life, and that we ought to fight to keep our newly minted freedom. Big data involves digital profiles of us all, which in turn produce a better understanding of our current and future behavior. "*Sie wissen alles,*" They Know All, wrote German data entrepreneur Yvonne Hofstetter in her German bestseller, referring to governments and the business models behind the large technology companies.[2] The fear held by critics of big data is that big data eventually might be used to patronize and manipulate people, business models and whole societies. It was US founding father and President Thomas Jefferson who said, "Information is the currency of democracy". The problem nowadays is that an immense amount of data, the new capital, is in the hands of a tiny number of people.

According to Gartner, we have now reached the stage where big data is widely practiced.[3] Within (web) retail, insurance, travel and banking, there are increasingly intelligent algorithms on consumer behavior — founded in big data — which translate consumers' individual preferences into the production of goods and services. Personality traits and recent buying patterns can both predict what the next interesting thing will be for the consumer. This is already happening using machine learning and deep learning techniques, which have been modelled after the human brain. Google taps into this technique to display its ads in the perfect spot. Amazon uses this kind of algorithm to show its customers relevant goods, Booking.com does the same to recommend hotel rooms, and Spotify uses the same technique to suggest music. International dating website eHarmony even uses these algorithms to match people to each other. It was *The Economist* who catapulted big data into being 'digital oil', when it stated "data are to this century what oil was to the previous one: a driving force for growth and change".[4]

In the future, this kind of technology will be able to improve its analysis and interpretation of even the most complex issues. Big data-based techniques will help answer questions like: is this person planning to pay back his loan? Consumers will also be able to benefit from big data. Making their information available to retailers is not as new as they might think — in the past, stores would make a note of their customers' personal information (name, address, etc.) to fine-tune what they sold. Now, they use the information to adjust their (in-store) supply based on actual buying patterns. The ultimate strength of big data in retail is to use the analysis of consumer data to benefit the individual customer directly.

The smart shopping city

Over the next few years, many cities will become smart. Already, smart technology has made city life healthier, cleaner and safer. According to Gartner, the number of *connected devices* in smart cities will increase from over 2.7 billion in 2017 to an immense 9.7 billion by 2020.[5] The cities of the future will see everyone involved in retail working together to make shopping downtown and in shopping malls more fun and more relevant. Local government, retailers, service providers and restaurateurs are all investing in creating vibrant inner cities and providing better service to the consumer. Innovative technology is what will help them.

Still, excitement about smart cities is not universal. They can easily be hacked, rendering the algorithms that manage the city out of control. Some researchers believe there is a very real risk of a smart city no longer regarding its population as citizens, reducing them to mere consumers instead. It remains to be seen if financially-strapped cities will be able to resist the urge to sell consumer shopping data to tech companies.

Shopping in a smart city has one simple premise: *beacons* in shopping streets are sensors that use Bluetooth to connect with the smartphones of shoppers. Monitoring their behavior is straight-forward. If they are keen to have a personal shopping experience, they just download an app (one for every street, shopping mall or store). Next, the smart shopping street can try to influence their behavior.[6]

London's Regent Street is one of the first streets in the world where over 130 stores are able to communicate directly with pass-ing shoppers. The stores use apps to try to lure customers inside. In the app, people have pre-selected what kind of information they would (not) like to receive.[7] There is no need to worry about being bothered by all kinds of offers, as it is up to them whether or not to download the app. If they do, they decide which parts of the app to use.[8]

Personally, I would hate for my phone to give a signal in every single store, trying to lure me in. What I do like, though, are apps like Starbucks, which allow me to order a coffee and pay for it be-fore I get to the store. When I go in, I can bypass the line, head straight to the barista and scoop up the latte macchiato with my name on it, with no need to open my wallet to pay, and my loy-alty points are automatically credited to my Starbucks account. If a store offered me a 10 percent discount or free coffee in exchange for bypassing the line, I might be inclined to get their app.

There is no turning back from the rise of smart cities and shop-ping streets. There are brilliant benefits, and they're not limited to retail: what about free Wi-Fi (Kansas City), an app guiding you to the nearest parking space (Boston), an energy-saving app (Bar-celona) or one to help you avoid traffic congestion (Amsterdam)?

Connected stores

In the future, literally every kind of store will be a connected store: supermarkets to hardware stores, travel agencies to banks, bakery shops to butchers. They're going to create all kinds of ways to navi-gate the customer journey, either at home or in-store, with options to order from a mobile device, in-store Internet terminal or other device. Every kind of digital technology will be used in connected stores to improve customer service. *Beacons* in the store will make sure online and offline shopping blend into a single shopping experience, allowing retailers and tech-companies to track customer movement in-store, monitor which departments they go to, and so on.

Traditional retailers are slowly and grudgingly adopting these new options. Physical stores make customers actively decide to install their app, or switch it on, for every visit. Several US department stores — including Macy's, Target and Walmart — have started using beacons with high hopes that it will make tracking customer behavior in physical stores more mainstream.[9] Customers who appreciate personal attention can opt to receive individualized messages on their smartphones, taking into account their in-store location, behavior and shopping profile. Time will tell whether receiving exclusive in-store offers, coupons and discounts overrules that feeling of being followed.[10]

There are actually new online in-store technological innovations ready to replace beacons. *Visible light communication* technology, a blend of Bluetooth, light and LED-lamps, narrows down a customer's location within 4 inches, including his direction, aisle location, proximity to a display, and so on. For this, customers need not install an app. After their initial permission, the app starts automatically. IKEA and Target are two retailers experimenting with this technology. An added benefit for retailers is that the technology can be installed "independently," without the need to share the data with Apple (iPhone), Google (Android) or Samsung.

STORES BECOME MORE DIGITAL THAN EVER

Stores are already tapping into all sorts of digital technology to involve their customers in their goods and services.[11] More and more stores (IKEA) allow you to check relevant product information by scanning a barcode or QR-code on your smartphone. Others (Target) have special apps that give extra value to in-store online shopping by offering discounts. Still others (Timberland) have a tablet desk to help simplify online shopping for customers in the store or provide extra service options (Argos).[12] [13]

Miniature smart screens on hangers can display dynamic product and price information and even show how popular an item is (the number of

likes it has on Facebook), as well as how many items are in stock. Norwegian firm Thinfilm has *smart labels,* equipped with computer chips, which can be used by supermarkets or other stores to track the freshness of milk. An app can warn customers against picking up anything near its sell-by date. Soon, your smartphone will be able to suggest which wine best complements the food in your trolley.
These smart technologies give customers a whole new shopping experience on the street, in-store and online – but seducing the customer is still an art. So, what else is new?

Internet of Things

Widely seen as the top technology of the future: billions of machines connecting and sharing chunks of data with each other and with people. The Internet of Things (IoT) is transforming every corner of life: the home, the office, city shopping streets and beyond. IoT may well be the exemplification of the smart economy. The rise of the personal computer, fax, email, mobile phone, smartphone, tablet and smart speaker were all similar: new technology seems to happen *to* people. Apparently, they have very little trouble adjusting to the new possibilities it provides.

We can already see the first instances of the IoT being applied: for the past few years, I have used a handheld scanner when I shop for groceries, and I often use contactless payment in stores. A while back, I bought a new TV set and paid little attention to the fact it was a "smart" TV. I have happily adopted most of its options, though I cannot seem to adjust (yet) to the hand gestures I can use to operate it. Some people are more proactive in opting for smart applications, such as smart door locks, bike trackers, kitchen devices, sprinklers, thermostats, lighting, plugs, etc. Smart home speaker devices and smart kitchen appliances with integrated voice assistants are flocking into our homes. Whether or not they are aware of it, many people seem to relish the benefits of the smart economy, and it is but a small step to use more smart machines.

The second that machines and people can connect anytime, anywhere, the possibilities for the economy, businesses and consumers become almost infinite. In years to come, continued exponential growth of micro-electronics, lower prices for computer chips and increased memory capacity are likely to be the driving forces for the IoT. New smart sensors and the adoption of photonics (i.e. the use of glass instead of copper as a conduit) will bring about a technological revolution, the effects of which are only just becoming visible.

THE END OF MOORE'S LAW

Moore's Law states that the number of transistors in computer chips is likely to double every two years.[14] It was Gordon Moore, one of the founders of chip manufacturer Intel, who described this process back in 1965. The law later proved to apply to how other technology developed as well, such as memory capacity and energy used by computers, or the number of pixels for digital cameras.

It remains to be seen how long chip manufacturers can keep up with Moore's Law. It is nearly impossible technically – not to mention very costly – to shrink silicon based electronics even further. As a result, people are searching for a replacement for silicon.

In fact, the demise of Moore's Law may be a blessing in disguise for today's consumer. "There will be no need to switch to a new gadget the second a faster chip appears! This might even encourage businesses to innovate differently and produce better goods, things people can actually use."[15]

In 2003, a mere 500 million large and small appliances were connected through Internet, whereas Cisco and Ericsson expect there to be roughly 50 billion by 2020.[16] Morgan Stanley, the American corporate bank, even predicts 75 billion connected appliances by 2020.[17] The research agency IDC has a prediction of the IoT reaching roughly 1.7 trillion dollars in 2020.[18] According to US consultancy firm McKinsey, the worth of the IoT will reach 3.9 trillion dollars by 2025, adding between 4 and 11 trillion dollars to the global economy.[19]

Retail will be impacted by IoT immensely: online shopping is to become even easier and more personal by linking appliances and accessories to your personal profile. Tech giants such as Amazon, Alibaba, Apple, Facebook, Google and Microsoft are able to delve deeper and deeper into our private lives, using data we provide willingly. "Private" takes on a new meaning. Apparently, we do not mind the acquired benefits of the IoT cutting into our privacy. Aral Balkan, American social entrepreneur and advocate for Internet privacy, has referred to the novel by George Orwell, *1984*, where privacy has gone from private to public. In his poignantly oppressive novel *The Circle*, Dave Eggers has one of the characters say: "Everything and everyone should be seen."[20] Regardless of these worries, we are seeing the dawn of a new revolution, of a data explosion, which will allow patterns and trends to be deduced for a whole range of business sectors, retail being one of the most important.

AN IPAD ON WHEELS

In 2016, I visited the Tesla plant in Fremont, California. I was simply overwhelmed by the experience. Tesla is manufacturing the very first fully electronic cars, where you fully realize the added value of the IoT. The Tesla – named after the Serbian-American engineer and inventor Nikola Tesla, who once worked for Thomas Edison – has also been called an "iPad on wheels." Virtually every option in the car is operated through the 15-inch (Model 3) or 17-inch (Model S) touchscreen and your smartphone; there are no dials on the dashboard. The doors can be locked remotely, and you can find a parking space, monitor the battery charge, or set the car's temperature before you get in – after you have located its spot using Google Maps, of course. No job is too hard for the Tesla.[21]

VR, AR and MR

Two technologies that will become invaluable for onlife consumers in several years' time are virtual reality (VR, special glasses that let you think you are somewhere else) and augmented reality (AR, which involves laying text and/or images on top of your smartphone visual). Ultimately, we will be able to carry our favorite stores with us non-stop by using VR and AR projections to access them anytime, anywhere.

AR, for example, could help you picture what the couch you are eying might look like in your own home. IKEA, Target and Amazon's apps let customers overlay, move and rotate an item in a live camera view mode to see how the item will fit and look in real time. Through the use of AR, literally any place can be transformed into a virtual showroom to look at goods, regardless of whether you are at home, in your kitchen or in the store. For every type of product, ranging from technology and electronics to clothing and consumer goods, customers are constantly on the lookout for more information. Using their smartphone, customers can point at any product and get augmented information. With AR information on products in-store, customers are more likely to grab a product on impulse, even if they've never tried it before.[22]

VR has matured, too. The new generation of glasses, made by HTC (Vive), Sony (HMD), and Facebook (Oculus Rift) are further mainstreaming this technology. The Microsoft Hololens (a hybrid of helmet and ski goggles) is combining AR and VR options. Even though I've been blown away by the experience of the Hololens in Microsoft's flagship store in New York City, putting on VR-glasses is still rather a nuisance. Maybe the next generation of glasses or the successor to Google Glass, designed to resemble "regular" cool eyewear, can rid us of that hurdle. Or perhaps we will switch to Spectacles en masse, such as the video sunshades introduced by Snapchat that let you make short videos you can share with friends in-app.

Both VR and AR are gaining popularity. Pokémon GO may well let Pikachu achieve what Google Glass failed to do. Marks & Spencer has started experimenting with Oculus Rift to let its customers compose their perfect living room.[23] A headset allows for 360-degree images to be projected in stereoscopic 3D with a 100-degree field of vision, truly tricking your brain into believing you are somewhere else. You can turn your head and the image simply moves with you without dizziness. Tommy Hilfiger showed his fall line in virtual reality to let customers experience what it's like to be on the catwalk. Travel is another business area adopting VR: there are hotels in Dubai that use VR to rent rooms and Marriot has a 4D option using low-cost VR glasses.[24] Spanish travel retailer Navitaire lets you book your entire trip in VR: select your hotel room, try out different rental cars and walk through the cabin of the plane.[25]

Mixed reality (MR) is where VR and AR meet. Other people can join in with MR and share the experiences of the person wearing the VR-glasses. On a secondary screen or by way of a video link, they can track the experience of the other person. Shopping is another option in MR: items on your grocery list would light up when you pass through the aisles of the supermarket, provided you donned your VR specs or popped in your MR contacts.[26]

A VIRTUAL SUPERMARKET

Yihaodian, China's leading online supermarket, uses AR to provide customers with a way to shop without ever having to enter a store. (Incidentally, Alibaba's largest competitor, JD.com, bought Yihaodian from Walmart in 2016.) They've opened virtual supermarkets in parking lots, parks and near popular venues. Our eyes cannot see them without using a smartphone or tablet. By using the app, the store springs into view to the shopper, allowing them to walk along its virtual aisles and take goods off the shelves with a simple click. The shopping is then delivered to the customer's home.[27]

Holograms

The advanced new hologram technology is a whole different ball-game. Letting you evoke 3D projections of goods and services wherever and whenever you please, this option is only being used by retailers in fashion and luxury goods — for now.[28] A few years back, the Parisian lingerie brand Empreinte used hologram technology to have models pose in glass display boxes on the street. Miss Sixty, the Italian fashion brand, projected models in-store trying on outfits after-hours. Another way luxury brands are using holograms is to enhance packaging and make it interactive.[29]

In the future, we will ultimately carry around our favorite stores in our pockets, thanks to VR, AR, MR and holograms giving us the option to visit a store no matter where we are. Just imagine sitting at home with a blend of visual recognition and an e-catalogue of furniture helping you project a virtual presentation onto a photo of your very own room, or virtually experiencing your next holiday destination through a 3D presentation at home or in-store. Fans of the *Back to the Future* movies will hardly bat an eyelid when they hear of this. After all, wasn't it Marty McFly who offered us a glimpse of 2015 back in 1989 — including printed pizzas and cinemagoers terrified by holograms of *Jaws 19*?

3D printing

Using 3D printing, machines operated by computers can produce unique items of every possible shape. How it works: a laser beam builds the object out of liquid or powder — usually a plastic or metal, though other materials are used too, including organic ones. Industrial businesses have started to experiment widely with 3D printing. Newcomers in particular are successfully turning whole industries upside down. Manufacturing companies have begun producing new prototypes and (spare) parts faster than ever before. Siemens, for example, now uses 3D printers to produce machine parts. Instead of ordering spare parts from outside suppliers, they can now simply print these onsite, rendering them less dependent on others while further disrupting the traditional chain of the manufacturing industry. Retailers and consumers alike will be able to benefit from faster, cheaper and more made-to-measure production of goods in the future. That is why 3D printing has quickly become one of the most talked-about examples of the smart economy. Many areas of business are reeling from its disruptive effect, or from their enthusiasm over its possibilities, depending on their own role within the value chain.

Gartner believes this kind of printing is likely to double — at least — every year. According to research site Statista the global market for 3D applications will go from 13.2 billion in 2016 to almost 30 billion dollars in 2020.[30] The medical industry, for example, uses this technology to print artificial heart valves. Gartner is convinced that hearing aids, hip replacements and artificial knees will soon be rolling out of 3D printers.[31]

Retail is likely to be revolutionized by 3D printing too. There are far-reaching effects for all kinds of (web) stores. Over the next few years, 3D printers will start appearing in stores, supermarkets and hardware stores. Shopping streets are going to see the arrival of dedicated stores for 3D printing, setting up shop in empty storefronts. Not only will they sell 3D printers for home use, they will also offer customers the option to print their very own designs in-store. Obviously, customers can choose to upload their design and have the printed item delivered to their home. These 3D-service stores will help customers design items, as well as give workshops on how to print at home, sell the required materials and accessories, and so on. In the UK, supermarket chain ASDA has already set up a 3D printing service. You can print a miniature likeness of yourself[32] — when I was at a wedding recently, I saw the bride and groom had a tiny version of themselves on top of the wedding cake. Dutch department store HEMA offers customers the option to print a miniature sculpture of themselves, as well as personalized smartphone covers and jewelry.

At the same time, there are scores of international 3D printing marketplaces where a host of new services are provided. Platforms such as Shapeways and Sculpteo let you order custom-made 3D-printed items. Creative Commons is a platform where you can freely share your designs, and Home 3D Printing allows people who have their own 3D printer to download various designs. There are specialized search engines — Yeggi and Fabforall are two — that search for 3D files online. There are also hybrid 3D web stores that offer all these options at once.[33]

Online retail titan Amazon has also set its sights on this new technology.[34] In 2014, it opened its own 3D web store, and the company currently operates on both Shapeways and Sculpteo. In 2015, Amazon applied for a patent for a *3D printing on demand mobile delivery truck*. With this, Amazon could simply send an STL file for each order to the nearest mobile unit, which would then print the item on demand, wherever. Amazon customers benefit from this, certainly, but so does the company itself by realizing savings in supplies, robots and staff.[35]

3D-PRINTING OF CLOTHING

Returns continue to be a costly part of business for consumers and (web)stores alike. The "Fashion that Fits" project by the University of Applied Sciences in Amsterdam is developing new ways of matching the correct size to the someone's physical measurements. After having a photo taken from the front and the side using a smartphone or tablet, a 3D image is calculated. The dress size can then be estimated and a 3D scan can be worked up. It will not be long before customers can select outfits on their tablets, view them on a digital copy of their own bodies and order the outfit right away.[36]

Shoe manufacturer Nike is certain that it's only a matter of time before consumers come to stores to print the Flyknit sneakers they designed at home to match their personal specifications.[37] In a few years' time, opticians are going to have 3D printers in-store to instantly produce perfectly made-to-measure specs after performing the usual eye scan. UK supermarket chain Tesco expects customers to soon start printing spare parts for household goods, such as a tube for the vacuum cleaner.[38] Zalando has high hopes of 3D printing clothing, which would be a service provided to small and mid-size clothing brands.[39]

In the future, 3D printing web stores will go beyond jewelry, toy figures and phone covers and actually start offering homewares such as lamps, picture frames and chairs. What about *objets d'art* or fashion items? These new online stores have two key characteristics: they offer small and affordable print runs and excel at personalizing their products. Possibly the greatest revolution brought by 3D printing is not the technology, but the possibility to turn production into something local and close to home. The effects for world trade will be overwhelming in due time. According to ING printed goods could already wipe out 40% of world imports in 2040 and world trade will be 23% lower in 2060 if the growth of investment in 3D printers continue at the current pace.[40]

Robotization

The robots are coming. Left-right-left, here they come, marching into the lives of retailers.[41] Distribution and fulfillment centers of large department stores, (web)stores and parcel delivery companies are the main areas for robots to work. On their own, they weave their way through the stacks, sourcing the correct items and needing no help packing them for delivery. At German book distributor Sigloch, there are so-called "Toru Cubes" zipping around:

automatically operated vehicles delivering books from the store-room to the packing tables. Quit Logistics — a US fulfillment company working for Zara and others — has turned to a range of robots to prevent staff from walking back and forth between stacks and packing tables. Similarly, these centers for distribution and fulfillment have security robots monitoring storerooms for missing pallets or using heat-detection cameras to scan at night for possible intruders.

Amazon has installed approximately 50,000 robots in its US distribution centers.[42] According to their own calculations, this reduces operational costs by one-fifth — every single order becomes 20 to 40 percent cheaper thanks to the use of robots. Amazon tends to use small, agile robots that can lift up entire racks at once and deliver them to packing tables. Warehouse workers no longer need to walk. Supermarkets, too, are introducing customers to robots. Segway-type robots like Tally can zoom past every shelf and scan all the barcodes in-store in less than an hour.[43] Robots can also restock empty shelves and replace checkout staff through the use of "self-check-outs". Walmart's robot Bossa Nova now roams the aisles in 50 Walmart stores in the US. It is able to perform tasks such as identifying when items are out of stock, locating incorrect prices and detecting wrong or missing labels.[44] Consumer electronics retailer MediaMarkt-Saturn even uses robots in German and Swiss stores to enhance in-store customer experience. Service-robot Paul welcomes customers, answers to simple questions and walks with you to the right aisle (more on this topic in Chapter 12).

It will not be long before robots come into our homes and help us with our daily chores. Robots like CLOi (LG), Kuri (Mayfield Robotics) and Buddy (Blue Frog) are ready to take on a pivotal role in households.

Artificial intelligence

Artificial intelligence (AI) is gradually seeping into all aspects of everyday life. Not to mention being a buzzword in the tech sector. At the base of AI are machine learning and deep learning. Whereas the human mind still provides the foundation for machine learning, deep learning involves self-learning computers taking over the work previously done by humans and machines. Smart software and flexible algorithms are on their way to relieve us of some of our work, and we should not be afraid of that, in and of itself. For example, routine and predictable questions for call center staff can easily be handled by a computer. Chatbots are becoming ever more prevalent in new *customer care centers*. Digital advisers are perfectly capable of handling most of the simple requests. More complex issues do still require humans, though not as many as before. Besides, the programs are gaining intelligence as we speak. AI is bound to help retailers improve, not just in customer service and customer engagement, but also in key performance indicators such as marketing, delivery times, fulfillment and analytic costs, to name a few.

Staples, the US company for office supplies, has started testing AI by having customers place an order by voice and answer simple questions.[45] Before too long, they will be able to answer the questions the customers have not even asked yet. The athletic gear brand Under Armour offers customers an app that provides them with insights about their sleep, fitness, activity and nutrition, thanks to AI. When providing recommendations on today's workout, AI-powered tools check on the weather forecast, considering factors like the expected temperature and likelihood of rain.[46]

> He who owns the interface, owns the customer.
> He who owns the customer, owns the data.
> He who owns the data, owns the future.[47]

All tech giants are wholeheartedly developing AI as part of their goal to become pivotal to our household, for one with their smart home speaker devices. Amazon Echo, Apple HomePod and Google Home are certainly going to stake a claim in the customer journey. It's part of a new revolutionary shift in consumer behavior from text to voice. "Voice is the next big thing," explains Werner Vogels, Amazon's CTO. "It is more natural than a keyboard, and makes technology more accessible."[48] Smart home speaker devices and digital assistants on your smartphone will effortlessly lead the way to the best restaurant or your favorite store based on their knowledge of your likes and dislikes inside out. In fact, they can invite your friends, send them a route to the restaurant and jot down the date in your calendar, all in one go.[49] These devices will become your personal assistant, thanks to AI learning from your behavior and taking care of you in a personal way.

The developments in AI are a particularly volatile topic of debate. Some people believe the intelligence of robots and computer programs will one day equal or even eclipse human intelligence. Ray Kurzweil, Google's own futurologist, believes that computers will soon be able to not only do the same things as humans, but actually do them better than we can.[50] He expects that most of our online searches can soon be done without us ever having to ask for them. The point in time when non-biological intelligence surpasses that of humans is otherwise known as *singularity*.[51] This often conjures up all kinds of horrifying scenarios. If I were to limit myself to the effect of AI on onlife retail, I imagine a world looming where people have come to depend completely on machines and computers, leaving us utterly at the mercy of a tiny group of technological superpowers.

Will we reach the point where manufacturing and service have little or no need for human input? In Silicon Valley, the phrase often used is *"software is eating the world."* Can humans even stop this development? Or should we turn to the humanisation of technology, where we attempt to allow people and technology to work together in a mutually beneficial and performance-enhancing relationship?

THE DARK SIDE OF AI

In 2015, a group of over 1,000 high-profile experts, leading scientists and entrepreneurs – among them Tesla founder Elon Musk, Apple co-founder Steve Wozniak and author Erik Brynjolfsson – issued a warning on the dark side of AI. Their concern: what would happen if big-data-based algorithms and AI fell into the wrong hands? What do we do if algorithms become smarter than humans? Musk and his peers believe that robots ought to act as they were intended. A robot is designed to serve people, and this should never change.[52] AI ought to be developed further, to serve a broad social interest, but we need to ensure that it does not reach the clutches of the wrong people, nor those of a mere handful of dominant companies.

In 2016, Amazon, Facebook, Google, IBM and Microsoft set up the

Partnership on AI. Its promise: to keep a check on the developments in AI.[53] Its goal: conduct research together and make pertinent recommendations. The group rejects outright any suggestion that they themselves are aiming to control AI without any government involvement.[54]

Blockchain

Blockchain is the technology — still very far from perfect — behind digital currencies such as Bitcoin and Ethereum. Odds are, the blockchain will have an enormous impact on the world of onlife retail. The blockchain is a mechanism to automatically guarantee the authenticity and integrity of transactions. It's done through an open network (best compared to Internet) in the cloud. Accessible for all and, just like Internet, nobody is in charge of it or can claim ownership.

When we take a closer look, though, we find that the blockchain is actually an advanced digital structure of data, constructed out of millions of blocks of information that belong together. You could imagine millions of blockchain configurations, each of them with their own data verification method and way of operating.[55] Onlife retail applications of this technology might be the exchange of information and documents involved in contracts or financial transactions.

Similar to Internet, everyone is free to add new information to the blockchain. Powerful cryptography ensures that it all happens safely. The key strength and unicity (setting it apart from Internet) of the blockchain is that you can only add new data *to* existing blocks of data. In other words, data that's been placed in existing and joined-up blocks of data cannot be adapted or deleted. For this reason, or so the theory goes, hacking the blockchain is close to impossible, as is manipulating it. Any attempt to do so would raise red flags for thousands of participants instantly. After all, they have the older blockchain. You could compare it to Wikipedia or Linux, where people are always monitoring and checking the accuracy and veracity of new information.

Even though blockchain technology is still very much in its infancy, the Bitcoin and Ethereum already use this technology. This has naturally caught the full attention of banks and financial institutions. Users in the blockchain are constantly exchanging information — and validating that information as they go — rendering any third party intermediary obsolete for the matching up of supply and demand.[56] Not only does the blockchain then present a real threat for traditional intermediaries such as banks, but what is left of the added value of businesses such as Airbnb and Uber if a blockchain-based platform allowed consumers to get in touch directly with an apartment renter or an on-shift cabdriver?[57]

In onlife retail, the blockchain mostly translates into a safe means of buying. Provided the technology develops according to plan, concerns of privacy will become a thing of the past, and we will be able to transfer money to each other without needing a bank. All the information in (web) stores on goods and services will be absolutely reliable. Marc Andreessen, co-founder of Netscape, the first commercial Internet browser, believes the blockchain is "the distributed trust network that the Internet always needed and never had".[58] Now, retailers need only tap into its potential operational advantages and start using it to offer even better personal service and unlimited safety guarantees to their customers.[59]

Privacy

All this new technology in the smart economy has one thing in common: the inconceivable amount of data it generates. A lot of people are very wary of the idea that so much information is being collected, correlated and analyzed, all supposedly for national security, science or commerce. The practices of American espionage agency NSA, the Facebook/Cambridge Analytica data scandal, the Chinese government attempting to monitor how trustworthy its citizens are, and perhaps most importantly, the unrestrained craving for data by the tech companies: many people find all these things abhorrent. They believe privacy to be a universal right, which cannot be infringed upon lightly. [60]

The difficulty is that while citizens may value their privacy, they also expect to be protected from terrorism and live free of computer hacks. Consumers want to shop online without having to keep filling out their details and download apps that are immediately relevant to them personally. Most people are fine with surrendering some privacy in exchange, believing they have nothing to hide, anyway. Ultimately, we are perfectly willing to share pretty much everything on social media. We give others access — sometimes without even realizing it — to our personal profiles, and we accept the ever-changing new terms and conditions of the big tech companies without bothering to read them.

Sure, it is a tough bind: accepting cookies might give you a better user experience online, but it might also result in being hounded by *tracking cookies* for weeks on end afterwards. Most consumers have given up on the option of declining cookie acceptance.

So, how do big data, big businesses and Big Brother interact? There are wildly different opinions on this issue when you compare Europe to, for example, the United States. In Europe, privacy advocates are the reason legislators try hard to regulate the matter with cookie laws, privacy laws and the like. Until the adoption of new, more stringent European privacy laws, there was scant pan-European supervision, a fact which was happily embraced by American tech giants in particular. With the comprehensive reform of data protection rules in Europe, in effect since 2018, people have the right to view their data, have incorrect information corrected, ask for the processing of data to cease and even have the right of being forgotten altogether.[61] This legislation has profound effects on American and Chinese businesses active in Europe, requiring them to ask for explicit consent to use data for advertising purposes, among other regulations.[62]

In the United States, the mood is more pragmatic; more *laisser-faire.* People assume that e-commerce needs the free exchange of data in order to flourish. The US Federal Trade Commission (FTC) does, however, take a firm stance against businesses who mislead consumers in their online privacy statements about what they will do with consumer data. Google and Facebook have lived to tell the tale of this.[63] The troubling thing is that we have no idea what companies will do in the future with the data we provide them with today.

Big data and privacy are controversial topics with a call to action for retailers, too. Offering privacy to consumers could be a new unique selling point for a business. After all, the mountain of generic data already accrued still leaves ample room to make relevant suggestions and offers to anonymous customers in a legitimate yet equally effective way.

By opting for a *data protection by design* principle, companies can decide to safeguard their customer privacy in procedures. This does, however, require them to embed personal data protection into their services from the get-go. A company could then have a label for their privacy policy to show consumers that they do, after all, have a choice.[64]

On the other hand, consumers have higher expectations of data protection of their bank than of their local supermarket, where they have loyalty cards. Their favorite web store needs to keep them happy by sending personal offers frequently. They ought to be given the option to decide if, and how frequently, they want to benefit from personalized commercial services at (web) stores, travel organizations, banks and insurance companies.

TARGET HITS THE MARK

Back in 2012, an irate father showed up at Target just outside Minneapolis, demanding to speak to the manager.[65] Why on earth was his teenage daughter being targeted with special offers for baby's onesies and cribs? The manager was at a loss for an answer and had no choice but to apologize profusely.

Target uses a range of data for its marketing, combining social security number, name, email address and prior purchases.[66] The system can then make certain predictions with these data. If a young woman buys in March a larger-than-average bottle of body lotion, a bag that could easily double as a diaper bag and a handful of supplements including calcium, magnesium and iron, the odds of her expecting a baby in August are close to 90 percent.

A few days after the incident, the manager reached out to the family again to apologize once more. Imagine his surprise when the father shared with him that his daughter had come clean: she was pregnant after all.

Interpretation

Algorithms can sometimes deduce facts about us of which even our own families have no clue (see the box on page 47). However, skeptics are adamant that big data always needs to be interpreted, most notably in the case of ethical issues. They believe this kind of data is an "instrument that can help us find answers that are good enough for the time being, until we find better methods and even better answers become available."[67] Scientists and statisticians strenuously argue that the correlations proven by big data are very far from patterns of cause and effect. They also emphasize over and over that overused and sloppy data is seriously flawed.[68]

Big data as a phenomenon is then not able to avoid the classic *hype cycle*. Its proponents are convinced that it will be the answer to practically every single problem in the world. It is unlikely, however, that these promises will uniformly be kept. Big data comes in all shapes and sizes, and not all data is good data.[69]

You

The search is on for the answers to big questions like: Who owns big data, the consumer providing the information or the retailer who stores them? And who owns the data digested from them?[70] In 2006, *TIME Magazine* was spot on — naming "YOU" as its "Person of the Year"[71] — in predicting that consumers will win big in the smart economy. Big data will produce an onlife user experience that just keeps on becoming more personal. Smart algorithms will recognize our behavior and make us perfect offers at exactly the right time.[72] There is much to be gained, despite the need for a serious debate in the immediate future on how big data affects privacy. "Privacy might deal with big data, but not all big data will deal with privacy."[73]

"*Sharing is to ownership what the iPod is to the eight-track, what the solar panel is to the coal mine. Sharing is clean, crisp, urbane, postmodern; owning is dull, selfish, timid, backward.*"

MARK LEVINE,
POET AND AUTHOR[1]

3
Consumers in the sharing economy

Traditional economy	Sharing economy
Buying	Sharing
Consumer	Prosumer
Encyclopedia	Wikipedia
Facts	Trust
Family and friends	Crowd
Individualism	Community spirit
Internet	Internet of Things (IoT)
Loan	Crowdfunding
Matching platform	Cooperation platform
Offline reputation	Online reputation
Own network	Crowdsourcing
Possession	Use
Profit margin percentage	Zero marginal cost
Recommendation	Screening and verification
Referrals	Reviews
Secrecy	Openness
Steady job	Flexible job
Toss out	Reuse
Websites	Peer-to-peer platforms

Not in the mood for cooking? Why don't you order a delicious meal from that foodie neighbor or have a top chef come and cook for you at home? Need a car or bike for a few hours, or even days? We're on it. Or do you feel like lending someone else your car on the days it would otherwise be stationary? We can do that, too. A blocked toilet or a garden cluttered with leaves? *No sweat.* How about exchanging homes with a French family? Need a cash influx for a special project or a new business? The so-called *sharing economy*, platform economy or collaborative economy has it all.

I will be describing the rise of the sharing economy in this chapter, and its impact on government, retailers and consumers. Some people believe it will incite a social revolution of sorts, not least due to the boost it can give local relationships between people and businesses. Others can barely suppress their skepticism towards the impact of the sharing economy. They question its business model and its true potential for making money. I will discuss the opportunities and threats of the collaborative economy for retail. Furthermore, how is the sharing economy going to build a more "social" society where retailers and consumers come together?

Is this sharing economy really a new idea?

The sharing economy is best described as a socio-economic system, which has sharing at its core: (temporarily) sharing untapped potential, goods, (work)space, money and services. Its principles are as old as time:

- Governments were early adopters of sharing. They did so by constructing railroads and setting up bus services for their citizens. National governments put energy suppliers in place, whereas local governments erected phone booths at inner-city hotspots.
- Businesses, motivated by making money, focused on sharing and reusing: examples include hotels, bath houses, laundromats and dry cleaners. The same concept applies to car rental companies, tuxedo rentals, and so on.
- People have always been happy to share and reuse goods, time and talent — not least as a quick way to save a few dimes.

THE SHARING ECONOMY HAS BEEN AROUND FOREVER

In the 1950s and 1960s, the sharing economy was fueled by the scarcity of goods. People would use each other's phones if they needed, and you went to the neighbors to watch TV or listen to the radio during a national event. Clothes were worn, mended, and worn again until they fell apart at the seams. Generations of children grew up wearing the hand-me-downs of their older siblings. Tapping into neighbors' talents and vice versa was so mainstream that no one thought to mention it. People simply helped each other out. Swapping homes with distant relatives or friends could hardly have been more ordinary.

The rise of the online sharing economy

Nowadays, the sharing economy is fueled by the opportunities provided by new technology. Thanks to mobile devices with GPS, social media, sensors and 3D printing, people and organizations can share theirs skills, stuff, space and services — just like that.

Back in 1995, two of the first instances of the online sharing economy were the ad network Craigslist and auction website eBay. In 1999, US music sharing platform Napster gave people a way to listen to music for free — aptly described by *The New York Times* as the "something for nothing economy."[2]

American economist Jeffrey Rifkin predicted in 2000 that new digital possibilities would create a society where the possession of goods would soon be replaced by *access* to goods and services.[3]

The 2008 financial crisis further boosted the sharing economy in Western countries. In the subsequent Great Recession, (consumer) trust in traditional business practices started to flag. At the same time, unemployment soared, leaving people unable to pay their bills. So too did resistance, even disgust, begin to soar against unchecked consumerism.

Today, many consumers are re-evaluating their lifestyles and the value of their possessions related to how infrequently some items are used. Why on earth buy a brand new drill hammer for 99 dollars if you'll only end up using it for 13 minutes or shorter?

Besides, a lot of people are eager to incorporate environmentally sound choices into their lifestyles.[4] According to research, 75 percent of consumers expect the sharing economy to reduce the production of waste.[5] However, this applies to user goods and cars more than anything else.[6]

Most importantly, sharing their stuff seems to make people happier. After all, possessions can cause stress, depression and even death, so says British trend watcher James Wallman. He believes consumers should stop trying to "keep up with the Joneses".[7]

Social revolution

While sharing may well have its economic and ecological benefits, there are plenty of consumers who are motivated by other reasons. More than anything, they are invested in creating a new and timely kind of community spirit; a smaller scale, a return to human dimensions. Others see this social benefit as simply an added bonus.

In their book *What's Mine Is Yours,* Rachel Botsman and Roo Rogers call this new sense of community "cooperative consumption." They talk of a new socio-economic *big idea,* the precursor of a revolution in consumer behavior.[8] In 2011, *TIME Magazine* named *collaborative consumption* as one of the ten ideas that would change the world.[9] The rise of the sharing economy does actually change the behavior of consumers.[10] After all, who could have imagined five years ago that we would get into a car with a perfect stranger (Uber, Lyft, BlaBlaCar, Didi Chuxing)? Or rent out an attic or spare room to people we've never met (Airbnb)? We advertise our own services as handymen (TaskRabbit, Helpling), but are equally prepared to rent our boats (Boatbound, Barqo), homes (HomeAway, VRBO, FlipKey), cars (Car2Go, Turo, Zipcar) or drill hammer (Peerby). Our most prized possessions, our personal experiences and our very lives: we trust people we have never met with all of it.

A key success factor in the sharing economy is the online reputation of its players. Reviews, screening and verification protocols all add up to make the behavior of all relevant parties in the sharing economy clear and transparent. They ensure a mutual sense of trust. We review the person renting us the apartment, rate the cab driver, and reward consumers whom we lend money or whose tool we borrow with likes or dislikes, as the case may be.

There are people who engage in sharing who expect something in return immediately. However, asynchronous reciprocity is just as common: someone who receives something is often inclined to help others at a later time. People who have shared cars often end up sharing other goods and services, too. They share bikes and often tend to use public transport more than before. The sharing economy, then, is not merely an economic breakthrough; it also causes social change.

JOIN THE CROWD

Possibly the best example of sharing among peers the world over is Wikipedia. This free online encyclopedia is run by volunteers and financed by donations from private citizens and businesses alike. The thousands of platforms for green energy, healthcare or crowdfunding are more successful examples of civil initiative by enterprising citizens, "prosumers" bent on co-creation, and groups of onlife consumers joining forces. Linux, the open software system, has IT developers working to make free operating systems for computers everywhere. Incidentally, Google is the largest global Linux user, with over 100,000 servers.

Local connections

Often overlooked as a driver of the sharing economy is the social aspect of it all.[11] Single-person households — a growing demographic — will need their neighbors and extended communities more than ever. Our very real longing for human contact makes us feel good about joining the sharing economy. People want a sense of belonging, of doing good for others, and of being part of a community brimming with social interaction. The literally thousands of peer-to-peer marketplaces that have popped up, the sharing platforms and the social networks are all ways of fulfilling that very need for community. Pinning up a note in a supermarket or library has now been replaced by an algorithm. Assuming personal responsibility is another wish that the sharing economy could fulfil. Collaborative consumption is a conscious choice for people, as is treating scarce resources sustainably. What people long for most is to build local connections, on their own street, in their neighborhood or on the block nearby. They want to connect with people within their own local community. Sharing, exchanging and reusing goods, services and talent — sometimes for free, sometimes for money — are the foundation for these new connections.

Business models

In *What's Mine Is Yours,* Botsman and Rogers have defined three different systems:[12]

- *Product service systems (PSS)*: consumers pay to use certain products, which means they don't need to buy these themselves. This model works equally well for businesses (laundromats) and consumers (loaning a neighbor your car for a small fee). Services which improve the lifespan of goods, such as repair and maintenance, are also part of this model. There are obvious advantages: making maximum use of a product while eliminating the need for (re)users to purchase, maintain, repair or insure expensive appliances themselves.

- *Second-hand markets*: social networks that help find a new owner for used goods. Sometimes they are given away (Freecycle), sometimes you need to pay (eBay), or a combination of the two (Craigslist). Sometimes, goods are simply exchanged for other goods. Their users feel it would be wasteful to simply toss the stuff if it can still be used — even if it's a new or different use than before. Reuse and reinvention, conceiving new product applications — that is where the sharing economy and the circular economy intersect. More on this in the next chapter.

- *Shared lifestyle*: this is a system for people to share immaterial things, such as time, space, talent and money. This kind of system tends to appear locally, in the sharing of workspace, parking lots or odd jobs, for example. There are global matches being made for the shared lifestyle, too, of which *couch surfing* (Couchsurfing.com) is a prime example. It is a hospitality network for people to set up overnight stays on the floor, couch, or wherever really, in the home of a stranger.[13] In a sense, even Airbnb could be regarded as part of the shared lifestyle.

Online marketplaces, platforms and networks are the key business models of the sharing economy. They tap into the resources of others in order to work. Airbnb depends on empty apartments and homes. Uber needs the spare time of drivers and the fact that cars would otherwise remain unused, immobile. Peerby and Poshmark count on people making their possessions available for others to use. Instead of breaking your back assembling a new IKEA bunk bed, you can find a good deal on eBay (and even find a handyman with rave online reviews).

The common thread: presenting consumers with an option to step off that tired linear path that is the customer journey. Suddenly, sharing, exchanging and reusing become real alternatives to buying goods and services.

Disruption

Not for nothing, then, that many sectors find these new sharing economy business models disruptive:

- The music business was taken off-guard at the turn of the century when downloading was introduced. Suddenly, the market was inundated by endless (illegal) websites where people could download music for free. Apple iTunes (started in 2001, growing to nearly 1 billion users worldwide today) and Spotify (started in 2006, with currently over 100 million users) are both legal options that *do* charge money.[14] [15] It has taken the music industry the best part of 20 years to come up with even a semblance of a response to these developments. The year 2015 was the very first time that digital music providers had more revenue than physical sales of music.[16]

- Taxi-sharing service Uber, founded in 2009, matches passengers and drivers through an app. Uber then earns a commission on every single transaction. Now, this company — with a staggering market valuation into the tens of billions of dollars — is being hit with lawsuits and claims the world over, amongst others on account of its disruptive effect.[17] The established industry (taxis) is begging for government protection instead of choosing to innovate and reinvent their own business models.

- Airbnb has truly turned things upside down in the hospitality industry. This marketplace is the facilitator of short stays in overnight accommodation, ranging from single rooms to apartments, whole houses or even castles. With its over 100 million users and over 2 million places to stay in over 200 countries, Airbnb presents a very real threat to hotels, hostels and motels.[18] There are now dozens of startups keen to grab their own piece of the pie (Wimdu, Roomorama, 9flats).

- The automotive business was completely blindsided by car-sharing and all its options. The numbers of shared cars

(Car2Go and DriveNow), parking spots (JustPark) and charging stations for electronic cars (PlugShare) have soared sky-high, as has that old faithful: carpooling (BlaBlaCar). Research in the US has shown that a single car-sharing vehicle results in 32 fewer new cars being sold.[19] PriceWaterhouseCoopers (PwC) expects car sharing turnover to cross the 10 billion mark in the year 2020. Others believe this number is more likely to be in the trillions. The number of worldwide users is set to increase from 7 million in 2015 to 36 million in 2025.[20]

Stores, travel organizations, banks and insurance companies all need to step up and take the opportunities the sharing economy has to offer. This means they need to embrace and adopt new business models. By integrating sharing and exchanging into the value chain, they could tune into the new behavior of customers. The Swedish home goods retailer IKEA entered the *gig economy* for that very reason with the acquisition of handyman website TaskRabbit in 2017. TaskRabbit uses its online marketplace to connect 60,000 freelance workers or "taskers" with people looking to hire someone to do chores like furniture assembly. Now IKEA customers can hire an experienced handyman with "IKEA assembling skills" directly on the IKEA website.[21]

Patagonia has already made this move. The specialist in outdoor gear has joined forces with eBay to set up a marketplace for the redistribution of used jackets, shoes, sweaters and equipment. Both H&M and ASOS have opened up marketplaces of their own on eBay, giving them a huge increase in customers, both new and loyal.[22] In New York, there's an online store called Rent the Runway where you can rent designer outfits and accessories. The web store has also opened several brick stores in New York, Las Vegas and Chicago, as well as a large in-store unit at luxury department store Neiman Marcus in San Francisco. The German former mail order company OTTO has introduced a rental platform for household appliances. German consumers can go to OTTO NOW and rent items for at least three months at a time. This online platform is aimed mostly at students, young families and early adopters who love trying out new concepts.

In the automotive sector, car rental firm Avis paid half a billion dollars for the acquisition of car sharing site Zipcar; BMW has set up its own car sharing service; and car manufacturer Daimler is experimenting with a car rental and sharing program in China. An app lets users check availability of cars and trucks, and they can even use their smartphones to open the vehicle's doors.[23] General Motors, Google and Mercedes are deeply involved in models for sharing self-driving cars. Those are just a handful of examples of how the business world has started to discover the sharing economy. The biggest investors are well-established companies, helping to accelerate the sharing economy through startups and incubator-type programs.

Consumer turned producer

As early as 1980, futurologist Alvin Toffler coined the term *prosumer* referring to the blurring of the lines separating producers from consumers.[24] Consumers now produce their own energy with solar panels on their roof or home-grown vegetables in their kitchen garden or allotment. Thanks to 3D printing, consumers and small businesses are able to create products of their very own, at home and through open software, if needed.

Author and businessman Chris Anderson predicts that so-called "DIY manufacturing" will take hold in a big way: any developer or keen amateur can use the appropriate software and 3D printing to create products that could previously only be manufactured in a factory, using machines. Anderson is convinced this will upend the manufacturing industry completely and bring about increased economic growth.[25]

Prosumers can join forces in cooperatives and/or opt to work with existing businesses. Better than most, they can easily solve problems *in the cloud*, write product reviews or criticize services, as well as come up with innovative ideas for new goods and services. Prosumers will prove to be important partners for online marketplaces, platforms and networks. Not to mention, they are perfect partners for those brave businesses, retailers and brands who dare to open up their business models to prosumer input.

The rise of the zero marginal cost society

Jeremy Rifkin believes the sharing economy and what he calls *the collaborative commons* are part of a new industrial revolution. In his mind, it is a new "economic ecosystem."[26] There are literally several hundred million people working together all over the world, in every realm of society. They have organized themselves into millions of self-managed small cooperatives, civil initiatives, organizations, clubs, and associations, but also for-profit social enterprises and social businesses. The Internet of Things is what Rifkin sees as the *soulmate* of the sharing economy.[27] People from every segment of society are connected with each other through these networks and platforms, which are, in turn, not centrally organized on purpose. It means that people the world over have the opportunity to work sustainably and share and reuse goods and services.

Businesses have long since — for centuries even — set themselves the task of increasing the efficiency of their goods and services. After all, every inch of marginal cost reduction could be the tipping point in the race with your competition. Rifkin believes we are now experiencing the dawn of an age where goods and services will be produced at virtually zero marginal cost, provided we disregard the fixed cost of production. There are examples to be found, such as Airbnb. They have little to no effort or cost when a new apartment is added to their online portfolio. The owner of the apartment does the hard work himself — for free, no less. Just compare this model to traditional hotel chains, who have to make significant investments if they want to increase the number of hotel rooms. Auction websites, marketplaces and platforms have a similarly easy ride: adding new goods or services, or even new manufacturers, can all be done for (next to) nothing.

Rifkin is convinced that the zero marginal cost society is going to be both inevitable and dramatic for everyone involved in retail. Producing goods and services with ever-decreasing revenue, to the point of no marginal yield, is surely a dead-end street. Turning over any profit becomes a nearly impossible feat. Then, the fixed cost of buildings and staff cannot be recouped. In the long run, so says Rifkin, looking ahead 50 years or so, capitalism will no longer be the dominant economic system. We are not there yet, though a collaborative economy does seem to be an irreversible given.

Skepticism

But is the sharing economy truly a new socio-economic model? Will it really revolutionize our consumer behavior?[28] There is certainly no consensus that it will be so. First of all, we need to ask ourselves if the self-professed proponents of the sharing economy — Airbnb, TaskRabbit and the like — are in fact in the sharing business. They collect houses, vacant rooms, empty cars, idle handymen and all sorts of goods and exploit the data generated. They do everything but share the money they make from their activities, though. There is a growing number of people who regard this as a problem in society: the fact that a small elite owns the generated data, the power they derive from them and the profits that are made.

Skeptics believe the rise of the sharing economy is in fact a result of growing living expenses; in other words, fallout from the recent economic crisis. A lot of people have turned to the sharing economy as a way to supplement their income. Critics say the sharing economy does little more than facilitate badly-paid freelance work, such as being an Uber driver. Some people are *ubering* for fun, true, though most of them are motivated by sheer financial necessity.[29] The irony of it all deepens even more when a company like Uber turns out to be charging their drivers extortionate *lease options* and has a work environment plagued by scandals.[30]

Online columnist Susie Cagle has described the sharing economy as a kind of disaster capitalism.[31] If we slightly tone down that rhetoric: profit in this economy is made at the expense of the current workforce, who would be wise to unite if they want to rise up and protest these working conditions.[32]

There are also scores of consumers who are very reluctant to share stuff. Why bother to get a drill in this manner (search it online, pick it up, pay $10 for a day, then return it again), if you can order one online for $30 and have it delivered tomorrow? The average consumer is not likely to jump on the sharing bandwagon unless sharing becomes fundamentally cheaper than owning things and reusing goods proves to be cheaper than tossing them out and replacing them.[33] Businesses operating in the sharing economy have begun to realize they must provide added value. At Peerby Go, you can now get a drill for $10 a day, including the search, delivery and pick-up.

Challenges in the sharing economy

In the future, the sharing economy is set to face many challenges. Is there sufficient trust between people and companies for the sharing economy of the future to fulfil its potential? How can we guarantee quality within the sharing economy? What positive effects will the sharing economy have on the workforce and employment? Can we prove that the sharing economy has more advantages than downsides? At what rate and to what extent are traditional businesses embracing the new business models of the sharing economy? Last but not least: how are governments dealing with sharing economy regulations?

Threat 1: distrust

Challenges and threats swirl around the sharing economy. Trust could very well prove to be the number one success factor. There cannot be anything more annoying than finding your car, apartment or drill scratched all over, filthy or broken after loaning, sharing or renting it. We have already determined that transparency on the part of the people involved is essential. Personal reviews and ratings are where you can go on record about how people have behaved. This sounds much harsher than it is; after all, don't we all do a quick Google check when we do business with someone for the first time? Similarly, searching LinkedIn is another way of protecting ourselves against dubious business partners. Online visibility of reputations has increased clarity and can be a strong encouragement for people to willingly take part in any given platform.

In addition to rating and review systems, companies in the sharing economy are introducing new services to further boost mutual trust. To name one, Airbnb now provides Host Protection Insurance against accidents during rental periods. Fueled by the international sharing website Peerby, insurance companies have stepped up to include loaning and renting in home insurance policies. When you rent something through Peerby Go, insurance is included. In years to come, we will see specialized platforms, networks and businesses focusing on quality control.

Of course, you can do some online screening, ID verification and checking of social media profiles yourself in hopes of finding out if it is safe to loan or share things with someone. Onlife consumers may be given a *trust ID* to prove they are trustworthy partners in the sharing economy. This way, online platforms, marketplaces and networks will be secure in knowing who they're doing business with and which people they can match up within their secure environments.[34] Just in case things *do* go amiss, they can take out insurance based on those identification measures at specialist insurance companies.

Is the sharing economy indeed going to succeed in gaining and holding the trust of consumers without the need for government regulation? David Brooks, columnist at *The New York Times,* thinks the evolution of new mechanisms for assessing trust will in fact be implemental in shrinking the part governments must play in the sharing economy.[35]

Threat 2: working conditions

One of the greatest promises of the sharing economy is the claim that it's going to create jobs into the 100,000s and make entrepreneurs out of people who fail to succeed in traditional businesses. Tapping into the unused talent of people who can work for lower rates is sure to lead to increased demand for those workers, which in turn will lead to more jobs.[36]

Skeptics then swoop in to point out the downside of the impact on jobs.[37] Is the creation of new and insecure jobs not a means of threatening traditional and secure ones? Are the responsibilities and risks of big business not being heaped on the rather less sturdy shoulders of the self-employed, the prosumer and the small-business owner? To name one example, what happens if Airbnb guests use your apartment as a brothel during their stay?[38]

Increasingly, self-employed people — sometimes called *microentrepreneurs* — are going to embrace the sharing economy and do so with a widely varied portfolio. They might drive taxis for Uber and Lyft in the mornings, followed by some gardening through TaskRabbit in the afternoons. The evening might be spent delivering groceries for Amazon and dropping off packages for MyWays on their way back home.[39] They will be expected to be fast, flexible and always available at a moment's notice whenever someone clicks their mouse or swipes their smartphones. Should an *independent contractor* of this description not be considered a *de facto* employee?[40] The jury is still out on that one.

The rise of the sharing economy is going to boost the trend for increased flexibility and micro-entrepreneurship. Companies see it as the best way to adapt to future economic changes.[41] Participants in the sharing economy can find a means of escaping the burden of being employed by someone else. Everyone involved can find opportunities of making optimum use of the unique and specific talents of different people. However, it's essential that there are sufficient guarantees regarding the intrinsic value of this labor and the financial and legal ramifications. Otherwise, it will never succeed in attracting all the relevant parties, nor will the sharing economy truly take off.

Pros and cons of working conditions[42]

+	−
Flexible work/part-time work	No guaranteed hours or income
Options, variety of jobs	No protection, no formal working conditions
Entrepreneurship	Need for paying income tax and value added tax oneself
Possible regular work	Often no control over fees

Threat 3: regulation

Another important bottleneck is how to fit the various new business models into the existing structure. After the breakthroughs of Airbnb and Uber, governments swiftly attacked these newcomers in the hospitality and automotive industries, largely wielding regulation as a weapon. It is an age-old reflex to do so. Governments and established institutions are keen to protect existing businesses and industries. Same old, same old: there should be a level playing field, buyers and vendors need protecting,[43] newcomers should be kept from monopolizing the market. The Rathenau Institute believes that sharing platforms such as Airbnb and Uber need to be taken down a notch before they become invincible.[44] All over the world, Airbnb and Uber are being knocked about by lawsuits regarding homes for rent as illegal hotels, violating taxi regulations, and so on. Even TaskRabbit has had its business fingers slapped by authorities, albeit in its capacity as a veiled employer.

These *disruptors* are actually not beyond reproach themselves, and they often court the boundaries of the law and ethics of doing business (not to mention the loopholes) as a conscious business decision.[45] There are sure to be people and businesses within the sharing economy who truly care about the world. They often launch thought-provoking ideas which gain the sympathy of people instantly. On the other hand, there are many people and businesses who want to earn money first — as is the case in every economy — or at the very least be compensated for their efforts. They are always on the lookout for the network effects of online marketplaces, peer-to-peer networks and crowdsourcing platforms. Does this mean that governments ought to set regulations pre-emptively? Why not simply welcome the new businesses and their business models without actually shirking or avoiding the tough questions that are raised?

This is precisely what the European Commission (EC) has decided to do. They have resolved to liberalize the legislation and regulations for the sharing economy in Europe.[46] The EC has warned member states that outlawing activities set up by new companies should be the very last resort.[47] There are other interests at stake, too — the tens of billions of dollars that the sharing economy contributes to wider European economic growth, for one. If the regulations were too strict, both established businesses and start-ups could easily opt to move to the United States. The EC is by no means alone in their belief that much is to be gained: globally, over 25 billion dollars has been invested in startups within the sharing economy.[48]

SHARING ECONOMY GROWTH

In 2015, Juniper Research estimated that the sharing economy had a 6.5 billion dollar turnover. It predicts that it will grow to 20.4 billion dollar in 2020.[49] In 2016, PwC estimated that the revenue of businesses in the global sharing economy will even grow to 335 billion dollars in 2025 – more than 20 times its current size and equal to the traditional rental market.[50]

Threat 4: slower economic growth

Sometimes, new business models *do* add value to the economy, thanks to the appearance of new economic activities. More often, though, there is merely a shift in activities: one kind of activity is simply replaced by another. In the sharing economy, we often see that new activities flourish at the expense of established ones: sharing information, news, entertainment, music, cars, homes, clothing and green energy all adds up to a decline of turnover in traditional business areas. Consumers tend to cut back on their spending.

Popular bicycle sharing services as we see pop up in China and in big cities all over the world is going to impact bike sales. When we allow people to park on our driveway or private parking lot, parking garages are going to find themselves with fewer customers.[51] Every single shared car means there is less demand for newly manufactured cars. When we start taking care of our parents ourselves, there is less demand for newly-built homes for senior citizens, which in turn means fewer mortgages. In Manhattan, tens of thousands of new visitors organize their accommodation on Airbnb, avoiding the hysterically expensive *Big Apple* hotels. We should not be too surprised if the sharing economy in fact produces a decline in economic growth in years to come.

Many startups in the sharing economy finds themselves struggling to mesh their idealist principles of the startup with the need to make money in order to realize those very principles.[52] People who take part in their activities may feel fulfilled in the knowledge they are contributing to the greater good in their own way, making society a more liveable place and making a difference with like-minded souls. Why should there be no financial reward for that? When we bear in mind the controversy of excessive salaries, bonuses, stock options, profits and wealth, we should realize that future generations need to discuss for themselves what constitutes a reasonable and responsible profit.

What's next

The engines for the current sharing economy are Internet, social media and GPS. New technology and apps will lift it to the next level. Today's disruptors will find themselves being disrupted in turn. Why do we need mediators like Airbnb and Uber if we can get in touch with suppliers directly for ourselves? The development of blockchain technology may well lead us to the point where we can bid platforms and networks — who run off with enormous profits — adieu, at last.

Would it not be wonderful if all the revenue of the sharing economy could be preserved for the actual participants of that economy? This has started to happen on a minor scale in so-called *co-op platforms* such as Stocksy (stock photography) and Coopify (for cleaners and handymen). They are standing up in protest to the big guns who do business unethically and tend to exploit their users to some extent.

Soon, the sharing economy is going to have a significant effect on the economic system. Consumers become prosumers, with the sharing economy bringing new lifeblood to the well-worn model of *homo economicus.* In the sharing economy, the ideal person is a micro-entrepreneur who is deeply motivated to turn all his time, money, talent and possessions into money-makers.[53] The sharing economy is about earning money too, then. Or, at the very least, asking for a decent fee for services rendered.

We simply have to wait and see if the sharing economy does shake up the economic order, spurring it on towards the creation of a more social, just society. A society where sharing, exchanging and (re)using are immediately beneficial to cooperating citizens and likeminded onlife consumers.

> *"If you want to be a great company today, you also need to be a good company."*

JEFFREY R. IMMELT,
CEO OF GENERAL ELECTRIC[1]

4

Sustainable shopping in the circular economy

Traditional economy	Circular economy
Buying	Using
Limited use	Optimized use
Linear business models	Cyclical business models
Manufacturing	Repairing and upcycling (cradle-to-cradle)
Mass production	One-to-one production
Waste	Resources
Wasteful	Sustainable

We are now experiencing the dawn of an immense shift, slowly unfolding over the next years and decades: linear economy becoming circular. Society is now faced with hard questions, following years of boundless consuming and the resulting harmful emissions. One person may see the increasing scarcity of resources and environmental damage as a call to action. Others could be more interested in all the possible new opportunities. Retailers in the circular economy have new roles to fulfill, after all — they can start developing new business models to become intermediaries between producers and consumers.

At the moment, retailers determine their profits based on the sales of many different goods. In the long-term future, this may change, and profit would be derived from offering new services. There is a trend — slowly, but surely — for producer, (web) stores and consumers to be increasingly prepared to take on the responsibility of a more sustainable society.

In this chapter, I will discuss the concepts of "circular" and "sustainable," which are often deemed inseparable. I will focus on the differences with the use of resources in the linear economy and how important it is for retailers to contribute to the design of a circular model. The ten-R's model will be the basis for my discussion. Furthermore, I aim to discuss the increased use of packaging, the growing number of delivery miles, and their effects on emissions and energy consumption. Next, I will turn my attention towards the changing roles for producers, consumers and (web) stores in the circular economy. At the end of the chapter, I look at what I call the *circular retail paradox*. Why on earth would retailers decide to participate in a circular economy where onlife consumers are intent on consuming less, while still requiring vision, investments and a giant dose of tenacity? What would it take to accelerate the current, rather sedate and gradual transformation into a more radical transition process?

Circular and sustainable

The words "circular" and "sustainable" simply cannot be separated. You could describe the circular economy as the business model for shaping a sustainable management of a company. This does not always apply, though. The aim might be to conserve resources for the cycle and yet the transport, deconstruction and reassembly of the materials are all going to affect the environment, too. For this very reason, we cannot treat circular and sustainable as identical.

You can define "sustainable retail" as "enabling consumers in making purchases that are both socially conscious and environmentally sensitive towards every possible aspect of the manufacturing process." On the other hand, "circular retail" is "conserving the value of goods, parts thereof and required resources through efficiency of use and facilitating and stimulating reuse." For sustainable retail, the social and technical-environmental impact of a business can sometimes outweigh the interests of the consumer. In circular retail, making the cycle possible is what matters most. The two concepts are intrinsically entwined, however, and are likely to have immense impact in future decades: every single part of the retail value chain will feel their effects.

Within the circular economy, the main focus is on producers and their use of alternative designs and resources. Onlife retail has instead joined up all the interested parties: government, producers, consumers, waste processors and — certainly — (web) stores.

Use of resources in the linear economy

Right now, our economy is based on a linear system: we take resources from our planet and turn them into goods that are destroyed when they reach the end of their lifecycle. Nearly 80 percent of all goods are thrown away after six months. In this so-called *take-make-dispose* economy, everything of value is systematically destroyed at the end of the chain.

In *Waste to Wealth*,[2] Peter Lacy and Jakob Rutqvist distinguish between four types of waste in the linear economy:
1. *Wasted resources:* non-renewable resources and energy being lost irreversibly after being consumed, i.e. coal and gas.
2. *Wasted lifecycles:* goods with a short lifespan, even though they can still be used. Think: mobile phones that are just a few years old, clothes or furniture that have gone out of style.
3. *Wasted capabilities:* inefficiency of use. The very best example are cars that stand still for 23 out of 24 hours,[3] or delivery trucks and storage facilities that use only half their capacity.
4. *Wasted embedded values:* these are elements, materials and energy derived from defunct, abandoned goods that are not going to be reused. Just think of packaging that has been made from new resources.

The main issue with the current linear economy is that future generations will have to deal with the consequences. Our own children and grandchildren are going to have to handle polluted soil, oceans and air. At the very same time, there is a crisis of resources looming in the future.[4] According to estimates by the United Nations, the population of the world is set to increase from 7.4 billion (2016) to 8.5 billion in 2030 and to 9.6 billion in 2050.[5] Based on our current pattern of consuming, we will need one-and-a-half planets by 2030 if everyone is to have sufficient resources.

HELP! WE ARE RUNNING OUT OF RESOURCES!
For centuries, an impending crisis of resources has been a topic economists love to discuss. Back in 1865, British economist William Stanley
Jevons stated that England would soon be out of coal. He was terrified there would be a huge economic crisis, which led to the advent of
the Jevons paradox. This would prove its own validity many times over
in the centuries that followed. When the production of energy is made
more efficient, this leads to an increase of consumption, not a decline.
Very few economists believe there is an absolute shortage of resources. Humanity will always keep on discovering new resources or
workable substitutes.[6] There are still a lot of stones unturned and
ocean depths to be explored.

Use of resources in retail

Of course, retailers never stop trying to improve efficiency. Traditional stores find this a more obvious strategy than fast-growing
web stores, as the latter are often overwhelmed by their own pace
and forget, for example, to consider the best packaging method for
their goods. Generally, retailers aim to prevent packing too much
"air" (by using a box that is too big) or using too much packaging.
Besides, they like to streamline the efficiency of transport — both to
minimize emitting pollution and to achieve the greatest possible
number of deliveries with the smallest possible number of delivery
miles. They further consider the IT systems they use on account of
energy use.

The ten R's
The linear model of the value chain grinds to a halt at the consumer; the circular model keeps going, optimizing and maximizing the reuse of resources and goods, minimizing the destruction
of value. The first step is a smarter design paired with an increased
product lifespan. The last step is reusing parts and materials. The
optimum cyclical model has resources being endlessly used and reused again, in perpetuity, as a way to retain their value. Goods that
would be written off in the current system will be repaired, taken

apart, given other dimensions and turned into something new.

IKEA is testing renting out furniture as part of an eco-friendly plan that aims to match shoppers' demand for a more sustainable business model.[7] IKEA has already started asking customers to return their old mattresses to the store. They found a recycling partner to help use nearly 90 percent of them to make new products. The mattress foam is used for isolation materials or as a lower layer of carpets and judo mats. Wood fiber can be used as a secondary source of fuel, whereas wool and cotton can be turned into cleaning cloths. American re-commerce business thredUP has specialized in sales of second-hand designer clothes, cleaning and repairing them before selling them on their own marketplace. Dutch brand Leapp has built a successful business through the refurbishing of Apple products.

In her book *Circular Economy*, José Potting describes the ten R's: ways of treating resources with more care, graded from 0 to 9 for increased efficiency.[8] The table on the following pages provides an overview of these methods. To make sure retailers see the relevance, I've included an extra column with practical opportunities for retailers.[9]

Packaging
Every day, hundreds of millions of packages of every size you can imagine are packed up in distribution or fulfillment centers before being shipped to consumers. Goods that already have their own packaging are then wrapped once more, in a cardboard box or sealed plastic bag, which are both often used for extra padding. Nobody can tell you exactly how high the mountain of waste is, resulting from e-commerce packaging. What we do know is that it is evidently a huge problem.

Consumers are becoming more aware of the need for change in e-commerce packaging. They've started to refuse goods that have been packed twice and are extremely annoyed by small items being shipped in large boxes. In some countries retailers and manufacturers have no direct financial incentive to use custom-made boxes with less air, because delivery prices are based on weights instead of volumes. In other countries *dimensional pricing*, based on the weight-to-volume ratio, stimulates efficient packaging and distribution.[10]

THE TEN R'S OF THE CIRCULAR ECONOMY

Application		Description	
Smarter production and use	r0 Refuse	Rendering products obsolete by refusing its use or providing an alternative that uses no raw materials.	
	r1 Rethink	Intensifying the use of a product by, for example, sharing.	
	r2 Reduce	Improving production efficiency.	
Prolonging the lifespan of the product and its parts	r3 Reuse	Reusing discarded but still working goods for the same purpose but by a different user.	
	r4 Repair	Repair and maintenance of broken goods for use in its former purpose.	
	r5 Refurbish	Refurbishing or upcycling an old product.	
	r6 Remanufacture	Using parts of a discarded product to manufacture a new product for the same purpose.	
	r7 Repurpose	Using parts of a discarded product, or the whole thing, for a new product and a new purposes.	
Finding sensible uses for materials	r8 Recycle	Recycling materials into goods of similar or inferior quality.	
	r9 Recover	Incinerate material for energy production.	

Besides the air in the packages, there is wasted space in delivery vans. Using standardized packaging dimensions could produce increased efficiency in how to stack packages. The result: less superfluous air. Manufacturers and (web) stores find customer complaints to be a great incentives for improving their packaging policy. Further, smaller packages, cardboard boxes and mailing bags cut to size are also a way to cut back costs, resulting in increased overall efficiency.

Recently, Amazon launched *small and light*. From now on,

Facilitator as	Efficient use of 'own' raw materials
Retail can provide a digital platform to eliminate the use of raw materials. Just think of Spotify, which has rendered CDs obsolete.	Doing away with packaging (as much as possible).
Retail can provide a sharing platform.	Cooperating with competitors in logistics.
Retail can offer or pre-select efficient goods.	Packaging products with less surplus room.
Retail can provide a platform for reusing goods and materials.	Offering inventory for reuse after it's been written off.
Retail can offer repair services or facilitate these by working with a repair service or producer. Retail can inform consumers on DIY repairs. Retail can provide spare parts.	Repairing inventory instead of instantly replacing it.
Retail can take on the part of information source and facilitator for consumers who wish to dispose of materials. Retailers process spare parts themselves and reuse them in discarded products.	Using discarded inventory for remanufacturing.
	Remaining materials (including packaging) are offered for recycling.

small items — stickers, screen protectors, USB cords and so on — will be shipped in an envelope instead of a box.[11] Since 2014, the Green Box Project by LEGO — conceived to pack LEGO products in smaller and smaller packaging — has achieved a reduction in packaging of up to 7,000 tons. So it can be done after all.

One of the main issues is that virtually all packaging is still being designed for displays in physical stores. The boxes are not strong enough to be used for shipping and delivery. The perfect solution would be if goods were packaged in such a way by their manufacturers that they could be sold in-store and online alike.

New types of packaging materials, packaging solutions using as little surplus room as possible, and reuse and recycling – all of these are possible future solutions. As yet, there is no one-size-fits-all sustainable solution for the outer packaging of goods bought online. Every company chooses its own solution, which often depends on the number of shipments and the kinds of goods they sell.

ALL WRAPPED UP

A few years back, I fell prey to credit card fraud: an enormous parcel from London department store Harrods was delivered to my home. Curious as to the contents, I started to unwrap it, with my wife and children sitting around me. Inside the large cardboard box was a smaller, sturdy cardboard Harrods box, swathed in bubble wrap. A stunning box to look at, with scents emanating from it that I'd never thought to connect with cardboard boxes. In that Harrods box, there were mountains of paper confetti surrounding yet another box, this one a Valentino shoebox. Inside this, carefully wrapped in layers of tissue paper, was a pair of vibrantly colored, wildly extravagant Valentino sneakers. I wrapped it all up again: the tissue paper, the confetti, the bubble wrap and the three boxes. Back to London it went.

Transport

Often, logistics are the linking pin between all the players in the retail value chain. The rampant growth of online shopping has made the logistical process immensely more complex and exacting. Every single consumer has their own preferences. The result: a veritable tangle of logistics moving from producers and sales intermediaries to distribution and fulfillment centers, then to the final delivery (usually) on the consumer's doorstep. In years to come, as we watch online retail continue to grow, the number of individual transports are going to increase in proportion to that growth. If nobody steps up, the efficiency of delivery will start to disintegrate.

From a sustainability point of view, people often ask me whether it's better to have something delivered at home or to pick it up at an (in-store) pickup point, or to simply buy it in an actual store. There are literally dozens of factors that influence this process. Obviously, every single instance of delivery traffic translates into emissions of harmful gases and particulate matter. However, a van driving around with a handful of parcels is bound to have relatively more impact (per parcel) than one that is packed full. Driving into town for the sole purpose of picking up something from a pickup point has more impact on the environment compared to driving past such a pickup point on the way home from the office. Variables such as where distribution centers are located, the efficiency of the delivery trucks and vans, the number of returned parcels and how many attempts a delivery person has to make before they can actually deliver the order: it all matters. This still doesn't answer the question if online shopping is better or worse for the environment than shopping in-store.

The next few years will call for research to clarify all the effects of shifts in logistics and distribution within the retail value chain. What's required is a fundamental understanding of all the aspects of the logistics operation. The real unknown is the behavior of the onlife consumer, though. Their wish to see their orders delivered within 24 hours, on the same day, or even within a couple of hours is in perfect sync with their onlife existence. At the same time, I've noticed that onlife consumers sometimes deliberately go for the cheaper (or even free) option of having things delivered slightly (or a lot) later.

GLOBAL WARMING

The Carbon Disclosure Project has estimated that the earth's temperature will rise by 4 degrees in the future, if we do not act now. There are in fact 100 companies causing 71% of global CO_2 emissions – with the coal industry the biggest polluter of all.[12]

US President Trump doesn't think much of climate change. Even though 13 US government agencies confirm climate change is real and human actions are having an effect on the warming of the planet, Trump has said often climate change isn't real.[13]

As online retail increases, so does its effect on our supply of energy. After all, every single website search uses a certain amount of energy. Whenever we open an email, at home or at work, there is IT capacity being used, somewhere in the world, using electricity. All the IT everywhere is now emitting more CO_2 than the global air traffic. If we listen to the worst predictions, we will need all the energy being produced in a few years – around 2024 – to handle all the data traffic and data storage.

The exponential growth of data consumption translates into huge challenges for governments, businesses and retailers, both large and small. On average, a data park uses the energy equivalent of 900,000 homes. Data centers used by businesses will need to become more energy efficient in years to come.

Many retailers have begun to reduce the carbon footprint of their brick-and-mortar shops and distribution networks, but few have examined how e-commerce trends are transforming their carbon footprint. When a consumer buys goods online, the main factors influencing the total carbon emissions – namely last-mile delivery and packaging – are more difficult to measure.

WALMART STUDY
Walmart studied the emissions generated by its own brick-and-mortar retail stores compared with its e-commerce channel to understand the relative impact of each, both on average and for specific types of purchases. It found that store purchase are more efficient on average, but when customers purchase fewer items and would otherwise make a dedicated trip to the store, Walmart.com is the more efficient choice.[14]

The onset of the Internet of Things (IoT, discussed in Chapter 2) will certainly mean an even greater increase of data use. Retailers are going to need the ability to facilitate increasingly complex connections between systems, all of which cost energy. On the other hand, IoT means that IT systems could become more efficient and reduce wastefulness.

A first step towards reducing energy consumption is a clear grasp of how much energy is used by online retail services, which can then be translated into a green IT system.

Apart from making sure IT is energy efficient, it's essential to have the energy harnessed in a sustainable way. I believe that IoT and big data have a huge role to play in being energy conscious. More and more energy companies are shifting focus to renewable energy, local energy production and distribution. All over the world, we can see initiatives appearing to make local solar, wind and water energy production accessible for nearby businesses and citizens. Thanks to their immense buying power, global tech players, platforms and marketplaces, (online) department stores and web stores can insist on lower prices. This power might just as well be accessed to make renewable energy mainstream.

New roles in the circular economy

In today's economy, I have defined the following players in the retail value chain, seen from the viewpoint of the retailer: producers, consumers and (web) stores. At the end of the chapter, we will examine the role of government. There are new players on their way in, such as mineral processors, that will move into a key position in the next few decades because they are able to turn waste into new raw materials for manufacturing.

What we know for sure: the value chain is going to become more complex than ever. The division of roles in the chain will be transformed completely: consumers becoming producers and possibly even waste processors, producers turning into retailers. It begs the question if there will still be a set division of roles or if each segment of the retail chain will write its own playbook.

Producers turn into service suppliers

Among the first to anticipate the circular economy effects on the value chain are the producers. They will need to be open to the new and cyclical business models. Entering into immediate relationships with their end users is also key. Philips has started offering its customers the option of leasing lights, *light as a service.* The company also accepts the return of old lamps in order to give them a second lifecycle. Other manufacturers have taken to buying back used goods at the end of the product lifespan.

In cyclical business models, producers and manufacturers

never relinquish ownership of the goods; consumers simply pay to use them instead of owning them. This is one of many instances where the circular economy and the sharing economy converge.

When I walked through the streets of Beijing in 2017 and Shanghai in 2018 it was impossible to miss seeing thousands of the — what have now become — tens of millions of colorful bikes deployed by Chinese startups in Chinese cities. They can be rented cheaply on a smartphone. Ofo (backed by Alibaba) and Mobike (backed by Tencent) are the most successful of the bike-sharing companies to date. They offer rides costing as little as 15 cents for 30 minutes. Users can park the bikes anywhere they want, they don't have to look for designated docking stations.[15] The popularity of bike sharing has backfired in big Chinese cities as the industry has grown too big too fast, with bicycles scattered across China's urban sidewalks, where piles of underused bikes have been dumped.[16]

In the circular economy, goods are designed and produced in a manner that makes it easy to take them apart at the end of their lifespan. The objective is to reuse as much as possible of them, with no loss of quality. Products that can be disassembled make it easy to regain the individual materials used or to reuse them in a more pure fashion. Non-durable goods such as toothpaste or laundry detergent should all be biodegradable.

The product performance is what determines its future success, which means that the right quality will become hugely important. This is another reason why the disassembly of goods is an essential part of product design. This translates into an easy way of renewing or replacing spare parts, which all adds up to an improved lifespan. Google has been cooperating with the startup Phoneblock to make the camera, battery and processor of its Android phones easy to replace.[17]

Consumer opportunities: buyers versus users

There are lots of consumers who recycle paper, glass, textiles and plastic. It helps them to feel they are doing their part to conserve the planet. They also faithfully take old and broken goods to their local recycling station. I know I always feel a sense of fulfillment after my weekly drive taking paper, glass and plastic to the recycling and old stuff down to the local thrift store. For years, people have sold off their old clothes, books and home goods at yard sales or markets. Sometimes furniture ends up being upcycled thanks to thrift stores. In our digital age, this has all been given an on-line makeover. Online marketplaces such as eBay or platform sites where you can give away stuff — think of Freecycle.org — are help-ing make reuse simpler than ever.

In the circular economy, the role of the onlife consumer is being seriously transformed. Consumers were accustomed to being the end user of products in the linear economy. Instead, they can now choose between three new additional product-service systems.[18] These new types of "ownership" are all ways of recycling raw ma-terials.

1 Pay-per-use

What would happen if people started preferring the access to and use of durables to ownership and possession? It could create a rad-ical breakthrough in society and be an incredible boost to both the circular and the sharing economy. Many young people are already used to the *pay-per-use* principle with their smartphone contracts. Businesses, too, are experimenting with this, or have even taken responsibility. The Dutch companies MUD Jeans and Bundles are putting pay-per-use into practice. Consumers can lease a pair of jeans for € 7.50 a month at MUD Jeans. The company remains the owner and takes them back after a year to be reused or to sell them on as "vintage" on their website. In pay-per-use the consumer (or the user, in fact) pays a set amount or a monthly fee to use the product. The producer retains ownership and stays responsible for maintenance and any repairs, and ultimately for recycling of the goods.

Or, what about the "clean laundry" service provided by Bundles ("We love laundry")? Bundles sets people up with Miele washing machines, and the users pay for each load through an app. The ma-chine is still owned by Bundles and can be sent back to the factory if need be for revision or upgrades. By analyzing user data, Bundles helps users do their laundry efficiently, saving both power and de-tergent in the process and reducing wear-and-tear to the machine.

Why should there not be similar services for clothes, DIY items, electronic appliances, and so on? Why should a service not replace a product? There are obvious advantages: maximum use of the product, with (re)users needing not spend any money to own, repair, maintain or insure it, all while helping make society more sustainable.

2 Buy-repurchase

Another interesting consumer option occurs when (web) stores or manufacturers offer to buy back the product after it's been used for a certain length of time. This becomes part of the sales agreement from the word "go". The (web) store or producer can then resell the product, renew it or use its parts to produce new goods.

3 Buy-sell-on

A third option is that goods are sold to a waste processor after they've been used. Obviously, this will mostly happen when goods have little or no further possible use to anyone. Consumers can be assured of still getting something in return and are secure in the knowledge that the parts and materials can find a new use, somehow.

(Web) stores

Stores will still be linchpin between producer and consumer, though the circular economy will turn them into caretakers who relieve consumers of their worries. Slowly but surely, we will see a shift from sales towards use. (Web) stores will become the sellers of service agreements provided by producers, for users. They can, of course, add on their own services, such as recovery, installation, repair or pick-up when goods have reached the end of their lifecycle.

Retailers have a part to play in nudging the circular economy along. The buyers at large (web) stores can force producers and suppliers to adapt to their production methods and become more sustainable. Swedish-based fashion retailer H&M will make all of its product from recycled or eco-friendly materials by 2030.[19] H&M has been launching an annual Conscious Exclusive collection of sustainable clothing for several years now.[20] IKEA has a "people, planet positive strategy" focused on providing customers inspiration to live more sustainable and healthy lives at home, including a business practice that strives not to depend on resources.[21] Walmart has announced plans to obtain 50 percent of its energy from renewable sources by 2025.[22]

Another option is that goods being bought back at the end of their lifecycle can actually provide a new influx of working capital. As a result, (web) stores, producers and consumers may, in fact, need to spend less. It's interesting for everyone involved to see if existing goods, or parts thereof, can be repaired or reused.

New business models

Lacy and Rutqvist describe five new business models:[23]

1. Circular input models. These are focused on producing goods through the use of renewable and/or biodegradable raw materials. Ultimately, this kind of goods will prove less expensive than things made out of traditional materials. Producers will find they are less reliant on the supply of materials from abroad. Online retailers can encourage the sales of these goods by adding "sustainability" to the selection criteria for searching their range.

2. Waste value models. This kind of model deals with creating materials out of waste through recycling or upcycling. Recycling is the breaking down of the original material to then produce something new. Upcycling is reusing an object or its material without taking it apart first. Recycling tends to use more energy than upcycling does. Both methods will mainly be done by parties which create and produce large amounts of waste. Retailers can then ensure their old and used goods end up at these waste processors.

3. Lifespan models. There are various ways to increase the lifespan of goods, including repair, upgrading or remanufacturing, or even simply re-selling them. Retailers have a part to play as facilitators by selling spare parts and providing extensive product information online about small repairs so that the end users can do those repairs themselves.

4. Platform models. Here, there are ways to better utilize goods by sharing them, renting them out or re-selling. This is a particularly interesting means of making money for retailers who have an online platform already.

5. Goods-as-services models. This is when the producer retains ownership of the goods and offers them to consumers as a ser-

vice instead. Retailers facilitate in this model by entering into, or selling on, contracts with consumers, or by providing an environment for consumers to use such services.

The circular retail paradox

The circular retail paradox is both a necessity — on account of scarcity of materials — and an opportunity, because it produces new business models and new jobs. McKinsey has estimated that a shift towards the circular economy can add 1 trillion dollars to the global economy in 2025.[24] In Europe, the manufacturing industry can take advantage of savings in (raw)materials, which could amount to 630 billion dollars in 2025. According to the action program Circular Economy 2020 Vision, the EU can benefit from an improved trade balance worth 90 million pounds.

New jobs will appear: brokers where consumers can get rid of their used goods, designers of products that are easy to disassemble, technicians who are able to repair durable goods or prepare them for reuse or disassembly, and administrators who can take stock of the raw materials. McKinsey believes there will be 100,000 new jobs in the United States and 160,000 in the EU in the next five years.[25] These are serious numbers to take into account, which further emphasize the importance and potential of the circular economy.

So they should, for the use of raw materials has doubled from 1980-2020 and is set to triple from 2020-2050 if we extrapolate from the current growth. As prosperity continues to grow, so too the use of raw materials will soar. The linear system will find itself stretched to its very limit. In 2012, 32 percent of small and midsized businesses were having difficulties with the supply of raw materials; 40 percent expects this to be a serious long-term problem.[26] There plenty of opportunities and an obvious need for change, yet there are many obstacles to overcome for all the parties in the value chain.

The paradox for businesses

Most retailers are not naturally inclined to committing to sustainable business. They tend to wait and see, lacking proactivity, and want to find out how innovations (often subsidized by government) by startups in the circular economy are going to turn out. They wait and see which way the wind blows, so to speak, because there are no business models available that will benefit their business result in the short term. Mostly, it remains to be seen how they can fit in between producers and consumers.

The immediate financial interests (both long- and short-term) of entrepreneurs and shareholders are, for the most part, not particularly enhanced by the circular economy. Rather, the opposite is true. Important principles of the circular economy — such as sharing goods or increasing their lifespan — are in direct defiance of the linear principles of increasing turnover and growing profits. Besides, recycling still costs money, especially since it is not possible to recoup 100 percent of the raw materials. How does a retailer make money when they're trying to give your products an extra long lifespan?

Traditional retail is based on replacement buys, which keep being postponed now, thanks to new materials and improved production methods (just ask car dealers and electronics salesmen). It was the political establishment, not the manufacturing industry, that decided to outlaw traditional light bulbs, which meant we all had to switch to low-energy ones.

Businesses will need to tap into their creativity if they are to develop new business models capable of reducing costs and providing added value to consumers. Until the urgency is upon them, until there is no profit left to be made, businesses are not going to hop on the circular bandwagon. Big businesses have to lead the way forward in the paradigm shift from linear to circular — tech companies such as Amazon, Apple, Facebook, Google, Microsoft and Alibaba. At the moment, Amazon is extremely committed to avoiding the whole topic of sustainability.[27] The tech giant is struggling with the issues of employee management, recycling and the lack of numbers on sustainability. Organizations such as Greenpeace and Climate Counts have stated that it's but a matter of time before consumers will start to judge them on these issues.[28]

Conversely, Apple, Google and Microsoft have incorporated sustainable thinking into their daily businesses. With its slogan "Our planet deserves our best thinking", Apple has been the teacher's pet for years. Liam the robot has been dismantling 1.2 million iPhones a year, 93 percent of their factories use renewable energy, and Apple has proven that using environmentally friendly materials can indeed be done.[29] It's even announced to work towards having all its products be made out of recycled material and reused products.[30] Google has been investing in cleaner data centers and has helped contribute to a cleaner planet by collecting data from Google Earth, Google Forest Watch and the Sunroof Project. Microsoft is also widely seen as one of the frontrunners of sustainable business. They consume over 2.5 billion kilowatt hours of renewable energy annually, with a 100 percent rate of renewable energy use at their US businesses, making it an even "greener" company than Apple or Google.[31]

The paradox for government

For governments the paradox is that they have work together to work towards a circular economy. Yet, their influences tends to be limited to their 'own' national policies, plans, regulations and measures. Within Europe, the disjointed implementation of European regulations for retrieval of large household appliances at consumers' homes by web stores is immensely frustrating. Web stores in countries that monitor compliance to these regulations still have to compete with web stores in those countries where implementation has been delayed to the long term. Besides, a sizeable proportion of national governments are unable to adequately oversee the presence of foreign businesses in their domestic market.

The role of national government can no longer be confined to their own country, though. The only real stimulus for the circular economy will happen when countries work together. In a glocal economy (more on this topic in Chapter 5), governments will increasingly be forced to transcend their borders to achieve agreements and shared policies with other countries. The results of the 2016 Paris climate conference are hopeful: for the first time ever, countries proved capable of reaching an international consensus on CO2 emissions.

Scaling up to an international circular economy requires the support of all the national governments involved. They can provide a stimulus by the dissemination of knowledge and raising awareness. They can use legislation and regulations to encourage minimal waste production and introduce incentives for manufactures who produce goods that are easier to repair, reuse, repurpose or dismantle. They can offer tax breaks to businesses that mitigate the ecological impact of their activities, stimulating the circular economy in the process. Last but not least, the government can be a network partner by uniting all the relevant stakeholders.

The United Nations were the ones setting 17 global goals for sustainable development, in 2015, to be achieved by 2030. Governments and businesses all around the world can use these goals as a compass for sustainable strategies and ways to run a business.[32] Things are starting to happen already: China has set up the CACE, a government-supported association to stimulate circular growth; Scotland has introduced its own circular economy blueprint, and the European Commission has set new and higher goals for all the 27 member states of the EU in its circular economy framework. Euro-commissioner Frans Timmermans, in charge of the European program for circular economy packages, plans to convince businesses to invest in the circular economy.[33]

The paradox for consumers

Most people do care about sustainability, but when it's crunch time, they often lack the money, time or effort to act on it. They would like to eat and drink organically, just not every day. They do realize that ordering a dress in three different sizes is not particularly responsible because of the need to return two, but still order it because it is so easy. They are very happy to reduce the number of plastic bags, but forget to take a bag with them when they go shopping. They recycle religiously and even use their bike to go places, just not every day. They might talk about purchasing solar panels, "green" energy or a more energy-efficient car, but often it is just that: talk. Besides, a lot of consumers are wary of this topic: how can you be sure that the energy really is renewable, or the food really organic?

Yet, I can see people's mentality changing, albeit slowly. On account of the greater transparency surrounding all the aspects of the retail value chain, people are now better equipped for informed decisions. Thanks to the Internet, they have constant access to information about where materials are from and how their purchases were manufactured. The growing popularity of second-hand markets, sharing platforms and online marketplaces is not just about saving money. In the past, possessions tied in with social success and status; now, some onlife consumers feel that using them suffices.

What's next?

Regardless of the decades of calls to action by civil society, no one really stepped up, certainly not on an international scale.[34] Until now, investment in sustainability has been relatively small, regardless of whether it was based on principles or on commercial gain. Sustainability architect Thomas Rau says the shift to the circular economy calls for nothing short of a mental transformation.[35] This could well be brought about by an event that emphasizes the need to change, and change soon. Large disasters or horrifying geopolitical movements could easily incite us to radically change course. For instance, the 2011 nuclear disaster in Fukushima clearly showed the whole world how vulnerable we are in our society and our economy.[36] Russia annexing the Crimean peninsula, and the subsequent economic sanctions by Western countries, roused us into considering our reliance on Russian gas.[37] For a short time, the West seemed willing to turn down the heating that winter. Who knows; perhaps the climate change denial of Donald Trump, the retreat of the United States from the Paris climate agreement, and the decision of the Trump administration to create millions of jobs in fossil fuel will all prove to be a wakeup call for countries, businesses and citizens.[38]

The big shift from linear to circular is not going to happen because we care so much about the environment. Ultimately, it comes down to cost benefits, simplicity of use and, most of all, the sense of just doing the right thing. If we manage to blend these key drivers of behavior change as a society, then sustainability will become the new normal.

"Internet is like a force of nature. It has four very powerful qualities that will result in its ultimate triumph: decentralizing, globalizing, harmonizing and empowering."

**NICHOLAS NEGROPONTE,
PROFESSOR OF TECHNOLOGY AT MIT**[1]

5

Winner takes all in the platform economy

Traditional economy	Platform economy
Ads	Metasearch engine
Department stores	Marketplaces
Free trade	Protectionism
Globalization	(De)globalization
Local retail	Glocal retail
Local stores	Worldwide shopping ecosystems
Monopoly	Monopsony
National economy	Global economy
Shops/webshops	Platforms
Store	Omnichannel
United We Stand	America First
Villagers	Global citizens
Villages, towns	Global village

All is well in the world. According to the Legatum Prosperity Index — an independent index measuring wealth, economic growth, education, health, personal wellbeing and quality of life — the world has never been in better shape than it is today[2]. New drugs mean a longer and healthier life for more people than ever. Education has a big impact on people managing to gradually break free of extreme poverty in emerging markets. Improved information and communication technology have turned us into citizens of the world, with the rest of the world at our fingertips at the click of a mouse. By 2020, almost 5 billion people are predicted to be connected through the Internet: truly a global village[3]. Over the past decades, developments in technology have been a huge boost to globalization, resulting in global free trade of goods, services, capital and labor. Similar to previous surges in industrialization, this has opened up new markets, led to an immense increase in productivity and provided billions of people with opportunities to improve their lives[4].

Yet, there are cracks in the perfect veneer as well. Large tech companies may have brought the world into our homes, but many politicians and citizens are concerned about the extent of their growing power and how much we depend on them.

All the gains in wealth cannot hide that the world is still suffering from the threat and impact of war and terror. National governments are buckling under the pressure from new political movements and groups. Their common denominator: disdain for established politics, the business establishment and its endless yearning for globalization.

Politicians on the right feel compelled to set things to rights within their country's borders. De-globalization has become a topic now. This compulsion is increasingly echoed by great swathes of voters, as Donald Trump's election has made abundantly clear. In Europe, the relentless river of refugees paired with an unpredictable economy has produced a frustrated and wary electorate, whose income has come to a screeching standstill and failed to improve for several years.[5] The ensuing discontent was a key factor in the unexpected Brexit vote of 2016.[6] The negative impact of globalization — exemplified by strict tax laws and regulations, structural economic reform and massive national debt — has lodged a profound sense of unease in people's minds that it will not benefit humanity as a whole.[7][8]

Politicians on the left are equally disenchanted by the growing differences in wealth and the huge concentration of riches for a handful of companies and individuals,[9] especially now that the economy in the Western hemisphere and SE Asia seem to be on the mend. The Global Wealth Report has estimated that one percent of the world's population possesses over half of all the property and wealth.[10] Silicon Valley giants and their CEOs have thus become poster boys and girls for extremely condensed power and riches.

Many politicians feel that, on top of this inequality, new businesses and technological developments are in fact destabilizing. Fearful of massive job layoffs in years to come, they worry about the social unrest that may well be the result of robotization, artificial intelligence and machine learning. Personal feelings of insecurity and distrust are everywhere, and they tend to zoom in on the political and economic establishment.

This chapter is about the "glocal" platform economy, with its pendulum swinging back and forth between the world at large (global) and individual neighborhoods (local). This economy, in fact, presents governments and retailers with momentous questions and unprecedented challenges. It also furiously insists they look beyond their own frames of reference.

In the first part of the chapter, I will discuss current and new global players in retail. Over the next few years , if nothing changes, they will expand their positions in the global market and create unforeseen monopolies of power. They are already firm favorites of onlife consumers, posing tough challenges for retailers and constant worries for national governments.

In part two, I will deal with the so-called prisoner's dilemma for local businesses. Do you try to keep up with the rat race instigated by the tech giants, or do you aim instead to build a strong market presence in your own local market by tapping into old-school retail methods of the past, where the customer was pampered with personal service?

In part three, I will delve into the various options for national and European government bodies to handle the glocal platform economy, as it slowly but steadily is turning into a winner-takes-all-economy.

The rise of shopping ecosystems

Over the course of two decades, we've watched numerous businesses ride the waves of the Internet to their advantages and global breakthroughs. Many of them had humble beginnings as startups in garages and college dorm rooms, where their founders tapped into opportunities for adding value to both existing and new markets and business sectors.

Since then, those early online pioneers have grown into global marketplaces and platforms (Amazon, Alibaba, eBay), search engines (Google), tech companies (Apple, Microsoft, Samsung), and shopping platforms with a focus on strong internal markets (Tencent/WeChat and JD.com in China, Rakuten in Japan and Southeast Asia). New international players have emerged in recent years, including social media giants (Facebook, Instagram, Snapchat and Telegram), sharing platforms (Airbnb, Etsy, Uber) and niche platforms for fashion (Zalando), travel (Expedia) and hotels (Priceline/Booking.com; Ctrip in China). Within two decades, these businesses have morphed into the top dogs in their own market segments. Thanks to immense domestic markets — China, Japan and the United States — they were able to grow at an incredible rate, creating staggering upscaling on the way. The time-to-market for these companies, as they took full advantage of the Internet and digitization, was nothing short of perfect. Their incredible savvy at shaping the new reality to fit their own specifications is nearly astounding.

EUROPE IS MISSING THE BOAT

Out of the 100 largest marketplaces and platforms in the world, 70 are from the United States, 25 from China and only 5 from Europe. There is no European Google, Facebook or WeChat. In fact, Booking.com, Spotify and Zalando are only a handful of European attempts at joining in.

The question as to whether these new businesses played fair on the way to gaining the top market position in their field is rarely a topic of discussion. After all, they simply played out the first-mover advantage in existing and new markets to its absolute optimum. Stunningly successful IPOs and annual turnovers — ranging from tens of billions to well into the hundreds of billions in dollars, euros, yuan and yen — have made these companies to the very top of the world. Alphabet (Google), Amazon, Apple, Facebook, Microsoft (the "Big Five"), plus Alibaba and Tencent (the "Seven Sisters"), keep on gobbling up more market share, profit and capital. Their profits and growth rates often manage to surprise market analysts, not to mention how they make the retail figures of more traditional markets pale into insignificance. Unsurpassed rates on the stock market and booming liquidity leave them free to make enormous acquisitions and further boost and strengthen their global market positions. Spreading their wings into adjacent markets — think: automotive, biotechnology, entertainment, financial services, healthcare, media and last but not least, retail — is a given.

Their shared characteristic is that they are essentially all tech companies. "Amazon is a technology company. We just happen to do retailing," is an oft-quoted phrase of Amazon founder and CEO Jeff Bezos. Billons of consumers have eagerly embraced the services of these platforms based on their ability to put the customer first, offer them unbridled advantages and never fail to deliver on their promises. Onlife consumers happily welcome the innovations of these businesses and experience no downsides of alleged monopolies in some countries occupied by these powerful companies.

These superpowers act as a kind of new intermediaries, bringing consumers together from different sectors, and they also have exactly what it takes to succeed when they venture into new markets.

Because of their involvement in almost every single step of the customer journey (see the table 'Global shopping ecosystems'), they have access to every single scrap of data of the end users.

Unprecedented scale, span of influence and accessible cash flow add up to the ability to shape and mold the infrastructure and value chain of retail as they see fit. They are expanding into shopping portals and platforms, opening up marketplaces and adding options to buy to their websites and apps. Over the next few years, we will see these global platforms evolve into true shopping ecosystems.

Shopping ecosystems are nothing more than global, interconnected technological networks with the ability to provide people and businesses with a perfect and never-ending customer journey in which the desired goods and services are always on tap. Being a *one-stop-shop* is part of their magic: onlife consumers can find just about anything they could possibly want. The shopping infrastructure has been personalized to the max. Manufacturers of brands and (web) stores alike can find all the required services of the retail value chain: fulfillment, payment options, cloud services or riding the waves of delivery and loyalty programs, all of which are part of the ecosystem.

GLOBAL SHOPPING ECOSYSTEMS

	Alibaba	Amazon	Apple
Own brand	JinglingX1	Kindle, Fire, Pinzon, AmazonBasics, Amazon Echo, Amazon Dash	iPhone, iMac, iWatch, Mac, iPod, Homepod
Delivery service	Alibaba Logistics, Cainiao	Prime Now, FBA, Amazon Flex, Amazon Prime Air, Amazon Fresh, Instant Delivery, Amazon Shipping	—
Cloud/web computing	Alibaba Cloud Computing	Amazon Web Services (AWS), Amazon Drive	iCloud
Mail service	—	Amazon Simple Email Service (SES)	iCloud
Shopping	Alibaba.com, Taobao TMall Global, 1688.com, Juhuasuan	Amazon.com, Amazon MarketPlace, Amazon Business, Amazon Go	Apple.com
Film/series/tv/ video/streaming service	TMall Box Office (TBO)	Amazon Video, Amazon Video Direct, Twitch	Apple TV
Music/streaming service	Alibaba Planet, Xiami Music	Prime Music	Apple Music
Photo service	Photo Bank	Prime Photos, Shutterfly (printing photos), Amazon Prints	Apple Photos
App Store	9Apps	Amazon App Store	Apple App Store
News service	UC News	—	Apple News
Advertising network	Tabao, Tmall, Alimama	Amazon Advertising	Search Ads
Payment system	AliPay	Amazon Pay	Apple Pay
Operating system	Yun OS	Fire OS	iOS, Mac OSX
Chat service	Laiwang, AliWang-Wang, DingDing	Anytime	iMessage
Tv/film/game producers	Alibaba Pictures Group	Amazon Studios	—
Loyalty program	—	Amazon Prime	iPhone Upgrade
Home Speaker Devices	Genie	Echo	HomePod

Facebook	Google	Microsoft	Tencent/WeChat
Oculus	Pixel, Nexus, Plus, Chrome, Google Home, Google Glass Enterprise, Nest	Xbox, Office, Windows Phone, Invoke Speaker	Weibo
—	Google Express	—	Ele.me
—	Google Cloud, Google Drive	Microsoft Cloud, Azure, OneDrive	Tencent Cloud
—	Gmail	Outlook	QQ Mail
Facebook Marketplace, Messenger	Google Shopping	Microsoftstore.com	WeChat
Facebook Live, Instagram Live, Facebook TV	YouTube, YouTube Live Streaming, YouTube Gaming	Azure Media Service, Mixer	sv.qq.com, Penguin Esports, Now Live, Tencent Video
Facebook Music Stories	Google Play Music	Groove Music	QQ music, Qzone, Kuguo
Facebook Moments, Instagram	Google Photos, Google Photo Books	Microsoft Photos	WeChat, Qzone
App Center, Gameroom	Google Play	Windows Store	WeChat Game, Ying Yong Bao
Facebook News	Google News	Microsoft News, News Pro	QQ.com, Tencent News
Facebook for Business, Facebook Ads	Adwords, AdSense, Analytics	Microsoft Advertising, Bing Ads	Tencent Social Ads, Tencent Open Platform
Messenger Payments	Google Pay	Microsoft Wallet	Tenpay, WeChat Pay, QQ Wallet
—	Android	Windows, Windows Mobile	TOS+
WhatsApp, Messenger	Google Hangouts	LinkedIn, Microsoft Teams	WeChat, QQ
—	—	Microsoft Studios	Tencent Penguin Pictures
—	—	Bing Rewards	—
—	Home	Cortana	Xiaowei

The global shopping ecosystems are unsurpassed in utilizing the platform and network economy and scaling up to their advantages. Their chosen method of providing their very own excellent services is precisely what keeps boosting and bolstering their market position, not to mention their power. Consumers (in particular) and smaller retailers can tap into the advantages, too, though the latter seem to struggle with the monopsony-type behavior of the shopping ecosystems.

MONOPSONY BEHAVIOR?

A monopsony can be described as a market with one single buyer: the monopsonist. This party is in fact the sole customer, the linking pin for all the other parts of the value chain. As a result, the buyer has such a powerful market position that they can dictate the price point for whatever they want to buy. Because individual sellers in the value chain are rendered powerless to influence their own prices, there is no true competition.[11]

Monopsonies are rare. Actually, governments are the only real ones we ever come across, as the sole buyers of road construction, for example. In a democracy, parliament provides a check to prevent the government from abusing its position of power. In business, this check is in the hands of supervisory bodies and politicians.

In a monopoly, the end users – consumers, most likely – are the ones losing out: they may be up against an unfair inflation of prices. In a monopsony, however, businesses feel the consequences. The increased power for shopping ecosystems translates into retailers becoming ever more dependent on these global superpowers, without whom they have no hope at all of reaching an equal number of customers.

"Some say Google is God, some say that it is Satan. But if they think Google is too powerful, remember that with search engines, unlike other companies, all it takes is a single click to go to another search engine."

SERGEY BRIN, CO-FOUNDER OF GOOGLE[12]

One thing is for sure: Google has the ambition to grow to become a global shopping ecosystem. I spoke with several Google executives when Eric Schmidt — CEO of parent company Alphabet — visited Amsterdam. For the first time ever, they admitted that they have reached a point of no return: in the years to come, Google will become a retailer of unprecedented dimensions. The subsidiary companies of Alphabet will make this come true: Android (cell phones), Google Search (search engines), YouTube (video services), Google Home (home speaker device), Google Apps, Google Maps, Google AdWords (ads), and last but not least, Google Shopping.

SHOPPING AT GOOGLE

Google Shopping is the company's retail platform, and it's rapidly becoming more popular. While Google Flights (airline tickets) and Google Hotel Finder (hotel bookings) may still be in their infancy, Google Shopping has already emerged as the go-to retail platform. You cannot miss the ad banner at the top of the page above the search results. There may be some small print hinting at the fact that it's sponsored by Google Shopping, but the layout and content easily beat the normal search results, which take a lower position on the page. Retailers are not given the option of buying similar ad banners with visually appealing product photos themselves.

Being included in the search results of Google Shopping is something businesses are willing to pay top dollar for. The auction system behind it pushes the price to a higher level yet, for which Google offers some optimization tools in return. What's more significant is the fact that when you are doing business with Google Shopping you're obliged to hand over to Google all the data your (web) store has collected. The search engine thus ends up with the very best (product) information in the world, free to collect and exploit it. Google hits it out of the ballpark, so to speak — nor does it have any inhibitions in ultimately opening up its own web store and fully integrating said product information into that store. Payments would then be processed through Google Pay and goods subsequently delivered through Google Express. In 2017, the European Commission fined Google with a staggering 2.7 billion dollars for abuse of power by displaying its own Google Shopping in its search engine results above other comparison sites.[13]

There is little mystery behind the developments at Google Shopping (see box), Google Flights and Google Hotel Finder. Through acquiring Nest (smart thermostats), developing the self-driving car, supplying users with its own web browser through Google Chrome and payment options through Google Pay, adding paid channels to YouTube to rival Netflix, offering thousands of e-books through Google Play, rolling out its own line of Nexus tablets and bringing Google Home into our kitchens and living rooms, the onlife consumer cannot help falling head over heels for Google.

Add access to the data of billions of search engine users to the data of more than 1.5 billion Android smartphone users, and retailers — European ones in particular — have no way around Google Shopping. Google's market share of over 90 percent in almost all 31 European countries, in African and Asian countries (except for China)[14] begs the obvious question: can retailers worldwide even manage without Google as their primary search engine?[15]

As Google feels other shopping ecosystems breathing down its neck, the road to retail may be inevitable. Amazon, for one, has started to nibble away at Google's core business of search engines. Every single country where Amazon has rolled out its successful customer loyalty program Prime has seen Google subsequently lose a significant share of the market. Loyal Amazon customers no longer turn to Google for their initial search for goods and services, opting instead to go directly to Amazon.[16] The name "Amazon" has even become the most frequently searched retail word on Google — in the United States, at least.[17] Germany, too, has seen Amazon become the top retail search engine.

"Amazon, the everything store that wants to eat global retail"
EUGENE WEI, AMAZON STRATEGIST FROM 1997–2004[18]

Over the past two decades, Amazon has transformed itself from online bookstore to global shopping ecosystem with no equal. Rightly so: around one billion items in-store entitle the brand to call itself the *everything store*. All sales are handled by its own warehouse and through Amazon Marketplace. Active in over 200 countries and holding over 300 million active customer accounts, the company is the definitive market leader in nearly all Western countries.[19] Amazon holds more than 40 percent of the market for online consumer sales in the United States[20] and between 20 and 30 percent in the United Kingdom, France and Germany. However, the government-protected market of China has only allowed Amazon to garner a 1 percent share.[21] On the stock market since 1997, the company has since seen year-over-year record growth of its turnover, making it the second largest retailer in the Western world after Walmart.[22] The annual growth of Amazon's warehouse and Marketplace ranges from 20 to 30 percent.[23] Possibly even more significant is the fact that for some years around more than 50 percent of the growth rate for consumer online spending is accounted for by Amazon's still-profitable business model.[24]

Much has been said and written in recent years about the alleged abuse of power by Amazon. Clearly, the company is slowly increasing its pressure on partners and businesses participating in the Marketplace. For years now, it has insisted that Amazon itself is entitled to offering the lowest price.[25] As a result, retailers need to swallow lower profit margins. It is not uncommon for Amazon's fulfillment services (FBA) to unexpectedly double or triple its compensation for the required mark-up on goods, such as, for example, during the American holiday season.[26]

Similar to Google, Amazon awards the best spot to the highest bidder, which means the first visible spot on the Amazon Marketplace. All over the world, retailers are jointly spending in excess of 10 billion dollars every year on commission and compensation. Many retailers feel this is a relentless *race to the bottom*, with Amazon emerging as the clear and only winner.

Competition from its own web superstore with the (web) stores and brands on the Marketplace has been evident for a long time. Whenever a product sells well in the Marketplace, you can bet your life that it will soon appear as one of Amazon's own products, sold through its own warehouse — at a lower price. Nor does the tech giant have any qualms in launching brands of its own to compete with retailers that opt to leave the Amazon ecosystem. Private labels for domestic appliances (Pinzon), tablets (Kindle), computer accessories (AmazonBasics), fashion (Society New York, Lark and Ro, Franklin and Freeman), coffee (Happy Belly) and baby food (Mama Bear) are all examples of Amazon continuing to expand its products: footwear, jewelry, watches and last but not least, food.[27] [28]

AMAZON'S WHOLE FOODS DEAL

For lots of food retailers, the news that Amazon bought Whole Foods supermarkets has given the incentive they've needed for ages to rethink how to reinvigorate the physical shopping world. Besides the given that Amazon wants to move ahead in the grocery delivery business, attract more premium food vendors, it provides Amazon the opportunity to play its innovation and integration card. It's able to truly link online and offline worlds and pull together a number of its products. For one, it gives the online retailer access to high-foot-traffic real estate and a knowledge base of how to run such a high-traffic business. Second, it gives Amazon a place to roll out Amazon Go as it builds up that technology. Third, it's providing a base to further expand its existing grocery options which are exclusive to Prime members, Amazon Pantry and Amazon Fresh. Fourth, it'll be able to make Amazon Alexa and Echo Dot more attractive as part of its "speak and spend" process as Amazon wants to secure its place in kitchens with its own sets of smart home speaker devices.[29] Finally and fifth, the big gain for Amazon lies in combining all the collected data from both online and offline customers.

Concerns

The huge tech companies themselves are vocal in their denial of any kind of monopoly or monopsony. After all, they provide consumers with the best possible information, an unparalleled supply with perfect sales conditions, and the best price. True, there are no signs (yet) of consumers suffering from inflated prices, which is a key characteristic in any monopoly. The companies are equally adamant in their denial of the abuse of power they were accused of by US market supervisors and the European Commission. No one is forcing retailers or brands into doing business with them; or are they?

They tend to adopt the line of thinking voiced by Venezuelan economist Moises Naím, who argues that it's simply a matter of time before new businesses and startups manage to reduce the power of the companies that are currently so powerful and make their rightful bid for power themselves.[30] Naím is convinced it has never been easier to reach a billion consumers, at no great investment to your business. Competing with the huge and powerful companies has never been easier, either, because businesses can start out as globally operating firms from the word "go".[31] It's simply a matter of time before someone discovers a new search engine algorithm, a 3D social media environment, a new virtual department store, a new concept for an out-of-the-box marketplace, or a new blockchain application that will blow the current global players right out of the water.

It remains to be seen, however, if this hypothesis will prove viable in a market where the big guns tend to define the future of startups. Can newcomers truly match the innovative ability, size and scale, not to mention the budgets, of those platforms? If the tech giants fail to keep the startups at bay, they can simply buy them — something that was hardly a rare occurrence in the past few years. Point of fact: Naím's book only caught the public eye two years after it appeared, when Mark Zuckerberg put the book at the top of his reading list.

The true threats for the open market and free trade are, in fact, not the monopolies held by the global shopping ecosystems. Instead, it is the role they play of monopsony within the retail value chain. The very essence of monopsonies is that they force others into a position of *dependence:* if retailers want to be found, or want to do business on a global scale, they have no way of avoiding these platforms. It's a position that few governments, retailers and consumers are aware of — let alone taking action against — though it should be grabbing everyone's attention.

The prisoner's dilemma for retailers

Should retailers regard the shopping ecosystems as a threat or an opportunity? Sadly, this is a deceptively hard question to answer. All over the world, tens of millions national, regional and local stores are vying for the attention of onlife shoppers in malls, shopping streets and online. The vast majority opts to go along with the business dealings of platforms such as Amazon, Alibaba or Google, despite the fact they might put their own business in jeopardy by taking part in these platforms. They have to — there is just no other way for them to reach the same immense number of (inter) national customers. Retailers everywhere need to scale up if they are to break even. They tend to regard the high advertising costs of Google, or the payoff to Amazon or Alibaba, as an inevitable investment.

Some of them ultimately find the price too high. For all the success stories of businesses who do well on these platforms, there are countless retailers whose experience is starkly different: the high commission fees and compensation they have to pay have chipped away at their businesses, with the strict conditions curtailing both their freedom to maneuver and their entrepreneurial spirit. Any (web) retailer selling through Amazon knows they are not simply competing with other retailers, but with Amazon itself and its ever-expanding portfolio of private labels. For clothing retailer Bare-Bones WorkWear, selling on Amazon since 2004, and many others it was reason enough to remove nearly all of its items from Amazon.[32]

Opting out is simply not an option for most retailers though. It is nearly unthinkable that there could be an alternative business case for (web) stores who choose to ride the global waves of the future.

Large chains chart their own course

All kinds of last-ditch attempts are being made by traditional department stores, chain stores and travel agencies to tap into their very own omnichannel options (i.e. using every conceivable sales channel) to reach consumer households. Setting up their own global, or even simply national, online shopping platform is unfortunately beyond the reach of most of these former retail superpowers. There are but a few large department stores, Walmart in the United States being one of them, who can manage to successfully serve their customers on a global scale.

Even global chains in established retail sectors such as fashion (H&M), home goods (IKEA), and cash & carry (Metro) find their options are seriously limited. Their only real alternative is to become specialist portals or platforms. In addition to doing so, they will have to stay focused on domestic markets, where they can harness customer loyalty with a proposition tailor-made for that particular country.

They could take a leaf out of the books of brands like Apple and Samsung, who have successfully built shopping ecosystems around their own brands. A well-established omnichannel retail proposition, blended with endless applications (Siri, Bixby), services (iTunes, iCloud, Samsung Music) and their own payment infrastructure (Apple Pay, Samsung Pay), they are the first among the next generation of brands that will firmly and without reserve take a position as a shopping ecosystem.

German retailer Zalando has similarly lofty ambitions, the first of which is to grow into a European retail platform for online *and* offline fashion retailers. Ultimately, the company hopes to become the go-to shopping ecosystem in Europe for fashion. Clothing manufacturers, fashion brands, physical fashion stores, (web) stores' stock, and fashion stylists should all converge on Zalando to exchange advice. In turn, Zalando hopes to make money by mediating between customers and retailers, helping companies fine-tune their digital strategy, and handling deliveries. It will have to settle for a lower margin on fashion sales, though it will also have lower costs and less stock needed onsite. An added benefit is that the cost of the (relatively high) percentage of returns will then be covered by individual retailers instead of by Zalando itself.

Nostalgia for local stores

Part of the trend – globalization versus deglobalization – is that people shift their focus towards the familiar in local, regional or national values and goods. Regardless of the benefits belonging to globalization, they yearn for honest human attention and commitment, from stores and brands to whom they feel connected.

Local and regional stores, then, will stand firm as part of the retail landscape for the next decade. They're good at providing personal attention and binding customers to them, and they're able to offer excellent and unique products, not to mention a superlative level of service. Villages and neighborhoods see their local supermarket, artisanal butcher, bakery, fresh produce or cheese store — all of which have locally grown goods — as social hangouts.[33] New digital applications lend a helping hand to this process. For instance, people in the neighborhood can use an app to find out about special offers or learn about home delivery. Cutting-edge local cooperatives and online marketplaces manage to bring retailers and neighbors together, all while increasing a sense of community and belonging.

Village stores that provide all sorts of services (often operated by volunteer staffers) are able to maintain a liveliness and vibrancy in small local communities. Book shops that are struggling to stay open in small and midsized towns are often transformed into co-operatives run by volunteers. In fact, I have set my sights on our local village bookstore — which I plan to take over and run with fellow volunteers when the current owner retires — and hope to keep it open for the benefit of our small town.

Large cities, too, have found their department stores, chains, supermarkets, travel agencies, and smaller retail businesses turn into new social hubs, particularly when they offer options to buy online inside the store, pick up orders the same day and enjoy a cup of coffee or grab something to eat. The physical store, then, becomes the ultimate place to connect with the customer — where you get to communicate and interact on a personal level, with no intermediaries.

Concept stores centered around experience, discovery and inspiration are also new. These stores blend a wide variety of goods (defying boundaries between sectors), such as fashion, interior design, animals and art, often focused on the lifestyle of its target audience or store proprietor. Concept stores succeed in carving out their own niche by aligning themselves to a particular kind of lifestyle and audience, or to the passion and vision of the owners.

Another new addition is the so-called mono-store, based on a particular theme. Just picture a city trip (everything from the city of your choice to the photo album afterwards) or wedding ceremony (everything from the wedding dress to the ceremony and dinner afterwards).

Shopping street redux
New kinds of technology including virtual reality, augmented reality and hologram (more about all of this in Chapters 2 and 7) all help turn an inner city visit into a full-blown experience of the future. This technology manages to provide experiences that stores normally would otherwise be unable to offer. Nevertheless, the number of actual stores (of every shape and size), travel agencies and banks will indeed continue to shrink.[34] This is simply an unstoppable global trend. For the Western world it will be, in some ways, a return to the 1950s, with retail concentrated in (midsized

to) large cities, often paired with other sights, such as historical architecture. It is a case of *l'histoire ce repête* — history repeating itself — at that time, countless small businesses had to make way for department stores, discounters and single-price-stores for supermarkets and shopping malls. In turn, those are now at risk of being wiped off the map. Today, people who live in villages and midsized towns have exchanged their catalogues of days gone by for online stores, marketplaces and shopping platforms that can deliver anything, anytime you like.

Some areas of business have been able to take advantage of the empty storefronts: the future will see more *farmers markets,* health stores, physiotherapists, training centers and DIY stores popping up in our familiar shopping streets. Large chain stores, generally located in the suburbs and retail parks (and will remain there), will start opening inner-city stores to be closer to their clientele. IKEA has started to experiment with this very concept in Germany, the UK, Canada and Australia. Well-known retailers and automotive brands have begun opening flagship stores and virtual showrooms in top-notch locations in cities.

Technological developments produce new retail concepts, too. New 3D print shops have made it possible to bring a local production scale back, be that in a regional factory or in-store. Smaller retailers have latched onto new ideas such as pop-up stores or shop-in-shops to maintain a physical presence.

Successful web stores have set up shop for like-minded people to meet each other, take part in workshops or trainings, and ask questions one-to-one. These stores are aimed less at sales and more at being centers of service and know-how.

Any retailer can tell you, though, that even the mundane shopping street is not immune to the competitive influence of the global shopping platforms. They will be opening up physical stores of their own in years to come. Apple and Samsung are focused on further expanding their so-called *experience stores* (in carefully selected locales, to be sure) on a global scale. Apple is planning to transform its stores into village squares where people come to meet each other. Samsung has opened its Samsung 837 store in New York, where a "digital playground" is blended with fashion shows and cookery demonstrations. Google is utterly enchanted by flagship stores, virtual showrooms and pop-up stores for self-driving cars, new VR glasses and Nest thermostats.

Amazon is planning to open even more (book)stores, pop-up stores and supermarkets of their own.[35] The cashless Amazon Go convenience store is no longer a pilot project and has opened for the public.[36] Amazon is even contemplating small supermarkets with drive-through facilities. All the Amazon Go experiences will certainly be incorporated into the business of the recently acquired supermarket chain Whole Foods. Amazon will then be able to not only deliver food and drink, but all manner of other goods as well, within mere hours, or offer in-store pickups in the United States and the UK.

TRUMP: A BLESSING IN DISGUISE FOR RETAILERS WORLDWIDE?

The election of Donald Trump as President of the United States may very well prove to be temporarily beneficial for retailers worldwide. National governments, the European Union and the like will be forced to re-evaluate their position in the new economy. They cannot afford to do nothing in the face of protectionist trade and labor policies, including high import taxation. Trump's economic policy might turn out to be a blessing in disguise, offering inner-city retailers, shopping streets and web stores valuable time and opportunity to reinvent themselves after all.[37]

The winner-takes-all-economy

The world would be a very different place than it is today without the vision and entrepreneurial spirit of the Internet giants. We owe it to them that we have unlimited access to information and communication, that we can shop anywhere we want in the whole world. They have made the world our oyster. Thanks to them, the world is now truly a global village.

On the other hand, their success has often meant the downfall of local economy. Now that we are on the cusp of retail morphing into onlife retail, national governments should feel the call-to-action to guide the glocal economy where it ought to be.

American economist and Nobel Prize winner Paul Krugman believes it is not a matter of whether the monopsonies have won their spot in society honestly, but only whether they are abusing their immense power. Krugman believes they are, beyond a shadow of a doubt.[38]

On a global scale, the need to act against the powerful global tech companies is gaining traction. This is fitting of the current political landscape, where national interests have taken center stage once more. Legislators, competitive trading bodies and supervisors are all voicing their concerns.

In the US, it took over 20 years for legislators to force Amazon into paying local sales tax and value added tax.[39] Japan has had its cartel bodies charge them with forcing retailers to offer their products on the Amazon website at lower prices than anywhere else. TripAdvisor, Expedia and Booking.com had also prohibited hoteliers from selling rooms on their own websites at a lower rate. Seven European countries subsequently initiated inquiries into market disturbance, which compelled Booking.com to adjust its "lowest price" clause in several countries. In the meantime, Turkey has banned Booking.com on the grounds of "unfair competition." In the United States, a 2013 investigation by the Federal Trade Commission into supposed abuse of power by Google may have ended in Google's favor after a few adjustments to the search engine. Still, the accusations have not vanished completely.[40]

THREE STRIKES AND YOU'RE OUT

There are three competitive trading suits pending against Google in Europe:

1. Google has been slapped with a record-breaking fine of 2.7 billion dollars for abuse of power. It has given preferential treatment to its own comparison site Google Shopping, and according to the European Commission, has provided insufficient opportunities for other (comparison) sites to display commercial offers in online searches.[41] The company is now required to take action, giving it less room to explicitly promote its own shopping facilities.

2. In another suit, Google might be forced to refrain from automatically loading Android smartphones with all kind of Google-owned apps, such as YouTube, Google Maps, Chrome and Gmail.

3. A suit brought against Google's advertising broker AdSense might mean the results of other search engines are awarded a higher online visibility.

Google is unlikely to lose much sleep over the possible fines of 6.6 billion dollars, but the damage to their image could be substantial.

European worries

In Europe in particular, international tech giants find themselves up against a wall of altered political relations and an anti-globalist sentiment. Google is still being sued by various European Competitive Trading bodies. Amazon is facing a lawsuit by the French government for unfair trade practices. It allegedly has been a huge nuisance to the suppliers on its own marketplace.[42] Facebook was fined by the European Commission for providing inaccurate and misleading information regarding the WhatsApp takeover.[43] At the time of the takeover, Mark Zuckerberg pledged to "absolutely not" transfer any personal information between Facebook and WhatsApp. In spite of this false promise and a 122 million dollar fine, the European Commission is still permitting Facebook to share data between the two services.[44] Further, European member states cannot stop complaining about the fair share of taxes powerful e-commerce businesses ought to be paying. For this very reason, the EU has started drawing up a new tax code, which should apply to non-European companies as well.[45] Another worry for the EU is the foreign interest in businesses like automotive, biotechnology, entertainment, financial services, media, ICT and retail. They are fearful of increased market dominance.

The United States is not wrong in accusing the EC of changing the rules during the game, for instance, with respect to the 14 billion dollar tax assessment for Apple in 2016. These Americans believe the current situation is clearly the result of endless discord and lack of uniformity and consistence of the European legislation and regulations. You cannot really blame the superpowers for taking advantage of this situation for years.

In 2014, the European Parliament passed a resolution to split dominant Internet companies into parts, separating search engines from the rest of the business. Threatening to divide a company has proven to be a successful strategy, as Microsoft remembers all too well from the early 2000s. However, it certainly remains to be seen if it would be just as effective in today's world. Dividing Google might be beneficial to the other tech giants (Apple, Amazon or Alibaba). In turn, Amazon took home the profit when a 2015 US Supreme Court Ruling decided Apple had been the ringleader of a conspiracy to force publishers into charging higher prices for e-books.[46]

Where American politics and companies are far too deeply entangled financially, Europe has to be the one to save us from the big tech companies, according to writer Jonathan Taplin: "The change has to come from Europe".[47]

Tipping point

Governments would be well advised to draw up binding terms for entering new business areas in order to provide some semblance of protection to the value chain in that particular market. This might prevent the rollout of monopoly and monopsony practices elsewhere. Expecting governments to enforce strict fines and punishments for abuse of power is a given. This means that politicians will have to widen their scope: not only do users need protection, but also businesses in markets dependent on third parties. If business fails to flourish in a country, the nation's economy will lose its substance in years to come, putting it at the beck and call of the global shopping ecosystems.

Right now, the glocal platform economy is at the tipping point between global and local. National governments all around the world will need to find an equilibrium between an open market with free trade on one hand and nationalist protectionist policies on the other. Then, and only then, will they prevent the glocal economy from turning into a winner-takes-all-economy.

"The reason it seems that price is all your customers care about, is that you haven't given them anything else to care about."

**SETH GODIN,
AUTHOR AND ENTREPRENEUR**

6

Power to the onlife consumer

Technology is developing at an unprecedented pace, and the rate at which consumers adopt new opportunities is just as fast. For the first time in history, businesses are having trouble keeping up with the new consumer behavior. Some examples: consumers have been ready and waiting for websites to automatically adapt to whichever device they happen to be using (PC, tablet, smartphone). And why on earth should we not benefit from a high-speed mobile 5G network for watching TV or Netflix endlessly, wherever we are? Why is my phone still unable to provide advanced options for augmented and virtual reality? Oh, and I would just love to have an advanced virtual personal assistant on my smartphone who can go beyond suggesting a good restaurant or scheduling an appointment for me.

What sets this industrial revolution apart from previous ones is that people are now in the driver's seat of the transition. It is not technology that's upending the world, but rather the behavior triggered, that serves as the foundation of the retail revolution. Citizens, customers, clients, patients, and so on are united in wanting more, better and faster service. Are there any consumers out there who do *not* want an easier, cheaper, simpler and more personal, service-minded and reliable shopping experience?

In this chapter, I describe the "new consumer" along the dividing lines of digital natives, digital immigrants and digital illiterates. The second part of the chapter deals with drivers of behavior change and four different types of onlife shoppers. In the third section, I will explain why new technology is turning onlife consumers into vastly more loyal ones. Big data and the information war between consumers and retailers will be discussed in the fourth part. Next, I aim to show that regular consumers are becoming the powerful consumers of the future, thanks to a new level of awareness and altered mindset on their part. Finally, I will leap forward into the next few chapters by describing the distinct steps that make up the new customer journey.

DESCRIPTION OF POSTWAR GENERATIONS

Post-war generations	Age	Era	Characteristics
Digital natives	**0-35 year-olds**	**Born after 1980**	**Tomorrow's consumers. Growing up with smartphones, tablets, wearables, etc.**
NEW! Onlife generation, Platform generation	0-10 year-olds	Born after 2007	Tomorrow's consumers. Growing up with smartphones, tablets, wearables, virtual and augmented reality, etc.
iGeneration, Generation Z, Selfie-generation[1]	10-20 year-olds	Born after 1995	Grew up with WhatsApp, social networks, network gaming. Feel globally and social connected. Extremely visually-minded. They work to live. Extremely interactive: early adopters of new technology.
Millennials, Generation Y	20-35 year-olds	Born between 1980 and 2000	Upcoming consumers. Grew up with text messages, chat, video games, online 24/7. Strong and open-minded multi-taskers. Technology is way of life. "Me-and-selfie-generation".
Digital immigrants	**35-99 year-olds**	**Born before 1980**	**Today's consumers. Grew up without smartphones, tablets, wearables, etc.**
Generation X	35-50 year-olds	Born between 1965 and 1980	Grew up with PCs, email and cell phones. Multi-taskers, product-oriented. Life is more than work. Biggest online spenders.
Baby boom generation (late)	50-60 year-olds	Born between 1955 and 1965	Grew up with television. Encountered PCs later and cell phones later still. Have caught up. Most are digitally savvy.

Post-war generations	Age	Era	Characteristics
Baby boom generation (early)	60-70 year-olds	Born between 1945 and 1955	Grew up with radio. Work is life. Are catching up fast digitally. Lots of time and money to spend.
Silent generation	Over 65s	Born between 1925 and 1945	Grew up with newspapers, later radio. Lots of elderly adapting fast to digital opportunities. Others however remain digital illiterates.

The future of digital natives, immigrants and illiterates

Every generation is, of course, a product of its own time: with unique social, economic and technological characteristics. Our generation defines our values, our outlook on life and the world, our behavior and — naturally — the way we shop.

The generations living today can be divided into digital natives and digital immigrants. There are various different definitions of these groups; I have opted to describe everyone born after 1980 as a digital native.

Millennials, sometimes called Generation Y, make up the first group of digital natives. Formative years full of computers, iPods, video games and cell phones. They knew about blogs, wikis and podcasts well before their parents and teachers did, as well as what the difference is between a PDA and a Blackberry. They are the first group to regularly buy goods and services online.

The iGeneration, or Generation Z, was born after 1995. They are the *selfie generation*, with 2.5 billion people worldwide in 2020.[2] WhatsApp, YouTube and Snapchat were all fixtures of their lives growing up. Irish psychologist Ken Hughes believes the iGeneration marks the transition from the pre-Google era into post-Google times.[3] These youngsters may not have much spending power at the moment, but they will be the onlife consumers of tomorrow.

The very youngest group of the digital natives are the ones I call the *onlife generation*. They were born after 2007, the year of the first-ever smartphone. These children are the first ones to have a fully onlife childhood, right from the word "go". From day one, online and life were completely blended. To them, there is simply no divide between online and offline. This generation is going to define what our lives will be like in the future: how do we live, how do we work and how do we shop?

The multitasking digital native

Back in 2001, education scientist Marc Prensky was the first to differentiate between the generations.[4] In the early 21st century, he began to notice that the education system in the United States was failing to meet the needs of modern students, all of whom had grown up with media-and-Internet-dominated worlds. Prensky believes the advent of digital technology in the late 20th century had an enormous impact on how students think and process information. This new generation of students, whom he named digital natives, crave new digital and media-saturated surroundings. According to Prensky, the brain of digital natives is structured differently. As a result, these young people would seem to be better equipped for multi-tasking.

Sometimes, youngsters appear to be doing several tasks at the same time: watching TV, chatting online, doing their homework and shopping online. Digital immigrants should take heart, though: multitasking does not really exist; our brains can only focus properly on one thing at a time. Young people do however switch more easily between topics, and are ever on the lookout for new input: at home, at school and when they're out and about.

On demand

Another key characteristic of digital natives is their need to be satisfied right now, not later, and certainly not tomorrow. This craving of instant gratification is what new distribution methods play to. Why go to an actual store to buy something if you can find it free online, instantly? These kids download *everything*: music, films, games, homework, book reports, papers, articles, summaries — the list goes on and on. They buy content, not stuff. Their parents may have bought books, CDs and DVDs and displayed them on shelves — digital natives prefer to read their books onscreen, listen to music through online platforms and stream TV shows and films to watch them whenever the mood strikes. Being able to use the goods bought online as soon as possible is essential to them. When I visited eBay in Silicon Valley in 2013, I already experienced a camera being delivered a mere 36 minutes after it was ordered. It doesn't get any more instant than that! In 2017 Amazon Instant Pickup was launched on campuses in the United States, delivering items like snacks, drinks and electronics to students within only 2 minutes after they have been ordered.[5]

The on-demand culture and instant gratification mindset are the foundation of a new kind of consumer behavior. Slowly but surely, a lot of digital immigrants will start adopting those very patterns themselves.

Digital immigrants

Everyone born before 1980, the digital immigrants, still remember life without cell phones and Internet. A lot of Generation-X (those born between 1965 and 1980) and baby boomers — those born after 1945 — know what it was like without a personal computer. The silent or traditional generation (over-65s) even lived awhile without TVs and telephones as household fixtures. In the course of their lives, these people went on to encounter Internet, email and text messages at some point. Like any true immigrant, they speak with an accent. Typical behavior of a digital immigrant is printing emails.[6]

The over-60s are the fastest-growing age bracket worldwide: these consumers are the biggest group within aging societies, and they are set to make up one-third of the population in Spain, Germany, Japan, Italy and Russia by 2050.[7]

Older digital immigrants can be subdivided into two groups. First, we have the slightly younger seniors: (former) professionals who are relatively wealthy. They see the appeal of the new technological opportunities and see the appeal of being connected online with their children and grandchildren. Online banking on their smartphone, tablet or laptop; tapping into apps like Skype and FaceTime; they are wired up in every sense. Do you think older people are all technophobes? Think again![8] A sizeable proportion of online consumer spending growth worldwide is accounted for by this group. In years to come, department stores, web stores, service providers, marketplaces and platforms will notice they are an essential and fast-growing group of consumers.

Digital illiteracy

The second group are slightly older and less affluent senior citizens. A relatively high number of health issues is part of their lot, as is being heavily reliant on other people on account of physical or mental discomfort. This group lacks both the required skills and ability to acquire them. These seniors are far less connected to the digital world and its opportunities — physically and psychologically.[9] They face a very real danger of becoming the losers of the new digital age. All the possibilities provided by new technology seem to be just beyond their reach.

We can expect this digital illiteracy to become a serious social issue. A group of people is appearing — senior citizens and the mentally-challenged — who can no longer access relevant (government) information, nor use the services offered by banks and insurance companies. There have always been people who were left behind in every era; it's the speed of digitization in society that's increasing the sheer number of them. Volunteers, family and friends are essential a safety net for these digital immigrants. We need to remember how to take care of each other and then act accordingly.

On the other hand, new technological applications can, in fact, be beneficial to vulnerable groups in our society. Older people can now keep in touch with their families more easily (albeit from a distance). The visually impaired can benefit from having messages provided in video format.

There is another group of digital illiterates, though their numbers are diminishing as time goes by. These are people who have decided to ignore the relentless onlification of society, a decision often motivated by rigid principles. They cling to the past and might refuse to do online banking on their smartphone (if they even have one). Their trusty old Nokia "does the job just fine, thank you very much". In the next few years and decades, they'll be confronted with less goodwill and understanding from people around them and will be consequently forced to move with society at least somewhat. A small number of them will likely choose to become digital outcasts.

TO THE AID OF JAPANESE SENIORS

All over the world, the elderly are growing in number, thanks in part to the improvements in medical science. Internet-based technology can actually help these people stay in their own homes for longer. In Japan, over 25 percent of the population is over 65, and several companies have joined forces to seize this opportunity. Apple, IBM and *The Japan Post* have set up the so-called "Watch Over" program. By 2020, they want to provide roughly 5 million Japanese seniors with iPads. On them, there will be apps reminding them to take their medication, or hinting at their attendance at exercise classes or sticking to their diet. The ideas is that mailmen regularly visit the elderly – for a small monthly fee – and help them use their iPad.[10]

This may be an extreme example, though it demonstrates how important it is that retailers ensure their web stores are easily accessible and legible for the elderly and visually impaired. The World Wide Web Consortium (W3C), an organization that codifies international (web) standards, has drawn up guidelines with the Web Accessibility Initiative (WAI). These are meant to ensure the accessibility for the visually impaired, mentally impaired and elderly all over the world.[11]

Drivers of behavioral change

Never before have scientists watched consumer behavior change as quickly as it has over the past few years. We often forget that being online 24/7, both at home and outside, and using services on our smartphone, tablet or laptop has only recently become the new normal. We quickly compare goods and services online, search for the best offer, use contactless payment methods, or even wander around the supermarket comparing prices online on our smartphones – at least, I know I often see people doing just that.

A similar shift has occurred in the way people of all ages access media, news and entertainment. We read the news on Facebook and collectively binge-watch shows on Netflix, or watch catch-up TV when it suits our schedule. The research agency Nielsen has shown a quarterly decline in the hours spent watching traditional TV, with the online streaming of news, shows and films – on our tablets, televisions or smartphones – steadily on the rise. In support of this trend, in 2017, for the first time ever, advertisers spent more of their budget on Internet than on television.[12]

I will define six principles of behavior change that help us understand the changes in our society's behavior as it goes through onlification.[13] As a social science graduate, I am aware of the limitations of social studies and its many possible research perspectives. For this reason, I have decided to limit myself to the perspective of behavior economics.[14]

The synergy between these six principles explains how consumer behavior changes if it can be:

1. Easier: it may cost time to be onlife, but people are willing to spend that time for the sake of ease;
2. Familiar: once people start to familiarize themselves with being onlife, they find it more acceptable;
3. Profitable: onlife behavior offers real benefits in time and money;
4. Enjoyable: people enjoy their new behavior;
5. Desirable: people are keen to join in and be part of something;
6. A habit: once they've adopted the new behavior, it soon becomes a habit, and people stop thinking about it.

Four types of onlife shoppers

The six drivers of behavior changes described above are universal to all of us, though our own uniqueness means that everyone has different tweaks in their behavior change. The so-called *shopper DNA* of people, or how they shop, is largely determined by their personality.[15] A few years ago, as part of a Shopping2020 research study, market researcher Gfk came up with a list of the different types of digital consumers. Basically, there are four different types:

1. The passionate onlife shopper: views shopping as a hobby.
2. The deliberate onlife shopper: views shopping as a sport.
3. The calculating onlife shopper: views shopping as a job.
4. The passive onlife shopper: views shopping as being similar to a dental appointment.

To be sure, no one fits these descriptions 100 percent; we all have a mixture of the types within us, but this classification is a good starting point. In the next chapters, where we will examine the customer journey, I will be using these four types to expand on the new shopping behavior of onlife consumers. For now, I will share some specifics for each of the types, including demographic information.

The passionate onlife shopper

Demographic: families, all age groups, relatively more women and young people, lower incomes and average education.

Shopping is a hobby for this person. Loves to visit physical stores, maybe uses a store app as well, and is generally sociable. A good vibe and unique experiences are crucial. They love being influenced by every conceivable digital technology: messages, reviews on social media, blogs and vlogs. They also shop online at home because of the endless options to choose from, the possibility of easy returns and the perception of lower price points.

The passionate onlife shopper regards shopping as rewarding and is happiest when he can be inspired in virtual showrooms or by augmented and/or virtual reality, either in-store or at home. A true bargain hunter. Brand image is vastly more important to this group than to the other types of shoppers.

The deliberate onlife shopper

Demographic: higher incomes, relatively advanced education.

This shopper relishes the competitive sport of shopping. Always prepared and definitely a *heavy buyer*. With an eye for quality, he has strong brand preferences (though familiar brands do not always have the upper hand), and cannot get enough of comparing goods and services. Product details, reviews and ratings are very important to him. Overly-interested in new product launches and high-end goods. Initial orientation happens digitally, though shopping in local and small specialist stores is another favorite pastime. Sharing goods and services is an option for this shopper too, as is frequently buying through platforms.

The deliberate shopper loves conferring with experts (if only to be recognized as a savvy shopper) online and in-store. What matters most: personalized advice, interaction and absolutely stellar customer service.

The calculating onlife shopper

Demographic: families, over 40s, lower incomes and lower education.

Shopping is like a job for this group: you simply do the best you can. Shopping often happens according to schedule, and generic brands tend to be favored, whereas fashion and trends are left aside. He never buys more than he needs. Price is a key decision factor, so there is a lot of price comparison before purchase via store flyers and price-comparison sites. Familiar stores within easy reach and with ample parking are preferred, but well-known web stores can be an alternative.

Online purchases are often electronic appliances, media and entertainment, books, and insurance policies. Reviews matter immensely, with personal referrals from families and friends making all the difference.

Warrantees, trustmarks, return policies, service and options for speedy delivery: they all matter.

The passive onlife shopper

Demographic: over 50s, mostly men, average income, lower education.

This type of shopper sees shopping as a necessary evil, akin to a dental appointment. If it can be put off, it will be. As a result, purchases tend to occur haphazardly, at the very last minute. Banking and sorting out insurance is done at home, online. He prefers one-stop-shopping to anything else, such as an actual shopping mall or online department store. Small, local stores and travel agencies are another favorite due to the personal attention, information and bespoke advice.

The ease and familiarity of trusted stores, brands, goods and services is what matters most.

WHAT KIND OF SHOPPER AM I?

On Friday afternoons, I feel like a deliberate shopper. My wife and I go round the local butchers, fishmongers, produce stores and cheese shops, stopping for a friendly chat wherever we are. I then pop into my local bookstore to mosey around and absorb the lovely bookish scents. Shopping feels like a sport then.

On the other hand, I absolutely despise shopping for clothes (as, I guess, many men do). When my wife insists I simply have to, I go to my regular local menswear store and stock up on slacks, sports shirts, Oxfords and sweaters. When it comes to clothes, I am surely a passive shopper. Walking through Amsterdam's 9 Streets or Manhattan's Meatpacking District, I enjoy shopping so much that I start behaving like a passionate shopper. Online, too, I can easily be persuaded into some impulse buying.

I prefer to sort out insurance policies online – like any true calculating shopper – carefully taking into account the lowest price and the best service. Besides, I try to be smart about our weekly bulk shopping run, often ordering these online and having them delivered. Our weekly fruit and vegetables are also delivered: I order them over the phone from our local market stall holders at our weekly market on my way to work, and they are delivered in a big box that same morning.

Loyalty

The new consumer generations, regardless of their type, are set to become more loyal than ever in years to come. The sharing of personal information and the use of smart algorithms means retailers can now provide a unique shopping experience to (mostly online) consumers, right down to personalized service and special offers. Onlife consumers are not happy to share their precious information with just everyone, carefully considering the handful of companies they will trust with their details – and then giving these businesses everything they want to know. As a result, consumers will become increasingly loyal to these few chosen businesses.

Several socio-demographic trends, most notably the growing number of single-person-households, double-income families and senior citizens, are going to further boost the preference for a chosen few businesses, helping people maximize their overly-busy lives. These groups of people are inclined to opt for the convenience and advantages provided by the shopping platforms.

Retailer loyalty programs tie into this trend. The best example is the unparalleled success of Amazon Prime. More than one hundred million households spend the substantial sum of $119 a year. Tens of millions of customers are "exchanging" their personal data and preferences for tailor-made services such as free two-day delivery and free photo, music and film services, amongst many other features.[16] It is how Amazon keeps you committed as a loyal customer and makes sure you do not stray from the Amazon ecosystem.

Businesses will need to stay deserving of their customer loyalty, however, through personalized attention, bespoke services and – of course – better prices.[17] Stores that slip up will find themselves vilified on social media in no time: onlife consumers have no mercy.

At the same time, shopping ecosystems are at risk of becoming too huge for the comfort in the minds of onlife consumers. Their loyalty may well be put to the test because of it. After all, losing loyal customers can happen in the blink of an eye. This is something traditional department stores and chain stores have discovered to their own detriment over the past years.

Information as currency

There is a veritable war on information going on as we speak between consumers and businesses. Who is going to know more about who in a few years' time? Increasingly, onlife consumers are aware of the very real value of their personal data. In the long run, this data is likely to become a kind of currency for which they expect something in return: the advantages of customer loyalty we discussed earlier could be the very thing.

A small but growing group of consumers is set on retaining control of their personal data usage. Thanks to *life management platforms* and *personal data systems*, they are looking forward to possessing a *personal ID center*. From there, they can determine what level of online security they want to use – an alias could be one of the options.

Other groups of consumers cannot be bothered with any of this. They are sufficiently annoyed by banners, adverts, pop-up browser ads, YouTube videos and so on that they install ad blockers. As a result, they can no longer be pursued by intrusive (web) stores trying to sell their products. These consumers relish the improved loading speed of webpages, love having fewer viruses on their computers, and are perfectly happy to undermine the business models of search engines, publishers, newspapers and other media. The number of people using ad blockers is increasing by the millions every month,[18] with the number of devices all over the world with ad blockers well on its way to 1 billion.[19]

The overall majority of onlife consumers, however, lack the inclination to take the trouble. They find managing their own personal data a hassle and installing an ad blocker far too involved and complicated. The information war between consumers and businesses has only just begun. At present, I would be wary of predicting who is going to win, though I personally still hope that consumers will always know more about businesses and their goods and services than vice versa. I might be indulging in wishful thinking, though.[20]

Ever more powerful, thanks to the smart, sharing, circular and platform economy

Awareness of the value of personal data in a smart economy is on the rise. One important reason for this are incidents where poorly-protected data ends up on the streets, both at government institutions and companies. Multimedia campaigns by governments, banks and insurance companies cannot stress enough that you should always be careful with your digital personal data. There is an ongoing call for teaching digital etiquette at junior schools so that very young children become aware of the impact of sharing information. More on this in Chapter 12.

In the future, consumers will be more careful with their data, making conscious decisions about which (web) stores they want to share data, as described earlier in this chapter. Thanks to the smart economy, onlife consumers can firmly step into the driver's seat of their digital lives.

In the sharing economy, social media are bringing people together from all over the world, making it possible to reach out to our families, friends and acquaintances with one easy click, wherever and whenever we please. New generations of entrepreneurs are stepping up to the responsibility of *social entrepreneurship*, in which "giving back to society" is just as important as turnover, profit and stock value.

New technology helps people create networks where they can be of service to each other. Simple neighborhood WhatsApp groups are one small example, whereas buying co-ops are on a larger scale — people can use these to purchase power (that is: energy) together or organize house painters for a whole street. This kind of cooperative group has more power than individual consumers. They can shake things up so that businesses become more competitive, something that economists believe will result in increased prosperity.

The sharing economy is where younger digital natives — who are less interested in possessions — can take older generations by the hand. Slowly but surely, people are beginning to realize they do not all need to own every conceivable durable item themselves. New technology means items for hire, rent or sharing are easier to find than ever before.

More than ever, consumers are becoming aware of the malleability of society in a circular economy. Purposely buying organic goods, preferably sourced locally, avoiding plastic packaging wherever they can, and purchasing electrical power from cheaper, greener and sustainable cooperatives, they are not afraid to tell (web) stores that making their business more sustainable is fairly easy. A new connection with retailers, who are often perfectly prepared to start using more environmentally friendly packaging, is the result.

The glocal economy is providing opportunities for onlife consumers to source and purchase goods and services from very far away or from super-local (web) stores. Large groups of consumers do opt for the convenience and advantages offered by the large shopping ecosystems, but there is equally a movement towards "old-fashioned" shopping, with artisanal goods and authenticity at its very core.

At present, we are still in a transitional phase. Now, consumers are gradually becoming more conscious onlife shoppers. Their very own onlife identity is taking shape, which in turn presents a very real value for retailers. As a result, consumers have a lot of power to wield. We are living in an era where customers are in the driver's seat more than ever before, and they are craving authenticity, newness, convenience, and creativity. We are living in a customer-driven economy.[21] Today's customers are, in fact, the powerful onlife consumers of tomorrow.

The customer journey of the onlife consumer

The customer journey can best be described as the shared journey of consumers and businesses during the purchase of goods or use of services. It consists of the steps consumers need to take to buy something and the possibilities businesses provide for them to take those steps. Belgian professor of marketing Gino van Ossel has termed this the *buying path*, though he also includes the actual consuming of the purchases, which I have decided not to do in this book.[22]

There are many different ways to describe the customer journey. I've found most of my inspiration from those by McKinsey & Company[23], IKEA[24] and Bonsing|Mann.[25] After adding my own twist to these three concepts, I've reached five separate steps.

THE CUSTOMER JOURNEY THROUGH THE YEARS

1. **Orientation** Then: radio, TV, newspapers, flyers, mailings. Now: search engines, comparison sites, social media, blogs, vlogs, videos Future: predictive personalized messages, virtual reality, augmented reality, holograms.

2. **Selection** Then: stores, travel agencies, insurance companies. Now: web store, influencer marketing, home speaker and ordering devices. Future: app (store), virtual and augmented store and showroom, holograms.

3. **Transaction** Then: identification, purchase, payment and delivery all happen simultaneously at the end of the customer journey; risk is balanced evenly between buyer and seller; virtually no risk. Now: identification, purchase, payment and delivery need not happen at the same time; risk is unevenly balanced between buyer and seller. Future: identification happens at start of customer journey; purchase, payment and delivery need not happen at the same time, virtually no risk thanks to blockchain technology.

4. **Delivery** Then: mailman, milkman, post office. Now: pickup points, same-day delivery, home delivery, office delivery, in-fridge delivery. Future: self-driving cars and delivery trucks, robot and drone delivery.
5. **Customer care** Then: service desk, by phone. Now: WhatsApp, (web) chats, Skype and FaceTime, virtual assistants and chatbots. Future: deep-learning chatbots and robot advisers.

Certainly, this is not a full reflection of our reality nowadays, where linear customer journeys are becoming increasingly rare. In years to come, the customer journey is inevitably going to go through an immense transformation. Onlification of society is certainly going to alter the way people look, choose and buy. Analogue customers will become onlife consumers who find completely new ways to shape their customer journey. In Chapters 7 through 11, I will discuss the separate steps of this new customer journey — from the perspective of onlife consumers. After all: the customer is always right.

"There is one critical difference between old-fashioned word of mouth and the digital version. Talking over the hedge is one-to-one. Digital word of mouth is one-to-millions. If you have a good experience, it's shared and re-shared with millions."

**DAVID REIBSTEIN,
PROFESSOR AT THE WHARTON SCHOOL**

7

Orientation: the N=1 effect

Can anyone remember what it was like to start looking for a product or service by leafing through the Yellow Pages or going through the newspaper ads with a fine-toothed comb? I can still picture my parents faithfully perusing all the weekly store flyers on the lookout for a good bargain. Saturday mornings were spent at the market, where my dad would let the stallholders guide him along as he explored his options.

Shoppers may have hardly changed in type, and while their motives may be roughly the same, their behavior when looking around has altered completely in just a few years' time. People of all ages increasingly look up product and price information digitally: on PCs, laptops, tablets, smartphones, smartwatches and smart home devices. In recent years onlife consumers have seen ever increasing new ways to explore new products and services at retailers, brands and service providers.

There are differences in how digital natives and digital immigrants each experience the customer journey as it evolves. Digital natives are no strangers to what the new customer journey has to offer: it is simply part of their onlife existence. Baby boomers and the silent generation, however, tend to need a bit more time as digital immigrants to get used to the new way of shopping. But beware: they are adapting faster than ever to all the new opportunities.

In this chapter, I will discuss orientation in three parts. First, I will examine the universal motives for shopping from the onlife consumer point of view. The second part deals with "finding" versus "being found;" new consumer generations expect (web) stores to be places where they can explore things in a context personally relevant to them. The third part discusses why it will prove insufficient for retailers to simply offer excellent customer service in-store; rather, they will actually need to blend into the lives of onlife consumers, a radically different way of thinking. After all, the on-life consumer insists on having goods and services offered at the perfect time, on the perfect channel, over the perfect medium and with the perfect sales conditions, the perfect service and last but not least: at the perfect price. Onlife consumers operate on the idea N=1.

Onlife consumer shopping motives

There are four general shopping motives, though they often occur consecutively and, at times, may even overlap.[1] These motives apply to both traditional and onlife consumers; the difference is how each group chooses to shape the motives. They are social, he-donistic, utilitarian motives and prior-experience-driven motives and experiences.

Social motives for shopping

Shopping has always been a social activity, meant to inspire. Going downtown with friends or family to wander around the shops or a mall can become a social hobby. Young people today have that same motive when they shop online: social media influencers are often the route to the stores, and friends frequently visit the same stores online at the same time.

Online and offline shopping, then, have a social element: you meet up and talk about your options, whether this happens in real life, at a sidewalk café or sandwich shop, or chatting online on your favorite social media platform. Watching vlogs together, talking about them and following the same popular vloggers is something that holds particular appeal to passionate young shoppers (see Chapter 6 for four different kinds of shoppers). In China, so-called *Wanghong*, a new group of online influencers, have become impor-tant. The thousands of Wanghong use Taobao, the Alibaba market platform, to recommend clothes and cosmetics which can then be ordered instantly.[2]

Hedonistic motives for shopping

At other times, we might want to be entertained and amused. Self-centered and hedonistic motives pop up then. During orientation, the full experience is a key motive. Of course, passionate shoppers see the appeal of this, but so do deliberate ones — they love to be triggered during their exploring by their senses and their imaginations. A calculating shopper might similarly be enticed by an exceptionally good bargain.

Shopping streets are the perfect spots to satisfy hedonistic motives. Many downtown areas are eager to become vibrant city centers once more, offering consumers the ultimate blend of shops, restaurants and bars, and movie theatres and historical architecture. Virtual and augmented reality will help to create new and inconceivably great experiences in-store.

For digital natives, watching a video blog or online fashion show — alone or with friends — can be just as tantalizing to the senses. At home augmented reality will help consumers try on new outfits and lets you place virtual furniture inside your home. Virtual reality will help you experience — while sitting on your couch — what your next vacation might be like.

Utilitarian motives for shopping

These are motives that are solely focused on solving a problem swiftly, effectively and efficiently. Shopping is something to tick off your to-do-list. Calculating and passive shoppers are particularly inclined to explore options online before purchasing an item or service. These groups of shoppers demand utilitarian values such as supply information, delivery times and the convenience of ordering 24/7. They are equally fond of buying items in-store, though, because that means you can take your purchases home directly without paying shipping fees.

Prior-experience-driven motives for shopping

Past experiences have a direct impact on future orientation. In particular, bad experiences influence calculating and deliberate shoppers to such an extent that they will not return to that (web) store again. Onlife consumers are inclined to go beyond their own (good and bad) experiences, letting reviews from others, vlogs or blogs also guide their decision-making process.

Finding versus being found

Orientation is the first step in the customer journey. In no time at all, the initial search for goods or services has shifted focus from the physical shopping streets to online. Ever since the advent of Internet, consumers have become inured to mass media (*push*). Instead, they prefer to actively look for relevant information on-line themselves (*pull*).[3] It is a completely different world and was brought about by all the possible — not to mention up-to-date — information available online 24/7; everything you need to know about the product, services, stores, brands and service providers is at your fingertips. Reviews, social media, apps, blogs and vlogs provide the means to share and swap experiences with like-minded fellow shoppers.

INFLUENCER MARKETING GAINING GROUND
Influencers can help raise brand awareness, drive engagement, and boost sales. When influencers vouch for your brand, they help you win the trust of your target audience while generating buzz. Influencer marketing is a form of social proof with a slightly bigger impact. Why? Because of an influencer's audience size and reputation. Retailers and brands are increasingly teaming up with influencers.[4] Amazon started recruiting social media influencers with big followers as part of its new Amazon Influencer Program. Selected influencers must post shoppable content, and they'll earn commissions on their posts that result in sales.

Consumers stay informed thanks to old-fashioned email campaigns as well. Retailers love these too, because the return on investment is excellent, especially for regular customers. These campaigns are becoming increasingly personalized, thanks to matching offers with the consumer's wish list or prior purchases. This trend caters to the consumer's every need through relevant information they have come to expect. Nowadays, roughly eight out of ten purchases begin with online orientation.[5]

Physical stores can provide consumer experiences that are harder to imitate online by displaying the look, feel and scent of a product.[6] This kind of sensory perception is no longer exclusively available in brick stores. Onlife consumers have begun ordering products to then examine them at home. At my office, I often see whole seasonal wardrobes being delivered at work for my staffers, who then proceed to dissect the outfits at length and then send most of them back to the store. This type of orientation is nearly free — sometimes there is a shipping fee — and less time-consuming than visiting several stores on the shopping street. Besides, there is no parking fee nor the annoying effect of items being out of stock.

Search engines
In the early years of the Internet, search engines could be tortuously slow and infuriating. They have since improved immensely, thanks in large part to smarter algorithms. Your search history is taken into account to offer you personalized, relevant information. Inadvertently, you're helping and feeding the databases with every single search word you type. No wonder search engines have become the stepping stones at the outset of the customer journey.

Small retailers have the most to gain from search engine marketing. Onlife consumers are being presented with the businesses that try hardest to be found. There is now a whole industry surrounding search engine optimization (SEO). A vital industry, according to the (web) stores who refuse to participate in the auction system preferred by the shopping platforms — there, retailers need to outbid each other to get their advert matched to a search word, commonly known as search engine advertising (SEA). Larger stores are particularly keen to lure in the consumer early on with a sponsored link. It still remains to be seen, however, how cost-effective this kind of ad is. People prefer to follow the advice of others than of a retailer: customer reviews and ratings are rapidly becoming more important than ever. So, too, have sites that compare prices, products and services, firmly winning a place in the orientation stage of shopping. They can be an irritant as well, though. Tracking cookies that follow consumers around for weeks on end with ads and outdated offers are simply annoying beyond endurance. In fact, the business models of these price, product and service comparing sites are under serious pressure. Because their revenue is based on the number of hits and/or sales they generate for web stores, they are no longer seen as independent or reliable.

THE ZMOT MOMENT

Nearly everyone can relate to this: the tiniest hint can compel you to grab your smartphone or tablet to quickly look up some information on goods or services. This is the moment of truth in the customer journey: that fractional second in which you make an implicit choice as to how and where you will look for something. In 2009, American research firm IRI called this the *zero-moment-of-truth* (ZMOT).[7] Procter & Gamble had already defined the instant in which a consumer – standing before the shelves or racks in-store – is on the verge of choosing a product as the *first moment of truth,* with the moment they start using a purchase as the *second moment of truth.* In 2011, Google decided to embrace the ZMOT in order to boost the orientation phase of smartphones.[8] A smart move, as it happens. Today, over 90 percent of all consumers uses their smartphones for shopping.[9]

New technology brings depth to orientation

Technology is likely to bring unprecedented possibilities in years to come to onlife consumers looking for ways to explore new goods and services.

More relevant search results

Ultimately, using search engines will be a completely different experience than what it is today. Already, consumers know that typing in a generic search ("washing machine") will yield other results to a more specific ("top-loading washing machine") or *branded* search ("Miele washing machine"). Smart algorithms will help turn search word combinations into better results. Onlife consumers will want even more and will no longer be satisfied by generic search results. Customers want individualized answers to searches, taking into account how urgent their question is, their location and the timing of their search question. What they would really love is to engage in dialogue in order to get a personalized recommendation that suits the context of their search question.

New interactive and dialogue-based software is going to enable this kind of thing. The typing of *keywords* will be replaced by *voice search*: recording a spoken question. Tech giants like Alibaba (Genie), Apple (Siri), Amazon (Alexa), Google (Assistant), Microsoft (Cortana) and Samsung (Bixby) have digital apps and virtual personal assistants (PAs) who can not only understand consumers but also learn from prior experiences.

IBM SUPERCOMPUTER WATSON

While in New York and San Francisco in 2016, I met IBM's supercomputer named Watson. With Watson attempting to virtually become the customer, IBM is well ahead of the pack in the field of personalized shopping. Words I once heard from IBM global retail leader Keith Mercier: *"You've got to be them."*

During my first encounter with Watson, I typed in the question, "I am looking for a lavish suit for my daughter's wedding." It then asked me a variety of questions, precisely what a sales assistant in a formal menswear store would ask: "Where is the wedding? What time of year? Inside or outdoors?" The conversation also covered the type of suit, possible colors, designs, sizing and price range. It was a pleasant "talk" between buyer and vendor, producing a highly relevant search result and personalized recommendation at the end.[10]

American retailer Macy's has already implemented Watson into its online app and ten physical stores.[11] Staples, Under Armour, 1800Flowers.com and outdoor titan The North Face have all started to experiment with similar intuitive and dialogue-based methods of recommendation.[12]

Virtual reality

Over the next few years, we will see whole new worlds of retail opening up, thanks to virtual showrooms and experience centers (see Chapter 2). In a three-dimensional setting, you get to view *and* experience the displayed products as if you were actually in the store instead of at home. You get to pick items up, lift them, spin them around, try on outfits and take photos to share on Instagram and the like.[13] Subtle sound and color effects will then show you related products to match.

Next generation VR glasses — such as advanced versions of the HTC or Oculus Rift — will help (web) stores further deepen their on-life relationship with customers.[14] You can count on this: your VR experience is going to be based on the data and preferences stored in your social media profile or your in-store account. You can even pick the surroundings in which you want to shop. Harry Potter fans might enjoy buying their clothes inside a castle like Hogwarts.

Upon their acquisition of Oculus Rift, Facebook started experimenting with an option to integrate VR purchases into its popular Messenger app.[15] The day Facebook can sell us clothes, homes or cars through its VR glasses is not that far off.[16] [17] In Beijing and London, you can already visit virtual showrooms for Audi. In downtown stores, this car manufacturer is providing the opportunity for potential buyers to assemble their perfect car, choosing from every conceivable model. Alibaba has been quick to build a full-service virtual store where Chinese consumers can use VR glasses to view items and then pay for them with Alipay.[18]

Augmented reality

Applications using AR (see Chapter 2) are becoming more popular as well. These involve improving, or augmenting, reality with real-time extras added to digital videos and photos.

Thanks to augmented reality, we can alter our methods of orientation. Well-known examples of AR are IKEA's app allowing you to place furniture in your home and the smart in-store mirrors in which you can see yourself wearing an outfit you selected. More and more department stores, like the London flagship store of John Lewis, have mirrors where you can "try on" the whole collection.[19]

SMART DRESSING ROOMS IN MACROPOLIS

Back in the early 1990s, we were already experimenting with virtual dressing rooms in our digital shopping city Macropolis. In the store of fashion retailer Peek & Cloppenburg, you could select a virtual mannequin resembling yourself, down to your hairstyle and color. If you dragged a sweater to the mannequin, using your mouse, the computer would then show matching skirts, jackets and scarves you could select to dress up the mannequin. The price of the outfit was displayed, too, of course. Macropolis even offered style advice on outfit combinations. Or, to quote an old article I came across: "Plus-size models can opt to get advice on outfits that make them look slimmer."

There are other uses for AR beyond department stores or travel agencies: you could even use it at home. AR is entering our homes with smart apps from Amazon, IKEA and Target (furniture). Checking to see if the chair you've had your eye on would actually look good in your room suddenly becomes an option. Amazon has patented a smart mirror for your bedroom, that could serve as an extension for its smart camera Echo Look. AR, VR, smart fabrics and machine learning will come together by giving advice which outfit suits you best.[20] In the future, we may be wearing sunglasses that not only shield us from ultraviolet rays, but also provide us with opportunities to step into an augmented reality.[21] At present, Google is working on Glass 2. Otherwise known as the Glass Enterprise Edition, it is set to be an improved version of the flopped Google Glass, this time tailor-made for the onlife consumer.[22]

Holograms
New and advanced hologram technology (see Chapter 2) can allow consumers to see and experience goods and service whenever and wherever they choose. Holograms are created by making them appear before us. For now, the retail applications of this technology are limited to product presentations, such as in the Shanghai Apple Store, where in 2011 the new generation of MacBooks was presented to shoppers using holograms. In 2013, Samsung used holography to project its new Galaxy S4 in stores. Kitchen manufacturer Lowe's opened a pilot store in 2016 using a Microsoft 3D HoloLens to let customers enter virtual showrooms. Here, they could get the full experience of the assembled kitchens and bathrooms while directly tweaking them to their own specifications.

The use of holograms in the orientation stage is most obvious at this point in time in supermarkets and in fashion, automotive, DIY and kitchen outfitters.[23] Or in advertising, where holographic displays will show customers different products and ads from various angles, allowing us to see the front, back and sides.[24]

N=1

Orientation for goods and services can be done anytime, anywhere. Day or night, wherever we are, we could be exploring our options: using a smartphone in-store, outside on the street or on our commutes in our cars, trains, buses or subways; even using a laptop, tablet or a smart home speaker in our kitchen. Busy lives mean that more often than not, utilitarian shopping motives tend to beat the social and hedonistic motives. For many, the convenience of online orientation simply outweighs the friendly atmosphere of a shopping street.

Onlife consumers expect retailers to adjust to *them* instead of the other way around. This goes beyond semantics or subtle distinctions; it is a fundamentally different perspective. Onlife consumers intensely dislike curtailed opening hours, the inability to reach customer service, or visiting (web) stores without recognition from the staff. The onlife consumer wants to be approached at the perfect time, on the perfect channel, over the perfect medium, with the perfect sales conditions, the perfect service, and last but not least: at the perfect price. N=1, remember? The reality of this is that I need to be seduced into starting a relationship with the retailer the very first time I visit their (web) store. The retailer needs to ask me just the right questions, at just the right time and in just the right context. It is then up to me how much information I want to share, depending on how well the salesperson manages to build rapport with me. I might be willing to start a conversation, which might move into a transaction. Maybe, just maybe, this could be the beginning of a beautiful retail relationship.

Repeat customers in the orientation stage of a new purchase should at least be given the option of being recognized and rewarded. Of course, this only happens based on the information they've (consciously or inadvertently) provided, which can then produce personal characteristics and behavioral patterns.

The upside of making a personal profile is that you get an individually-tailored experience brimming with convenience, added value and (price) advantages. Onlife consumers dream of stores performing a total reshuffle for their visit. They also very much appreciate being inspired in a personal and direct manner in between retail transactions. If that happens, they become far more inclined to keep choosing their faithful online department store, marketplace or platform whenever they start orientation for a purchase again.

Profound conversation

Subliminal messages and signals emanate from onlife consumers to retailers, too. Each time they use their smartphone, tablet or similar device, their actions produce information about their wishes, emotions and preferences. Inadvertently and unconsciously, they are actually engaging in a profound conversation with the vendor based on their identity and present mood. The very moment that businesses master artificial intelligence (see Chapter 2) to pick up these signals is when search results will reflect how we feel by translating and using all our signals.

Nearly all the big tech companies and shopping platforms have apps currently in development that think and learn like humans. Smartphones and apps can do so much more than simply store data. They're on their way to becoming far smarter by making connections and having the capacity for learning. DeepMind — the AI subsidiary of Google — is working on the creation of more and more powerful algorithms that will be able to, for instance, find photos using image recognition searches.

The downside, of course, is that tech giants are going to know an awful lot about our personal lives. Some people are fearful the world will become like the one depicted in the deeply dark dystopian Netflix hit show *Black Mirror*. Ariel Ezrachi, Professor of Competition Law at Oxford University, is worried that tech companies are secretly attuning their algorithms together. Further, skeptics are convinced that Internet companies will show no qualms in selling this data to third parties, resulting in our most private and intimate secrets becoming public.

For now, the onlife consumer isn't losing any sleep over this. Plenty of people appreciate receiving specific information when performing an exploratory search ("I need black sneakers, size 12, right now"), telling them which store with the desired item in-stock is the closest, including directions to get there *and* a quick calendar check to see if they're free right now ("You have time to pick them up!"). To these consumers, this new way of shopping brings back memories of going to the town store, where you knew everybody and felt happy, safe and secure doing business. Onlife consumers do not differ that much in their wishes and desires from consumers in the past. They just want some personal human attention. If all these developments are giving you the creeps, however, rest assured: Google is working on a "big red button" to halt self-learning computers and machines for when things threaten to become out of hand.[25]

"*Thus, in the future, instead of buying bananas in a grocery store, you could go pick them off a tree in a virtual jungle.*"

**YASUHIRO FUKUSHIMA,
HONORARY CHAIRMAN OF SQUARE ENIX**

8

Selection: new paradigm of choice

We all know the feeling of sheer overwhelm that sweeps over us when we must choose between all the vast different types of teas, laundry detergents or cookies. That very same feeling washes over us when we go online to find a hotel, washing machine or insurance policy. Not being able to see the woods for the trees, we feel lost in a veritable maze of options. Not exactly knowing what we want can make selection even more complicated and time-consuming.

Selection is part two of the purchasing process, after orientation and before payment. To be fair, though, selection and payment sometimes mean the same thing nowadays. More about that later on.

In this chapter, my first outline will be the paradox so many onlife consumers face: they love having options, but they quickly get lost in the humongous number of them. Next, I will delve into the various ways onlife consumers complete the selection process: by rote, comparison, research or on impulse. After that, I aim to determine the conditions retailers must meet — that is, if they want the onlife consumer to choose *them*. What instruments are retailers utilizing, based on the type of shopper, to convince the consumer to buy? What are shopping platforms, web stores and physical stores doing to help consumers during the process of selection? I will then round off the chapter with an introduction of the new paradigm of choice: onlife consumers want to choose from an infinite number of options presented to them in a way that resonates personally.

Paradox of choice or paradise of choice?

The immense number of options triggers infobesity in some people: they desperately, obsessively scour the Internet, fearful of missing relevant information. Research in the United States has proven that having more options does not necessarily constitute *better* options. Having too many might force a person into hasty decisions or, worse, even no decision at all.[1] Psychologist Barry Schwartz described how people experience more stress if they have too many choices before them — with disengaged buyers as a result.[2] I once heard him speak at a conference in New York, where he explained that this paradox of choice in fact reduces customer satisfaction.[3]

Chris Anderson, the former editor of US tech magazine *Wired*, believes Schwartz's theory is only confined to the physical world. There, consumers lack the required information to come to a proper decision. To Anderson, the virtually endless supply on the Internet is a paradise of choice.

Onlife consumers want the *best of both worlds*: to find their own perfect match in the realm of infinite possibilities. Being able to search far and wide matters to them. They feel confident that smart navigation technology and algorithms will present them with an offer that fits their personal wish lists perfectly. They also feel happier, though, with the simplicity of choosing from ten options instead of 150.

Choosing by rote

There are certain goods and services where we balk at the idea of even ten options. We simply want to get the same item as before, or, at the very most, a variation on that theme if it's new and improved. Most of our routine choices occur at the supermarket or local store. We just buy the same as before — no (online) orientation whatsoever. The smart economy provides us with the tech opportunities to deal with these purchases swiftly and smoothly. Online supermarkets store our previous purchases and line up a shopping list for us in advance.

Despite the fact that online daily purchases make up but a fraction of all purchases, we should expect to see online grocery shopping boom in years to come. McKinsey has stated that this phase of infancy doesn't mean consumers lack interest. Rather, it means the conditions haven't yet been met to make it sufficiently appealing to them.[4]

Saying that online grocery shopping is on the rise would be to wildly understate the facts. With British supermarket chain Tesco leading the way, many global supermarket chains are in the process of developing online propositions. They have no choice, really. New market entrants are hot on their heels with new retail formulas. To a lot of experts, the takeover by Amazon of Whole Foods represents nothing short of a turning point for the supermarket sector. It can simply not afford to sit back for another second.

New food concepts

When we decide what to eat, we want to have our every wish granted. Pizza and other meal delivery services have transformed the food and beverage scene for good. New concepts of food delivery are entering the market, disrupting it as they come. Key new players are Takeaway, Foodora and Deliveroo, and they are going to war with each other to conquer the European market. In China, around 1 million couriers of Ele.me are standing by to deliver meals. Out of the Chinese people using online platforms, over 60 percent order food to be delivered more than three times a week.[5] The shopping platforms are hopping onto this bandwagon, too.[6] Amazon Hot Wheels is the latest meal delivery service of the retail titan. Amazon Prime members can have groceries delivered within the hour, using Amazon Fresh, in selected cities. Further, Amazon Pantry is how the company is playing to customers who like a full store cupboard. Again, Prime customers get a good deal: they can order up to 15 kilos of non-urgent groceries, such as rice, shampoo and pre-packaged snacks.

Meal boxes — a grocery box filled with the ingredients for one or more meals — are playing to the dynamic consumer behavior of "convenience, healthy living and no fuss." The German brand Hello Fresh, currently operating on three continents, actually gets to decide what will be on their customers' plates that day.[7] We can expect to see this kind of meal box subscription grow to around two or three percent of all grocery shopping.

If customers give their permission, they could be instantly recognized upon entering the physical supermarkets and local stores of the future. Doing weekly food shopping will have never been easier. Using *smart robotic shopping carts*, little trolleys with digital screens can zip through the store, making speedy decisions that are — this is what counts — personally relevant. Their shopping list is displayed on the little screen, as is their most convenient in-store route. Using Bluetooth technology and in-store beacons, the store can make them personalized special offers.[8] Items are scanned as they are put into the trolley so the customer can see how much they have spent. Checkout happens automatically, too, by pushing the trolley to the parking lot. Selecting an item is now equal to paying for it. The smart carts are energy-neutral: by pushing it around, the customer is, in fact, recharging its 24V-batteries. Customers with reduced mobility can find little electronic cars to drive around, with all the options described above, of course. In the future, the shopping trolley will become your virtual assistant, guiding you towards the right decision.[9]

At Amazon's Go, Alibaba's Hema and JD.com's 7Fresh you need not even grab a shopping cart. Shoppers simply scan their smartphones when entering the store. With Amazon's "just walk out" technology, whenever they take something off the shelves (or return an item), it is detected.[10] Big data analytics are now used in all stores, to provide tailormade product offers to shoppers.

The smartphone tracks which items you've bagged and which were already in the bag you brought with you. When you leave the store — no cash register! — your Amazon or Alipay account is instantly debited for your purchases. With the 7Fresh app from JD.com you can pay with facial recognition. In the new Chinese supermarkets you can also buy fresh seafood an meats, have them cooked in store for immediate consumption or for delivery within 30 minutes within a 3 mile radius of the store.[11]

Comparing, then choosing

Some goods and services are worth a little more effort: we don't mind some comparison shopping for clothes, shoes, coffee makers, washing machines or TVs. Though we might not feel compelled to get every possible scrap of information, we do want to compare a few different options before deciding to buy. In brick and mortar stores, we want to try on several different pants, dresses and tops. Retail guru Paco Underhill coined a phrase for this selection process: *"see me, feel me, touch me, buy me."*[12]

The advent of Internet has added a whole new dimension to comparison shopping: we now compare goods and services online according to characteristics, price, delivery options, extra customer service and conditions, and if the web store has a trustworthy certificate or trustmark. We also consider the experiences of other consumers before we decide what to buy.

Thanks to Internet, comparison shopping has become mainstream. Especially true of the travel business, where massive comparing of airline tickets, hotels, camp sites, package holidays and trips is the new normal. My wife and I used nothing other than Booking.com, Airbnb and TripAdvisor to organize our 2017 summer trip to the stunning coasts of France, Spain and Portugal. Using reviews, ratings and references as our guide, we would book a hotel, B&B or rustic *chambres d'hôtes, casa* or *pousada* every morning.

Banks and insurance companies have also noticed a measured increase, with over 70 percent of insurance policies taken out by people who checked comparison sites first.[13]

SMART SHOPPING IN MACROPOLIS

Helping consumers to find and select goods and services online is by no means a new idea. In the late 1990s this was the very basis of our webstore portal Macropolis. You got to view and compare products in over 20 categories, at more than 5,000 (web) stores. Macropolis became one of the first ever online venues in the Netherlands where you could, for example, compare supermarket items.

Dialing the Macropolis Hotline on your mobile phone was another option – quite useful to do a quick in-store price comparison of washing machines or televisions. A one-guilder-a-minute menu lists all the prices of the washing machine or TV you were interested in, and the best web store to buy it at, through Macropolis of course. No one called the, far too expensive, Macropolis Hotline though, and the full-page newspaper ads in national papers were too big a hurdle for traditional retailers. They refused to advertise on Macropolis, with its link to the cheapest web store.

Choosing online, buying in-store and vice versa

Our online comparison activity has shifted in recent years from PCs and laptops to our smartphones. Another interesting shift is from "home" to "in-store" and back again. Now, over half of consumers in China and South-Korea do an in-store price-comparison check on their smartphones. The percentage in the United States is roughly one-third and in Europe one-fourth.[14] In the future, onlife consumers will stop thinking about this; it will be second nature to compare as they shop, wherever and whenever, even though Amazon may prevent them from doing so. The tech giant was granted a patent that would prevent in-store shoppers from comparing prices on a competitor's website. Instead, it would re-direct the comparing customer to its own website or distract the customer with a coupon or salesperson attention.[15]

Soon, we will likely be able to scan an item in-store — using a barcode, QR code, quick photo or a scan— and then simply swipe our phones or say "buy now" to our smartwatches to drop it into the checkout basket of our favorite online ecosystems. Or, we will just point our Google Android phones to an item and Google Lens[16] will tell us not only what it is, but also how to buy it and have it delivered to our doorsteps with Google Express. Looking around and choosing in-store before buying online is also called *showrooming*.

The reverse happens a lot, too. Onlife consumers are perfectly happy to compare goods and services online before going to a store to buy them. This is called *web rooming* and has now become part of the omnichannel strategy favored by many *bricks-and-clicks* stores in hopes of seducing onlife consumers online so they'll visit the physical store later.[17] Sports brand Nike sometimes lets customers know there will be free fitness classes in selected stores. Similarly, fashion store Rebecca Minkoff has taken to using *magic mirrors* in-store with the aim of getting customers to come shop. Its magic mirrors serve also as touchscreens, allowing customers to browse looks, colors and sizes.[18]

You choose, you buy

Comparison shopping is slowly moving away from "traditional" comparison websites to retail ecosystems and platforms. There, regular customers can wander through the full customer journey for nearly every conceivable item or service (read Chapter 5 for the pros and cons of this).

In 2015, Google added a "buy" button to Google Shopping.[19] Thanks to the Purchase on Google app and Google Lens, the onlife consumer can access product information, ratings and availability of items in web stores *and* in physical stores nearby. By hitting the "buy" button, they activate a *one-click-buy*. The payment is then charged to the credit card linked to their Gmail or Android profile.[20] By the way, Google has nothing to do with the actual stock or shipping of items; the fulfillment process is carried out by (web) stores who take advantage of the immense reach of the search engine by paying for advertising online.[21]

Social media platforms such as Facebook, Pinterest, Instagram and Snapchat have all added buy buttons to their mobile apps. For example, (web) stores can now show their products on their own Facebook pages before offering the option of buying items through the integrated payment options (or through a link to their own site).[22] Pinterest has implemented *Buying Pins*: items can now be purchased with a credit card or Apple Pay.[23] For Chinese social media platform Tencent/WeChat, these are all well-established practices. Around 1 billion consumers already use the immensely popular WeChat app to buy items instantly and pay for them with WePay.

Choosing after research

Exploration-through-shopping is a thorough approach utilized by many consumers. They examine all the facets of their proposed purchase extensively and often online. These kind of detailed decisions are part of buying complicated goods and services, particularly for the first purchase. However, there are certain types of shoppers who enjoy being this thorough more frequently.

When planning to purchase complex goods and services, most consumers prefer being prepared. The websites of brand manufacturers are the go-to place for product descriptions and specifications. Reviews and ratings are perused to discover others' experiences with the item or service. This kind of information is known as *user-generated content*. Next, comparison sites are valuable sources of manufacturer specifications, brand information and user reviews. There are also online forums for interested shoppers to engage in conversation with their peers about a potential purchase. People swap experiences and ask and answer all sorts of questions. Social media, where bloggers and vloggers share their stories and videos, is yet another way for the onlife consumer to find input for their decision-making process.

User-generated content is swiftly becoming more and more important. Onlife consumers are very fond of ratings and reviews, meaning that customer reviews will gradually become more significant in search engines and comparison sites. When thousands of consumers have reviewed an item, the review itself becomes more credible. It's that much harder to manipulate, not to mention the fact that being caught in the act means completely losing face.

An almost infinite number of information sources is now available regarding goods and services. There is no longer a monopoly of information for traditional (physical) stores, travel agencies, insurance intermediaries and banks. Manufacturers of branded goods have become more powerful due to the wealth of information at their fingertips: specifications of tens of thousands of items. It's but a matter of time before all this information is made to fit into a standard terminology, which in turn will be a huge boost to exploratory and comparison-based shopping styles. Brands are now building their own relationships with onlife consumers, something that will soon translate into direct sales with no need for a go-between.

Choosing on impulse

We are inundated by seductive stimuli all day long, all of them meant to entice us to look, choose, and ultimately buy this, that or the other. For that very reason, I came home with a bulk of garden waste trash bags and a grass clipper when I set out to buy a lawn mower. None of us are immune to the impulse buy, nor are these buys confined to physical stores.

Responsive mobile sites and shopping apps mean that onlife consumers can shop till they drop, 24/7. Pressing "buy" on a smartphone or saying "add this to my shopping list" is that much easier than logging onto the desktop version of a store website at home.[24] Shopping for fun in a beloved web store or app is no longer just the shopaholics' domain.

There is no better way to constantly show onlife consumers new, relevant and personalized offers than via smartphones and shopping apps. Amazon already tailors its advertising to the search history of its customers. Zappos, the footwear subsidiary of Amazon, even matches individualized offers to the type of smartphone someone has: Android users are given different options than people with iPhones. The smart carts we mentioned earlier can also be used to encourage impulse purchases.

Where do onlife consumers buy?

Selection is about goods and services, certainly, but the provider thereof needs to pass the test, too. Onlife consumers have come to expect specific things of retailers. These seven basic needs describe consumer deliberations as they decide whether to use a particular (web) store.[25]

1. Convenience: how much time and effort will it take for me to buy? Routine purchases need to be swift and efficient, whereas consumers are prepared to make more of an effort for complex purchases. At present, that is — in years to come, we can expect the need for convenience to grow steadily.

2. Choice: the depth and width of the product range, or selection of services, is what matters. Customers want access to every single thing while still expecting retailers to help them make the appropriate choice. Tailor-made is the word. Remember that N=1 (see Chapter 7). If a (web) store knows "everything" about a customer, they have less trouble tailoring their range to him, and the customer then needs less time reaching the best decision.

3. Price: onlife consumers are no less (or more!) price-conscious than consumers today. Yet, the price component is bound to take on new meanings due to the overwhelming range of goods and services presented in new, non-traditional retail environments. Besides, price is one of the driving forces of the sharing economy: how to spend less on comparable products and services.

4. Experience: the latest buzzword in retail. Contrary to popular expectation, offering sensory experiences is not limited to

SELECTION ACCORDING TO ONLIFE SHOPPER TYPE

	Customer knowledge	Customer range
Passionate shopper	– VIP privileges – Social media – Profiling – Videos, forums, blogs, vlogs – Multi-channel recognition – Brand apps	– Personalized range – Video reviews – C2C interaction – Lifestyle tips – Role model / Celebrities – Recommendations through app
Deliberate shopper	– Pro-active personal shopper – Personal profile – Store reviews – Blogs – In-store experts – Multi-channel recognition – YouTube advice	– Previous purchases – Personalized and ranked reviews – Extensive product information – Comparison app
Calculating shopper	– Shopping lists – Personalized brochure	– Ranked reviews – Price comparison – Extensive product or service information
Passive shopper	– Personal profile – Reminders – Recommendations – Price confirmation – Previous purchases	– Reviews – Video instructions – Fewer options – Summaries – Filtered range

physical stores. Who knows, someone might manage to create the *Internet of smell.*[26] In 2013, Google played an April Fool's prank by introducing Google Nose.[27] Atmosphere, experience and emotion are all going to be given new dimensions in future years. New applications of virtual and augmented reality will bring new experiences to physical stores and to our homes.

5. Service: there are two kinds of services – soft (attention, care, help, empathy, kindness) and hard (advice, installation, repair), and both will become ever more important. Service flows from experience; in other words, future onlife consumers want

Customer experience	Customer service
Surprise me!	– Virtual dressing rooms
– Entertainment	– Pop-up stores
– Group shopping	– Trendsetters
– Themed shopping events	– Free Wi-Fi
– "Customer knows best"	– Invite-a-friend
– Experience	– Group shopping
– Workshops	– Virtual reality
– (Group) tutorials	
– Virtual reality	
– Augmented reality	
– Holograms	
Seduce me!	– Location-based information
– One-on-one advice	– Reservations
– Buy one, give one	– Best buys!
– Personalized product page	– Cut to the chase
– Video instruction	– Delivery by subscription
	– Customer service
Affect me!	– Simple navigation and routing
– Personal profile	– Click & collect
– Coupons and discounts	– Delivery options
– Swift procedure	– Free and easy returns
– Expert on call 24/7	
Help me!	– Free returns
– Ranked reviews	– Pickup and home delivery (free)
– Keep it simple	– Lowest price guarantee
– Easy ordering	– Monthly subscription
– Confirmation	
– Contact by phone	

friendly and personal service, but it also has to happen in a timely and effective manner.

6. Confidence: this is where promises matter about convenience ("order today, have it delivered tomorrow"), choice ("biggest range anywhere"), price ("cheapest deals"), experience ("feel the difference") and service ("unhappy? cash back"). On the other hand, the onlife consumer is well aware of how valuable their personal information is. Which (web) store can instill enough confidence for them to store personal data there?

7. Transparency: onlife consumers expect a comprehensive understanding of the way they can do business with a retailer. Every single step of the customer journey needs to be clear and concise. Thanks to independent reviews, good and bad experiences can be taken into account before a purchase.

The onlife consumer will always choose businesses that have an excellent record of meeting these basic needs. More often than not, these will be the shopping platforms where the consumer can go through the full customer journey, confident in the knowledge that their every need will be anticipated and met. Still, smaller (web) stores can pull it off, too. Particularly in niche markets, they have an excellent chance thanks to factors like giving personal attention, being approachable as unique entrepreneurs who know their customers, having artisanal and authentic products, using local suppliers while offering a fair price.

How do onlife consumers buy?

The onlife consumer expects retailers to use different approaches to help the consumer decision-making process. This is a decisive element in how they buy. They insist that (web) retailers do the following in order to unequivocally convince them:[28]

1. Customer knowledge: use what you know and make everything personal to me.
2. Customer offer: only offer me relevant and accurate information.
3. Customer experience: surprise me, seduce me, affect me, help me!
4. Customer service: make it easy for me to decide.

Which of these four wishes prevails, and how to fulfil that wish, depends partly on what kind of shopper a consumer is. The table on the previous page clearly displays which tools a retailer can best match to which type of shopper.

How shopping platforms aid the selection process

Shopping ecosystems and platforms like Amazon, Apple and Google inspire shoppers with new sophisticated technology to help them during selection. Amazon (Echo), Apple (Homepod) and Google (Home) are taking home shopping to the next level with their immensely popular smart home speaker devices and their interactive *voice-response systems*. Take Amazon Echo (who answers to "Alexa") which is available in three sizes: Echo, Tap and Echo Dot. They are all 360-degree, sleekly-designed tubular smart home speakers with Wi-Fi, one or more speakers and up to seven microphones. Of course, all the Echos connect to the Amazon cloud. In the United States, the United Kingdom and Germany it's already possible to use Echo for adding items to your online Amazon shopping list ("Alexa, please put garlic on the shopping list"). For now, I use Echo in Dutch at home in my kitchen to ask questions ("how many teaspoons constitute a tablespoon?"), listen to the news or request music through Sonos. Routine purchases can be bought using the simple *voice command* or pressing a button, and they are paid for instantly. It will not be long before we can ask Echo what would be the best washing machine, where I can get the best price for it (Amazon, no doubt!), and what the possible delivery times are at the store I decide on.

Smart home ordering devices are also entering the homes and kitchens of households around the world. Take the Wi-Fi-connected Amazon Dash, a one-touch button that instantly orders an item online. These Dash Buttons are just big enough to show the manufacturing brand. You simply stick them on your fridge (paper towel roll), bathroom mirror (razor blades), washing machine (detergent) or office desk (printer ink), and one push is all it takes to add the item to your Amazon Fresh shopping list (*Place it, Press it, Get it*).[29] Sure, you may not want to deck out your entire home in these buttons, but they are still awfully convenient. The Dash Replenishment Service even has machines ordering items on their own accord by making a note that goods have run out and simply placing the order. Over 250 brands have signed up, including Kraft, Illy, Schwarzkopf, Coca Cola, Red Bull, Whiskas and Persil. Members of the popular Prime loyalty program can have Amazon Dash Buttons for just $4.99 a button. Prime members can also create their own buttons for free on the website and in the app.[30]

In 2016, Amazon introduced the AWS Internet-of-Things (IoT) button, to be used mostly for tasks and services. You can use it to call someone, open the door to your garage, order a pizza, and so on.[31]

These new opportunities offered by Amazon — and other shopping ecosystems and platforms — make life immensely convenient, though in the case of Amazon it does beg the question whether the tech giant might be getting a bit too powerful in the process. Might consumers be bringing a kind of Trojan horse into their homes by allowing the full tech wizardry of Amazon in the door?[32] After all, why on earth would you still shop anywhere else than on Amazon?

How physical stores aid the selection process

Traditional retailers are slowly but steadily implementing new technologies in the selection process. When we were on a field trip across China in 2015, we went to see a Metro pilot store in Shanghai. Loyal customers are given a discount on selected products through the use of in-store beacons and a WeChat app.[33] The latest app at the American retailer Target also uses beacons[34]; if customers have given permission, they can use a unique homepage in each store with a range of possibilities. For example, the app provides you with suggested routes through the store (depending on where you are in the store at any given time) and helps you find the items you want. It also presents customers with unique coupons or offers on products at the very moment they walk past them along the aisles. Sometimes, these *news alerts* are matched to social media topics: you might receive an offer for dresses that are *trending* on Pinterest as you walk through the women's wear department.

The new paradigm of choice

Onlife consumers of the future will have all manners of digital aids at their disposal to help them make choices in a simpler, more pleasant and — above all — more convenient fashion. Who is going to offer me the very best service, utmost convenience and best bargain out there? Which retailer is worthy of my confidence? The paradox of choice and the paradise of choice will blend into what I like to call the paradigm of choice. The paradox will resolve itself, for retailers now have sufficient information on their customers to take them by the hand, one by one, and guide them through their selections.

Retailers do have sufficient technology at their fingertips, though, to offer consumers the sense of being able to tap into the unlimited range in the paradise of choice.

The power in this new paradigm of choice belongs to the onlife consumer. He gets to decide who is allowed to help him and how much help he wants as he reaches his decision. Providers of goods and services will need to stop limiting the choices for people (paradox of choice) and rather present the consumer with the theoretically infinite and boundless range of options (paradise of choice) in a way that's smart, organized, personal and relevant.

"With the blockchain, billions of people can not only become connected, but more important become included in financial activity, able to purchase, borrow, sell, and otherwise have a chance at building a prosperous life."

DON AND ALEX TAPSCOTT,
AUTHORS OF *THE BLOCKCHAIN REVOLUTION*[1]

9

How to pay: no-click buying in the blockchain

The decision to buy something, the subsequent payment and finally receiving the item: for as long as we can remember, it all happened at the same time, in the same place. The risks for buyer and vendor were shared equally. Someone chose a dress in the store, paid for it, and took it home. Developments in technology have completely upended traditional payments in less than two decades' time. Online shopping has become nothing out of the ordinary. As a result, entering into an agreement, paying for the item and delivering the goods or services no longer have to take place at the same time or location. In the age of Internet, the risk has shifted to either buyer (advance payments) or vendor (payment on delivery).

Never before have we seen a transformation like the one now unfolding in the field of payments as part of the customer journey. Changing consumer needs and expectations requires new retail and payment applications. What these have in common is that they fit seamlessly into people's lives and match the way consumers purchase goods and services. New methods of payment are essential right now. Onlife consumers insist that payment blends in perfectly with the rest of the customer journey.

Payment is the third step in the customer journey. After orientation and selection comes the time to actually pay for the item or service. In doing so, the buyer becomes the owner. In this chapter, I discuss four different trends that are set to determine how onlife consumers will pay for their purchases:

- Contactless payment
- The *War of Wallets*
- Identity is the new money
- The blockchain revolution

Contactless payment

At present, most consumers still pay with cash or a debit or credit card. The number of cash payments is rapidly shrinking, though. We are slowly but surely on our way to a cashless society.[2] The strong encouragement to pay with debit or credit cards is the reason for this. The introduction of contactless payments is a further boost to this trend: briskly tapping a payment point with your card or smartphone; no need to enter a pin number.

Contactless payment — for small amounts especially — is quickly gaining ground in Western countries. In Europe, we can expect to see this kind of direct payment, where a smartphone is simply swiped past a payment point, to increase fivefold by 2021. This will constitute 16 percent of all mobile payments.[3] China, however, is way ahead of everybody. Roughly 86 percent of Chinese people use contactless payment, compared to 43 percent globally.[4] As of 2018, one in three mobile phones will support this technology.[5]

A SUPER-SMART CARD

In 1990, futurologist Alvin Toffler predicted the advent of the "super-smart card" or "electronic bank for the wallet." It was to be a plastic card with a microchip which you could use to check your bank balance, trade stocks and book airline tickets.[6]

A smartphone is really something of a Swiss army knife. Apart from using it for information, contacts and entertainment, it will soon have a fourth use: being a mobile wallet.[7] The speed of adoption for this new application is truly unprecedented. In over 20 African and Asian countries, there is more money in mobile money accounts than there is in bank accounts.[8] There is literally nowhere with as many mobile money transfers as Africa. Over 50 percent of all mobile transactions involving money take place south of the Sahara.[9] Market analyst Juniper Research believes, however, that 90 percent of all contactless payments will still be done using (debit or credit) cards for the foreseeable future.

Paying in physical stores

Retailers are becoming more attuned to consumer wishes for simpler payment methods. In years to come, traditional checkout systems (*Point of Sale* or POS terminals) will gradually be adapted into or replaced by mobile systems (MPOS terminals). These new cash registers have wireless software operated from an onsite PC or directly from the cloud. As a result, new checkout systems are cheaper, more flexible and easier to update. Using the Apple Store Checkout could not be simpler. The sales assistant just uses her smartphone as a POS terminal. Regardless of where you are inside the store, he can pop your credit card into a little gadget connected to her smartphone. No waiting lines at checkout. The sales desk becomes a customer service hub. In Amazon Go supermarkets and in convenience stores of Alibaba (Hema, Taocafe), JD.com (7Fresh) and Tencent (We Life) in China there are, in fact, no checkout points at all. Your groceries, snacks and small meals are simply debited from your account as you walk out the door. Using various combinations of facial recognition, QR-codes and radio-frequency identification, checkouts are being eliminated while data analytics is being boosted.[10]

NFC and RFID chips, QR codes and other technology

Thanks to new NFC chip technology and QR codes, authorization at these new checkout systems is a piece of cake. Another option is using a smartphone scanner to scan a dynamic (in-store or online) QR code, automatically guiding you to the transaction in your preferred payment app. South Korean Home Plus began experimenting with this in 2011. This supermarket chain hung up posters in busy Seoul subway stations displaying their best-selling items, ranging from orange juice to meat. People passing by could then scan a QR code with their smartphone to check the price and availability for that item. If they wanted to, they could then pay for it directly and have it delivered to their home.[11]

In China, WeChat Pay and Alipay use QR codes to process tens of millions of transactions every day, both in physical stores and online. QR codes, which previously failed to catch on in the West, are now slowly but steadily catching on as a result of the current Southeast Asian success of the technology.[12]

Bitcoin payments sometimes use NFC chips or QR codes too.

This is the currency based on blockchain technology (more on this topic in Chapter 2 and later on in this chapter). Users just scan a code to transfer money to each other, with the QR code or NFC tag referring to the recipient's "wallet address." The money is then transferred through the blockchain swiftly and at negligible cost.

Soon, brick stores will be using so-called "VIP Wi-Fi" to serve their very best customers. Given excellent service from the word "go", they can bypass the checkout by scanning their items with a smartphone or *wearable* and use NFC chips for instant payment with their digital wallet. Retailers are perfectly happy to have customers take home their purchases without actually paying for them — after all, they have the personal data of that customer already.

THE SMARTEST CARD IS NOT A CARD AT ALL

One of the most sophisticated smart card payment systems is the Octopus Card, which is immensely popular in Hong Kong. It can be used both online and offline (in stores, restaurants, parking garages, taxis and public transport). It tops up automatically whenever its users connect to their bank account. There are now over 30 million of these cards in circulation, and they're being used for identification purposes as well. Schools use them to check student attendance, for example. In 2014, online retail titan Alibaba enabled the Octopus Card for use on its marketplace Taobao for its Hong Kong clientele.[13]

In Sweden, the national transport company SJ has been experimenting with implanted microchips for train travelers. These are not only handy for checking in; when you board the train, you simply hold up your hand to the train conductor's smartphone and "bleep", you're checked in. The NFC chips — roughly the size of a wheat kernel — not only work on trains; they can open your office door or work as identifiers for the office copier.[14]

Why should you use a transport chip card if you can travel and pay with your debit card or smartphone? Or easier yet: what about having an artificial nail on your finger with a built-in RFID chip? London fashion graduate Lucie Davis developed an acrylic nail during her degree with the colors of London Transport Oyster Card and an RFID chip to match. She no longer needed to look for her actual Oyster, nor her smartphone, if she wore the nail, and she could get past the turnstiles in the tube in London, no questions asked.[15]

Feels like instant payment

The onlife consumer still wants to feel that these new money trans-actions are like cash payments. Their account should instantly be debited for that sum of money, and they insist upon instant con-firmation from the vendor upon receiving the payment. They ap-preciate this user convenience and feel comforted by it. There is a sensation of getting icing on their cake, and they like that a lot. For (web) stores the world over, though, the reality is not quite so idyllic. They tend to receive a notification from the bank saying the amount will be transferred (later).

Financial institutions have started to develop infrastructure for instant payments which do just that: transfer money the very instant it is paid. This is a highly significant development for retail-ers. It means they will have instant access to their actual turnover and revenue so they can meet their own financial obligations. On the other hand, it can also act as an accelerant for other payment innovations. The sharing economy, in particular, could benefit immensely. Instant payment (or transfer) is, after all, the digital equivalent of a cash payment without the nuisance of crumpled bank notes and other downsides of actual cash.

Paying with aliases

An alias is a nickname or code name for someone. Aliases are used mostly for payments between consumers, and they've become a regular occurrence on social media. They can be matched to a cell phone, Facebook address, email or Twitter account, all thanks to the use of these extra account names. The numbers or addresses are then linked to bank account numbers, which makes it seem like you're sending money to (for example) a mobile number with its own email account. These payments are known as person-to-per-son payments, or peer-to-peer (P2P). More people than ever have started using the apps of banks or new market entrants to make and receive speedy and easy money transfers. It's hardly surprising that the P2P apps of WeChat and Alipay in China are so popular. PayPal has even gone so far as to add consumer protection to its P2P payments. In doing so, the old-fashioned money-back guarantee is given a digital version. More and more companies are guarantee-ing customers a full refund if something goes wrong. In England, work is being done to better facilitate payments between customers (C2C-payments). Now, the company Payments UK uses a user's mobile number as an alias for their bank account. The advantage: you no longer need to jot down the full bank account number, and the instant transfer goes through a trusted third party, your bank.

Vulnerable people

A cashless society may prove challenging for small businesses and the poorest citizens. Cities all over the world, from Sweden to India, are working towards becoming completely cashless. Indian Prime Minister Narendra Modi firmly believes that limiting cash will be a way to combat corruption and "black money." Sweden may become the very first completely cashless society in the world by 2030. According to *The Guardian* reporter Adam Forrest, this presents a very real threat of excluding people from society.[16]

There are, of course, vulnerable people, such as the handicapped, elderly, underage, or those with financial problems. For them, being able to pay without "the need to think about it" poses a real danger. Through the new *seamless payment experiences,* they can fall into the trap of ordering items (too) easily and getting themselves into financial trouble unless they are properly protected. To be sure, this is first and foremost a responsibility for parents, guardians and voluntary caregivers, but retailers are stepping up to the plate as well. By using digital recognition tools and automatic credit checks, they are successfully preventing problems before they occur.

Notorious shopaholics can protect themselves with new technology. In Detroit, people who know their bad habits can install the Splurge Alert app. It uses geolocation and can warn a user and a pre-arranged buddy against overspending if they enter the danger zone.[17]

There are other ways to help vulnerable people: advice, implementing thresholds for contactless payments, and requiring age checks when purchasing certain goods. "Smart money" is yet another option: this money can only be spent on certain, predetermined items. For example, the monthly stipend I give my college children can only be spent on study books and daily foodstuffs, not on games or beers at the bar.

The War of Wallets

Luckily, onlife consumers are beginning to understand that transferring personal data is part of the payment process. In exchange for their openness, they expect to be able to pay swiftly and easily. Startups and shopping ecosystems alike are playing into this consumer desire for paying with *digital wallets* and payment apps.

These are digital payment services accessible from a laptop, tablet or smartphone, be that at home, on the road or in-store (online and offline). The wallet is a kind of digital emulation of the physical wallet crammed with coins and bills, a couple of credit or debit cards, a theatre ticket for that evening and some store loyalty cards. In a payment app, there is generally just the payment option; in other words: you get to sync all those cards into one, translating into payment at just one provider, in one type of currency.

Both the wallet and the app need to be "filled out" with relevant personal information and a bank account number upon first use. The proper name for this is "payment by default setting." Some wallets and apps allow you to transfer money in advance, so as to cap your spending amount. After that, there is no need to fill in any personal details when you make a payment.

Wallets and apps are also a popular option for all kinds of other business, such as tracking loyalty points or verifying someone's age. The onlife consumer gets convenience thanks to a speedy monetary transaction, but they also help aid the process of orientation and selection by contributing to store conversion and customer retention for (web) stores.

PayPal, Apple Pay and MasterPass by MasterCard are the most familiar and well-known examples of wallets that let consumers do online and offline payments all over the world. Globally, the payment apps used most are the ones belonging to Uber, Starbucks and those used by Chinese people everywhere, run by Alibaba (Alipay) and Tencent/WeChat (WeChat Pay). In China, Starbucks and WeChat have joined forces: you can use the WeChat app to pay in the Starbucks stores and to buy a friend a latte using so-called *social gifting*.[18]

A lot of web stores have great difficulty keeping up with the sheer number of new initiatives. Confused and baffled by them all, they instead retreat into wariness, not adopting any of the latest *game changers.* This also applies to physical stores — they, too, have trouble keeping pace with the fast changes in the world of payments. Carefully taking a wait-and-see approach, they hold off on making necessary investments. A great many payment points in stores today are simply not equipped for the latest chip technology that digital wallets and new payment apps require.

The War of Wallets is bound to produce some fierce battles over the next few years. Banks, platforms, marketplaces, (web) stores, search engines and brand manufacturers are fully aware that having access to a customer's digital wallet equals the perfect commitment of the consumer relationship and trust. Further, wallets and apps offer opportunities to sync up loyalty programs. Because they are effective forms of identification, retailers can then use wallets and apps for personalized customer discounts.

It's a given that wallets and apps will become an essential part of doing business for new and existing global shopping platforms. As we have seen in Chapter 5, these systems form the ultimate new retail power blocks. No one has a better grasp of the need for swift and easy payment than these giants. It's a sure-fire path to long-term consumer loyalty and helps reach optimum conversion. All the ecosystems have now more or less developed their own payment propositions to bolster their reign over the retail value chain: Amazon has Amazon Pay, Alibaba has Alipay, Apple has Apple Pay, Facebook uses Messenger, Google has Google Pay, Tencent/WeChat uses WeChat Pay and Samsung has Samsung Pay.

Banks and credit card companies: their role in the War of Wallets

A frenzy has taken hold of traditional banks and insurance companies that are now desperate to make up for their late entry to this game. The fact that creating a wallet involves so much more than developing a payment app — something most banks do have — represents a gargantuan challenge for banks.

Interoperability between banks is further complicating matters in the US and Europe. Countries with many different banks find it harder to get everyone to cooperate. For this very reason, banks all over the world have been struggling to stay in the race.

COOPERATING FOR SURVIVAL IN EUROPE

It was in 2002 that I met with the major banks of the Netherlands to discuss the combination of online banking and online payments in web stores. Why not work together in an interoperable way to facilitate online payments based on Internet banking? The process would be drawn out until 2005 before Dutch banks became the first in Europe to actually begin working together – not least thanks to pressure by the Dutch e-commerce association Thuiswinkel.org, which I headed.[19] The interoperable payment system iDEAL, based on online banking, was launched and has since become the leading method for online payments in the country, with a market share of around 60%, giving online retail in the Netherlands an incredible boost.[20]

Inter-bank cooperation is slower to be adopted in other countries, with cross-border cooperation between banks lagging even further behind. It wasn't until 2012 that a banking consortium launched MyBank in Europe, a conduit for the very first international payment pilots.[21] For anyone mindful of a strong internal market, it's truly baffling that EU banks seem incapable of setting their priorities straight: putting long-term customer interests – which are, of course, in the best interest of the whole banking sector – before their own short-term concerns.

A vast majority of banks are making attempts to adapt their old products to fit the new reality. Fintech startups are now proving far more agile in their response to the altered payment "desires" of (young) consumers. For banks and credit card firms, there is often no alternative to joining forces with these vibrant new businesses, as they face the imminent danger of losing touch with their customers in the immediate future. Ultimately, they risk becoming nothing more than back-office payment administrators for the handling of financial retail transactions.[22] They are already being treated as wallflowers in the digital payment dance, which is fast turning into a kind of tango between customers and (web) stores. At present, services like Apple Pay still need banks, but the actual bank has become an (almost) invisible actor within the transaction. The big tech wallets and apps are the ones in charge of the "front-end" of the payment.

Reaffirming their customer relationships by tapping into the trust they've been granted by those very customers is surely the way forward for banks. They can then enter the realm of online identification, working alone or with startups, and help (web) stores move from *few-clicks-buy* to *one-click-buy* or even *no-click-buy*.

Credit cards

For decades, credit cards have been the preferred method for online purchases of goods and services. However, they are also a great irritant for consumers. The system requirement of entering the full credit card number dates back to the 1970s. Apparently, credit card companies have not managed to move much beyond minimal improvements (think: 3D secure code) to meet online criteria. These businesses are now realizing that consumers are becoming increasingly disenchanted, something that has finally compelled them to simplify their verification procedures. *Tokenization* is a prime example here: this is an encryption of payment and identification data into a single unique code. It's an improved method for storing and protecting sensitive data. Paired with the development of wallets such as MasterPass, it's obvious that people will continue to use credit cards a lot. The possibility of collecting loyalty points and other card services are added benefits. The fact that credit cards are accepted internationally means that they are — for better or for worse — important drivers of international trade and business.

Who will win the War of Wallets?

The future of wallet and payment apps is by no means fully defined yet. Are they going to become a real fixture in the world of payments? Time will tell. For now, consumers are opting to use just a handful of wallets and payment apps on their smartphones. Wallets and apps that combine several payment options are particularly popular, as are those that can be connected to loyalty programs and other services.

The wallets and apps that successfully build consumer loyalty are the ones set to win the War of Wallets. For onlife consumers, borders do not truly exist, so why should payment methods? A wallet that can incorporate every possible (international) payment option — from banks, debit cards and credit cards to QR code scanners, NFC chips and in-store beacons — is the one that will conquer all.

We simply have to wait and see if wallets and apps stay confined to smartphones. It's conceivable that a physical appliance might become superfluous to the payment process. After all, we always have our own bodily characteristics "on" us, so why could they not be used with an in-cloud debit card to pay at an in-cloud checkout point?

A EUROPEAN STANDARD FOR PAYMENTS

The European Union places great emphasis on the harmonization of member states' payment standards. Having a single digital market ought to create a *digital level playing field* for payment, combat fraud and cybercrime, and, not to mention, boost consumer willingness to do business internationally.

The so-called "PSD2" has been a first step towards making payment accessible to both current and new information and to transaction service providers. This will bring a whole range of opportunities for new fintech businesses and big (non-European) tech companies to remain in or enter the market of (online) payments.

As of 2018, the Access-to-Account ("XS2A") is in place, giving businesses access to consumer accounts — after receiving permission, of course. This means banks are obligated to share payment dates and account information with third parties at the explicit request of consumers. Amazon and Facebook can be such third parties, or, in fact, any other player interested in the financial sector. Paying online in a web store is possible without any obvious interference of banks. In the process, Europe has been flinging open the door for new fintech market entrants and retail titans of China and the United States.

Identity: the new payment

If you think about it, you'll realize that in-store card payments are sort of data payments already. They're a digital solution in which data is used as part of the transaction. The true value for retailers lies in the personal data of these consumers shopping. The more you know about your customer, the more specific and tailor-made your offers can be to them. This increases the odds of a successful transaction immensely.[23]

The business models for all the huge tech companies are built upon a foundation of data acquisition and exploitation: the data is valuable personal data ranging from names and addresses to viewing patterns, online searches and previous purchases. In exchange for the free use of the goods and services provided by these companies, onlife consumers have grown to accept the usage of their data and now even willingly go for this option. For instance, Spotify lets you listen to music for free in exchange for your personal information. Personal data is the currency for using Facebook or LinkedIn; your login gives you free access to other sites as well. Google, WhatsApp, WeChat and Twitter all use that same currency of data. No one is under the illusion that things are free; instead, onlife consumers care whether their personal data will give them a good deal. For the moment, the answer is apparently "yes" for the billions of people using the services mentioned above.

There's a growing consumer awareness that personal data is of significant value to retailers. Personal data not only produces free access to goods and services for consumers; it also reaps benefits and discounts. Why not pay in "likes" and "followers"? In the future, the data provided by demonstrable *social selling* will effectively be a means of payment. In the end, it's the powerful onlife consumer who determines whether the added value they represent for the retailer is sufficiently interesting before accepting the retailer's offer. Similarly, retailers need to identify the consumer before them and ascertain that it is actually the consumer they think it is.

In other words, properly functioning online methods of identification are essential for payments with personal data. After all, the vendor needs to be sure that data is worth it before accepting it as currency for goods and services. Retailers need to be absolutely convinced that the data is productive, useful and — most importantly — verified.

In the near future, the battle over "who can identify the onlife consumer" is bound to define the rules of engagement in onlife retail for years to come. Are we all going to indiscriminately use the open logins of the big social networks, or will we start using new and secure logins provided by national governments? At the very least, consumers ought to have the right to choose between the two.

Online identification: the key to personal data

Determining a buyer's identity has become essential to the customer journey, especially the payment stage of it. By checking the veracity of an identity card or having the consumer link a tidbit of information only they themselves could know or own, the vendor can verify if someone really is who he says he is. Consumers needing to constantly retype information as part of the identification procedure before making an (initial) online purchase is hugely annoying for the onlife consumer. As a result, retailers lose business in the conversion.

In the years ahead, having an online identity, also known as eID, will become the new normal. These so-called eID systems might create new breakthroughs in adopting onlife and consumer behavior. They can become game changers in the onlification of society.

Governments need to supply a free online identification system for their citizens, which public organizations and the private sector can then use. As a result, people will simply have one single digital identity, providing them access to a range of services, varying in their levels of (required) confidence and security. You might use it to open a bank account, deal with your local authority or do some online shopping.

There are already instances of national eIDs being adopted and implemented successfully, most notably in the countries of Scandinavia. Norway and Sweden both have a BankID, and the banks and government are working together in Denmark. An electronic identity card in Estonia allows people to travel, vote, and log onto bank accounts and official government databases to, for example, look at their own medical records.

Biometrics

Using biometric identifiers such as fingerprints, facial recognition, retina scans, and voice recognition — all of which may or may not be supported by behavior traits — is actually closer than people might think. Until recently, it was something straight out of James Bond, but new technology is making payments through biometric identifiers more and more popular.

Fingerprint recognition has been used since 2015 in mobile banking and payment apps. It's the biometric technology used most and is supported by both Apple's iOS and Android devices. Every single high-end mobile device has a fingerprint sensor. How to use the sensor can vary, though. The latest sensors take a 3D-image of one or more fingerprints, thus increasing their reliability.

Paying with facial recognition or a selfie is easy to do with a smartphone camera; in other words, it is already widely available. Gradually, retina or facial scans have been added to the latest high-end smartphones (Samsung S8, iPhone X). Facial recognition does usually have a "liveness check" built-in. In order to prevent deception, Mastercard uses a centralized check for its "selfie pay." The unlocking of a Samsung S8 or iPhone X asks for a decentralized identity check.

Using voice recognition to enter instructions or commands into a smartphone is becoming more popular than ever. Authenticating personal identity is being done through voice recognition more often, too. ING (Direct) Bank's "voice banking" is but one example. Using voice recognition, a payment order is given, which can then be confirmed with a fingerprint, pin number or facial recognition in the banking app. Voice banking offers the opportunity to analyze vocal patterns to check if it is indeed the right person giving the order.

And finally, the behavior of paying customers is increasingly being used for payments. *Behavioral biometrics* is the generic name for checking several characteristics of behavior, such as the speed of typing words or how the mouse or touchscreen are used. Banks are using these behavioral biometrics in addition to old-school or biometric authentication more and more frequently.

No-click buy

When personal data and biometric characteristics are used for payment, that means the no-click buy has arrived in online and physical shops. Google is gradually phasing in no-click buying taking advantage of all of the learnings of its Google Hands Free app.

In a pilot, the app allowed Android users to do in-store payments instantly through a link with their credit card. It couldn't be easier to use: you simply told the sales assistant that you wanted to pay using Google, and he then checked if you had a Google Hands

Free account that matched your photo and initials. Next, the Hands Free app on your smartphone confirmed you were indeed in the store — you need not even remove it from your pocket or purse — and the assistant then okayed the payment. Google stopped the experiment in 2017, but will undoubtedly bring the best features of the program to people and stores in due time.[24]

At a later stage, a facial recognition camera is sure to replace the sales assistant doing the verification. Identity will have truly become a currency, then.[25] It might be any day now that we can all *wink-and-pay*: pay and complete the verification with a selfie and a blink of the eye.

Shift

The actual result of no-click pay is that the process of identification moves forward from the end to the very start of the customer journey. Onlife consumers will start receiving personalized offers and bespoke advice during the orientation and selection stages. Some people might think payment methods involving biometrics and personal data are still futuristic with little basis in reality; the truth is they provide staggering opportunities for consumers and retailers alike. Onlife consumers are thrilled by the convenience, retailers love the reduced risk.

DANGERS OF BIOMETRIC IDENTIFICATION

We should, however, take stock of the possible dangers involved in identification and payment through biometrics — in other words, not get completely carried away by euphoria over the new developments in technology. The most important risks are safety and privacy. A stored fingerprint must be a 98-percent match with the one being scanned to ensure safety, meaning there is a "degree of probability" involved. This is different to a pin number, where there is only right or wrong. What is essential, then, is a proper so-called "liveness check." This check will ascertain if there is a "live finger" and a "live facial recognition" (smile, wink).

The privacy risks of biometric authentication are that the stored data could be leaked or be used inappropriately and illicitly. The weakest link in the process are the intermediaries, who are — unfortunately — still essential. All the biometric data will be stored on heavily guarded servers owned by large players in the international market. Be that as it may, the data has not lost any of its appeal to thieving terrorists or political operatives interested in misusing it for their own gains.

Biometrics are actually safer than pin numbers, user names and passwords – things which consumers are notoriously sloppy with and frequently forget. Then again, they would prefer to lose their password than their fingerprint or retina scan – that biometric data can never be changed once lost or stolen.

The blockchain revolution

Another technology likely to affect our future means of payment is the blockchain (more on this in Chapter 2). Some people even regard the blockchain as the new Internet.

The key characteristic of a blockchain payment application is that it constructs, codifies and commits every action, payment or transaction into a "block" of data. These blocks, once joined together to form a "blockchain," then guarantee safe transactions. Breaking into them is simply impossible.

It is also a highly suitable technology for identification; for example, in a transaction between buyer and vendor. The blockchain is potentially a replacement for the intermediaries in payment traffic, bringing the retailer and consumer closer together. They are both receiving information directly and no longer need a go-between. This means payments can take place in real-time, day or night. The blockchain is different to banks, as its payments can be done anywhere and anytime you please. Nor does it have the limitations of huge and highly-vulnerable server parks, which require *downtime* for maintenance or in the wake of a DDoS attack.

In the infrastructure of the blockchain, it is frankly impossible for anyone to alter data illicitly. There is a downside to this, though: once personal data has been added, it can never be removed, which might lead to annoying or even troubling situations. It is, then, absolutely essential that protecting user privacy is a key aspect of the blockchain construction.

NEW BLOCKCHAIN APPLICATIONS

There are new blockchain apps appearing left, right and center all the time. For instance, there are already blockchain alternatives for YouTube and Wikipedia. Cloud storage and peer-to-peer payments are other examples being transformed into blockchain solutions. The UN is currently researching how smartphone-accessible solutions using blockchain can provide payment options for the poorest people in the world without third-party interference. Over 2 billion people in the world without access to a bank account are, at present, unable to participate in the global financial arena. Will smartphones, the blockchain and crypto make a difference to them in the future?

According to the World Economic Forum, the blockchain will wreak havoc on the financial world.[26] David Yermack, a professor at the NYU School of Law, even believes that the advent and rise of the blockchain will ultimately wipe out banks all together.[27] For the moment, the blockchain is still wildly imperfect, as the hurdles surrounding the bitcoin — the currency based on blockchain technology — have proven. Now, criminals can take advantage of the unique opportunities offered by this technology. In a way, this is similar to how the porn industry was one of the first business sectors to fully grasp the potential of the Internet back in the 1990s.

People are working around the clock to eliminate these growing pains. Universities have joined forces to map out the applications of the blockchain. *Venture capitalists* and fintech businesses have started to look for a new killer app to put bitcoin to shame, and banks all over the world are desperately considering their own role in a decentralized bitcoin-centered economy. Six of the largest global banks currently have a new currency of their own in development, based on blockchain technology, called the Utility Settlement Coin.[28] They are fully aware that they cannot afford to miss out on another opportunity like this. Governments and legislators are — as they were in the early days of Internet — struggling with their response to the blockchain. The future will require laws and regulations to guide the technology along the right course.

For most consumers, the blockchain is basically science fiction, just as the world wide web used to be in the early 1990s. Sure, we had heard of it, read about it, but in our wildest dreams we could not have imagined how it would totally alter our lives. If the blockchain does live up to its promise, the road to the no-click buy is wide open.

BITCOIN ACCEPTANCE

Many retailers all over the world have begun accepting cryptocurrency like the bitcoin as currency: Amazon, Target, Tesla and Zappos are among them.[29] The volatile nature of cryptocurrency in general has made many retailers wary of accepting it: because in the time it takes to process a transaction, the cryptocoin may have gone up or down in value by a few percentage points.

Pay without noticing: on the rise

Onlification affects payments. The onlife consumer is eager to have an integrated omnichannel customer journey, accessible 24/7 and 365 days a year, no matter where they are. They are completely fed up with needing a different payment option, with its own codes, tokens or passwords, for every different channel they use. Regardless of how innovative something is, a consumer is interested in only two things. First, does it solve their problems (cut down on lines at the cash register or eliminate disruptions with card transactions)? And second, does it make life easier for them (does it relieve them of that crammed-full-to-bursting wallet)?

In years to come, we can expect payments to become more and more passive. The Uber taxi-app is a good example: by giving permission to charge a credit card before using the service, customers can step out of the cab "without paying" on arrival.

This doesn't mean consumers lose the moment of purchase altogether. It just means this slides forward to the very beginning of the customer journey. Regular customers will effectively give permission to charge a certain amount at the start of their orientation. This shift translates into a reduced number of actions at the end of purchasing. Onlife retail is likely to be accepted more swiftly through measures such as this.

Retailers and other stakeholders will need to commit to simplifying, speeding up and removing hurdles from the payment process in the very near future. Consumers can scarcely imagine anything that drives them to despair faster than the egg-timer icon telling them to wait for the transaction to be processed. In the meantime, they have to wonder out loud if the payment has succeeded. Retailers know that slow checkout equals a disaster for conversion: if you keep customers waiting too long, they will cancel the payment instantly. If you want your customers to stay, you must ensure more than just easy payments — it's essential to have extra-top-speed payments, too.

"Amazon delivery drones will be as common as seeing a mail truck."

**JEFF BEZOS,
FOUNDER AND CEO OF AMAZON**

10

Delivery:
the last mile dilemma

How can retailers have all those billions of goods delivered the world over? To what lengths do they need to go in order to solve the so-called *dilemma of the last mile*, working together with all those mail and parcel delivery businesses, both new and familiar? The aim: to deliver purchases right on the doorstep of the consumer.

Delivery is the fourth step in the customer journey. This includes both home delivery and pickup points, the information regarding delivery, and the various related services, including return policies.

I've decided to limit myself in this chapter, simply discussing the delivery of goods by (web) stores at a pre-arranged address for the consumer. First, I will offer a description of this stage of the customer journey from the onlife consumer's perspective. What are their options? What are the expectations held by the different kinds of onlife shoppers?

Next, I plan to describe delivery from the perspective of the (web) stores. What's involved in having parcels delivered to a consumer's home address, what are the challenges relating to doing so in other countries, and finally, how future-proof is the model of free delivery and free returns?

The third part of the chapter is where I turn to the biggest challenge faced by (web) stores and logistics service providers: the eponymous last mile of delivery. What role can the Internet of Things (IoT) play here, and what are new business models for parcel delivery companies and (web) stores? I will discuss the rise and value of so-called *social delivery*, the increase of drone delivery and the actual shopping street functioning as a distribution center. The third section ends with the dilemma of returns: some (web) stores see this as a service, whereas others find it a costly bane of their existence.

In the fourth and final section of the chapter, we will examine the sustainability of the delivery process: the dilemma of the *last green mile.*

Delivery options

What onlife retail needs is a complete overhaul of traditional logistics. Onlife shoppers insist on service, speed and convenience, not to mention that they prefer it all to be free. They want their purchases "ordered today, delivered yesterday," so to speak. More often than not, they now have the option of determining how they have their goods delivered. The table below provides an overview of the various options. Each of these will be discussed at length in this chapter.

FOUR DELIVERY OPTIONS[1]

Attended home delivery	Unattended home delivery
– Home delivery – Drone delivery	– Delivery at neighbors – Mailbox delivery – Delivery in a dedicated "parcel box"
Attended intermediate delivery	**Unattended intermediate delivery**
– Pickup point delivery – In-store delivery – Delivery at work	– In-house – Delivery to a "locker wall" – Trunk delivery

Each delivery method has its own price tag. Consumers frequently have the option of specifying blocks of time for delivery, give permission (or not) to have items delivered at their neighbors, or choose extra-speedy delivery.

Some retailers decide to waive the separate shipping fees, though it's wise to remember that there is no such thing as free delivery. Retailers simply mark up their prices to recoup the cost of delivery or decide to accept a smaller profit margin (more on this dilemma later on).

Another aspect that influences the method of delivery and its options are the product dimensions. Not every delivery option suits every single item. Size matters. Nearly everything can be delivered at home or be collected at a pickup point. Small items might fit in the mailbox. Fresh and frozen food needs to be delivered promptly. Other items, however, may require an actual person to accept the delivery (and sign for it). For everyday groceries — including fresh and frozen items — it makes sense to accept delivery in person. Signing for receipt of delivery or having an obsolete item (a dishwasher or fridge perhaps) picked up are other options.

As the number of single-person and double-income homes continues to rise, personal home delivery is becoming more of a challenge. That is why pickup points on the outskirts of cities, in residential areas and in stores are growing more popular.

Expectations paired to shopping types

Onlife consumers might have completely different reasons for choosing any given delivery method. The table on the next page shows the various stipulations for different types of shoppers.[2]

Retailer considerations

Within the value chain, retailers are faced with the customer's desires, the fulfillment of goods — from order picking to packaging — and finally, the transport of their products. As a rule, they do business with the large-scale national mail and parcel delivery companies. As a result of more countries freeing the market constraints in the parcel sectors, there is generally no monopoly for the national companies. However, they tend to still dominate their home markets.

Virtually all the large department stores and web stores choose to work together with large-scale and frequently (inter)national mail and parcel delivery companies. Smaller (web) stores, on the other hand, are starting to take a different route by joining forces with other small businesses and working together in new platforms and networks. Together, they purchase logistics, collate the parcels

PREREQUISITES ACCORDING TO ONLIFE SHOPPER TYPES

	Delivery service	Customer receipt
Passionate shopper	– Wants options for delivery and return. – Wants (limited) options for delivery location. – Wants to track order on an app and likes getting alerts: fun!	– Wants speedy delivery, preferably same-day. – Wants delivery to happen where the item is to be used (home or office). – Wants exclusive packaging and other services that add to a high-end retail experience. – Wants special offers and extra attention.
Deliberate shopper	– Wants delivery options. – Wants to track the order on an app and to get an alert.	– Wants exclusive or breakable items to be treated with extra care (extra-safe delivery, for instance). – Does not mind waiting a few days, provided delivery is within a timeslot. – Wants to choose between various options for receipt.
Calculating shopper	– Wants comprehensive information on delivery options. – Wants to monitor delivery using track & trace.	– Reaches a calculated decision based on effort and price, wants an amended price for pickup location, speed, etc. – In-store pickup, storeroom pickup or other delivery pickup options. – Services need not be included.
Passive shopper	– Wants to decide on delivery location, timeslot and speed. – Wants his preferences to be stored in order to get personalized offers.	– Wants the order to be delivered at home and even taken upstairs if needed. – Is prepared to wait several days. – Would like items to be installed/assembled.

to be mailed, and offer a range of delivery options to their customers by way of several logistics service providers. Advantages of scale are created in the process, and the (web) stores garner lower prices and higher service levels at the same time.

Most (web) stores have a lot of difficulty in switching their logistics providers. To them, the existing agreements can feel like a *lock-in* which has them trapped. A lot of delivery companies demand exclusivity. Besides, the lack of technical compatibility between the infrastructures of different logistics service providers is another obstacle. Truth be told, customers often have very little choice as to which logistics firm is going to drive up to their home.

Customer returns

- Wants a simple and speedy return procedure.
- Is interested in a "returns subscription".
- Wants to be able to return the item instantly to the delivery person if it doesn't meet expectations.

- Wants a simple and speedy return procedure.
- Wants to make no effort himself when items are picked up for return (the pickup person takes care of repacking, taking item apart, etc.)
- Wants several options for returning items.

- Is willing to make some effort for returns if it gives him a price discount.
- Wants his money back ASAP.

- Wants a simple and speedy return procedure.
- Wants to be able to return the item instantly to the delivery person if it doesn't meet expectations.
- Wants to make no effort himself when items are picked up for return (the pickup person takes care of repacking, taking item apart, etc.).

OWN DELIVERY

More and more (web) stores and shopping platforms have begun to manage the delivery process themselves, completely or partially. They believe the effort and costs required are easily outweighed by the option of having personal contact with their customers. In the United States, Amazon delivers its own groceries for both Amazon (Fresh, Pantry) and Whole Foods customers. Items ordered from retailers advertising on Google Shopping are subsequently delivered by Google Express.

Niche delivery companies

New and specialist logistics service providers are popping up left, right and center in niches of the logistics chain. Delivery of heavy goods by two delivery people, or the handover of fresh and frozen foodstuffs, are examples. Some manufacturers have specialist delivery services of their own, too. So-called *drop shipments* are a means of delivering washing machines – for example – directly from manufacturer to consumer.

Other niche delivery companies are occupied by deliveries in busy inner-city areas (bikes, mopeds, cargo bikes), car trunk and geolocation drop-offs, home deliveries at the neighbors instead of your own home, or in-house or even in-fridge home deliveries when you are not there.

Young businesses tend to be the ones focusing on *last mile delivery* niches, all the way to your front door. In so doing, they've managed to undermine the market position of traditional logistics firms. They think outside the (delivery!) box when it comes to transport, staff, delivery hours, distribution locations, delivery options, sustainability and information providing. New innovative concepts are being developed, benefiting customers and (web) stores alike. The table on the next pages gives you an idea of the most recent developments in the field.

ROBOT DELIVERY

Artificial intelligence, too, is becoming more real than ever before in the realm of deliveries. The British-Estonian startup Starship is already experimenting with tiny robots who can collect small parcels from several flexible pickup points and take them to the consumer.[3] In Amsterdam Domino's Pizza is delivering pizza's with Starship robots.[4] In Norway, the online grocery store Kolonial has even started to deliver food in self-driving cars.[5]

Do-it-yourself or tag along?

In their strategy of outsourcing the fulfillment and logistics services to the shopping ecosystems and platforms, (web) stores get to benefit from the expertise and know-how that's been acquired, not to mention the lower delivery charges. The downside: they're coming to depend on the platforms more and more. What can they do, though? Tagging along comes down to relinquishing some customer ownership and subsequent loss of entrepreneurialism. Still, it's to be expected that retailers will increasingly sign up for these and other logistics platforms and intermediaries. For most (web) stores, it's the only way forward in the glocal economy.

Amazon and Alibaba — in the United States and China, respectively — offer the retailers on their platforms a full range of advanced delivery options with the logistics networks to match. They store goods in distribution centers, parcel and ship items for retailers and even provide customer care.

Through Fulfillment by Amazon (FBA), the fulfillment and distribution services of Amazon are not merely available for the goods sold on the Amazon Marketplace, but also for all the other products of any particular (web) store. The store's (or brand's) own packaging is then used. Amazon offers users of FBA the option of having their parcels delivered just as fast as Amazon's own deliveries to the tens of millions of loyal Prime customers. Retailers on Amazon Marketplace not only get to take advantage of the bargain bulk rates that Amazon has negotiated with United States parcel delivery companies. With Shipping with Amazon (SWA) it is launching a new courier delivery service for business customers selling goods on the Amazon Marketplace. Thanks to setting a lower price point than familiar and established names like FedEx and UPS, Amazon is keen to tighten its relationships with retailers and brands alike.[6]

Alibaba has made equivalent investments in its own logistics network. In 2013, the company set up the transport and logistics network Cainiao with a consortium of logistics companies, connecting (regional) transport businesses to storage facilities and distribution centers. Every day, this network delivers around 50 million parcels to roughly 250 Chinese cities. In ten years' time, this number will have grown tenfold to 300 million a day.[7]

Shopping platforms are becoming logistics service providers, too. For a long time, Amazon was the very best friend of these busi-

DELIVERY INNOVATIONS[8]

Means of transport	Staff	Delivery times	Supply locations
– Car fuel/ electronic	– Citizen	– Weekend	– Distribution center web store
– Car self-driving	– Commuter	– Evening	– Distribution center manufacturer
– Bicycle	– Employee	– Narrow timeslots	– Physical store as distribution center
– Pedestrian	– Neighbor	– Same day	– Store
– Drone	– None	– One-hour delivery	– Sharehouse
– Tube system/ Hyperloop		– Thirty-minute delivery	– Consumer's home
– Internet			– Flexible outpost (bus, container)
– Robot/drone			

nesses, though it has now fast become a formidable *frenemy,* gobbling up percentage chunks of market share which belonged to the national logistics service providers.[9]

Google Express has been delivering non-food items for Costco, Walgreens, Toys"R"Us and other retail partners.[10] Google is desperate in its attempt to stay relevant following the loss of market share to Amazon in retail-related searches in the United States and Germany.[11] Even Uber, the cab service, has taken to delivering groceries through UberRUSH,[12] meals through UberEATS and outsize parcels through UberCARGO.[13]

International deliveries

Many (web) stores are discouraged by the incomprehensible maze of options for overseas deliveries. Retailers tend to favor their national logistics carrier, who has partners abroad, to deliver parcels in other countries. Others decide to work with some of the new intermediaries in this field who are able to print the required shipping labels for any conceivable country. A third option for retailers is to hook up with foreign logistics providers directly.

Delivery options	Information	Cost
– At the front door	– Email	– Free
– In a box by the door	– App	– Free above
– Service point	– Photo	certain
– Pickup point	– GPS	amount
– Physical store as	– Exact time of	– Subscription
distribution center	delivery	– Pay
– Store	– Possibility	
– Office	of altering	
– Locker wall	location	
– Current consumer	shortly before	
location	delivery	
– In the car or on		
geolocation in cities		
– In-home/in-fridge		

Business models

In general, retailers lack the necessary information about all the different options. Another obstacle is the lack of transparency regarding pricing structures. Whereas delivery habits are familiar in the retailers' own country, these might vary wildly abroad. For example: in the Netherlands, over 80 percent of parcels are delivered at home, and in Germany, people are far more inclined to use *pickup points*. Estonians, too, have a strong consumer preference for pickup over home delivery. In many other countries, having something delivered to the neighbors' is just unheard of.

European deliveries

The Digital Single Market in Europe has created a commitment to further the transparency of the European market as a whole, the operability of the parcel service market in particular. Research has shown that retailers struggle with the scant information, too-slow deliveries and lack of track & trace facilities. The impenetrability of pricing is another hindrance (a parcel sent from the Dutch city of Maastricht to nearby Belgian Maasmechelen, a 10-km distance, is almost as expensive as the 1,000-km journey of a parcel going from the North to the South of France), as are the differences in legislation and regulation, not to mention the problem of returns.[14] Europe is working hard at resolving these issues by developing the new information platform Deliver in Europe. This is meant to simplify *cross-border* operations for retailers.[15]

In order to improve intercountry cooperation, Europe agreed on a standardized parcel label and matching technical specifications for parcels.[16] The use of a single common parcel label will enable interoperability between parties, and makes webstores more flexible, as they are no longer required to tie themselves to the IT integration of one single logistics service provider. As soon as the standardized label is widely adopted by the market, web stores will be able to choose any logistics service provider they want. At the same time, the logistics service provider can read out and subsequently deliver any package all across Europe. (Web) stores also instantly gain insight into where a parcel is at any given time. In the process, Europe is focusing on speed, affordability, flexibility and market transparency for the mail and delivery business. The effects of these policies will start to pan out in the near future and give the market a formidable boost.

Free delivery and return

For as long as we can remember, free deliveries and free returns of parcels have been important international online retail trends. In 2005, Amazon was the first company to offer this benefit, with Zalando following their lead in 2010 in Europe.

For onlife consumers, this is one of the key prerequisites of online retail. Over half of American customers actually cancel their order if the shipping fees are too expensive, with a similar proportion cancelling an order if it doesn't reach the minimum amount to qualify for free delivery.[17] Over three-quarters of all European consumers describe "free delivery" as the number one option during checkout.

In recent years, the large shopping platforms, department stores and web stores have turned free delivery and returns into the way to go. Thanks to its size, Amazon can offer customers free delivery options at (virtually) no cost at all. Zalando has made free delivery and returns into a cornerstone of its marketing strategy to capture a top position in the European market.

Regardless of their size, (web) stores face immense challenges through this policy of free delivery and returns. For large (web) stores, there is the expectation that they will simply comply with this new standard. Research has shown that pairing free deliveries with a lengthy viewing period is a key contributor to customer loyalty.[18] Small(er) and midsized retailers find themselves pushed into a *race to the bottom*. Particularly for items with little market value, free delivery and returns are just not feasible. They would love consumers to realize that in this context, there is no such thing as "free": someone, somewhere has to cover the cost. They believe that this trend, in fact, undermines the added value of the service of delivery.

Retailers can take heart when they hear of recent developments in the UK. Free delivery has taken a nosedive there. By offering a range of options to customers, free delivery is now only available for items with a longer delivery time or with a value exceeding a certain amount. Customers ordering items in a hurry, or small orders, simply have to pay for their delivery.

Challenges in the last mile

How in the world can we succeed in delivering those millions of orders and parcels to customers' homes as effectively, affordably and — preferably — as sustainably as possible? It seems every single (web) store owner is breaking his head over this. Similarly, consumers find it baffling to manage being at home at all the different times they need to be in order to receive all their orders. Surely, this could all be accomplished in an easier way, as well as better, faster and cheaper? Frequently, the last mile of delivery is what causes the most issues.[19] [20]

Every single parcel sent has required hours of clever thinking. There's a huge number of variables to take into account: delivery locations, product attributes (size, weight, etc.), time windows, cost, express delivery. The algorithms that calculate routes based on zip codes and possibilities for delivery are geared at optimizing customer service.

In densely populated cities, socio-demographics such as increased urbanization, the growth of single-person households, double-income homes and an ageing population keep presenting web stores and logistics service providers with new challenges. As online consumer spending continues to grow and the need for efficient logistics of returns intensifies, we can see pressure increasing on inner-city distribution. At the very same time, people are insisting on sustainable logistics more and more.

Finally, is seems odd that logistical service providers only deliver packages on the busiest 12 hours of each day. It should be feasible in due time to find ways to deliver packages at homes when inner-cities are at rest, streets are empty and people are at home. Perhaps the Internet of Things (IoT) can help to create time and space in inner-cities — think designated parking lots for vehicles — for the effective delivery of packages.

The Internet of Things and the last mile

Apparently, the IoT and use of big data might well be part of the solution for all those last mile obstacles. Logistics companies and parcel delivery businesses might take advantage of this in their planning and optimization of routes. It is vital to process real-time information both at top speed and until the last possible second during delivery.

UPS now offers its customers the option of altering the delivery time and place every second of the way. Even when the delivery person is already on his way, the chosen route is recalculated based on up-to-the-minute traffic, but also to process the fact that consumers might want to switch their delivery address at the very last minute and have something delivered at work instead of their home.

In years to come, we can expect to see the whole logistics chain undergoing digitization. Remotely tracking the path of a parcel will become an option by using the sensors fitted to the parcel itself.

INTERNET OF POSTAL THINGS

The United States Postal Service mentions the *Internet of Postal Things.* In it, an average piece of mail or parcel is scanned 11 times, give or take. The very moment the US Postal Service has outfitted its trucks, mailboxes, cars and bikes with sensors, they will have a wealth of information at their fingertips. By using that information, they can create opportunities for better and faster service, reducing the costs and environmental impact at the same time.

New business models

Now, there are suddenly opportunities for logistics service providers to utilize new goods and services to offer improved levels of service to retailers.[21] Examples include mailboxes outfitted with sensors (as discussed above) or the use of "home delivery lockers," which is something the US startup Postybell has been experimenting with.[22] This company sends the consumer a message on their smartphone telling them of a delivery to their mailbox. More and more, we are seeing both startups and traditional parcel delivery companies providing standalone parcel-locker-walls where consumers can go collect (or even return) parcels from a range of suppliers. An app provides the consumer with information, and they can open their locker using a code they've received through the app.

You could also opt to have items ordered online delivered to your hotel — no reason why not — as UberRUSH has started to do in large cities. Or, what about the trunk of your car at the office, an idea introduced jointly by DHL Parcel, Amazon and Audi? Commuters could certainly find this option of *trunk delivery* interesting.[23] Yet another option is to have parcels delivered by self-driving electronic vehicles, as Apple and Google do. Ford and Mercedes, meanwhile, are working on intelligent last-mile-buses, including matching delivery drones.[24] The Swedish supermarket ICA has started an *in-fridge-delivery* experiment, where the groceries are delivered into the customer's actual fridge. A digital lock on the front door provides entry for the delivery person. When the groceries have been delivered and the front door has been locked again, the customer receives a message.[25]

Social delivery

With high-tech solutions being concurrently developed by the big logistics firms, I've noticed a burst of new *crowd-based pickup & delivery* ideas. Why can't cab drivers, commuters, college students and senior citizens deliver parcels (even if they need to use a bike or electric moped to do so)? The IoT and big data can certainly help to make these new and crowd-based initiatives part of a more sustainable delivery process.

The first few such ideas are being expanded upon as we speak, with serious market players behind them. Flex is the Amazon program which has "regular people" delivering parcels.[26] These independent delivery contractors decide when and where to pick up and deliver a Prime order assigned to them.[27]

The smart economy and sharing economy cross paths here. An added benefit of solutions like this is that delivery becomes more personal. They are often referred to as *social delivery services* for that very reason.

In China, I witnessed these new and more personal delivery services bringing people together. In Beijing and Shanghai, everyone with a bike and smartphone can participate in this kind of social delivery.[28] Frequently, older people deliver the parcels in the hutongs, the traditional residential areas of large cities. When I was visiting the head office of JD.com, I was able to track the many delivery workers — using sensors and chips — in real-time from the information hub of the web store. Based on big data and geolocation, parcels are assigned to delivery workers depending on their availability, location and the delivery destination.[29]

Drone delivery

The opposite end of the spectrum is drone delivery: airborne mini robots like smartphones with propellers capable of depositing parcels on your front lawn. It sounds too good to be true, having an order delivered at home within 30 minutes. All you need to do is step outside and accept the delivery — even in remote areas (or perhaps *especially* in remote areas) that would otherwise be difficult to reach by car.

Drone delivery may prove to be an enormous disruption to e-commerce in the next decade. For now, drone delivery is limited to only the largest parcel delivery companies and shopping ecosystems due to the high cost of development and execution. They are the only ones who can afford it.[30]

Amazon, Google and Walmart have started experiments with drone delivery. Alibaba and SingPost have conducted trials in China and Singapore, respectively. Almost every single large mail and parcel carrier — ranging from DHL and PostNL to Swiss Post and UPS — is looking into this innovation. In 2016, Amazon carried out its first experiment of drone deliveries in the UK. In New Zealand, Domino's Pizza has started delivering pizzas with drones.

They fly at 20 miles per hour and can deliver pizzas in a 1 mile radius of the Domino's branch.[31]

Where Amazon's delivery ambitions are concerned, the sky is the limit.[32] With Shipping with Amazon (SWA) and Amazon Prime Air it is working towards delivering parcels within the half-hour to their Prime customers. The Amazon "Airborne Fulfillment Center" (AFC) is the patented flying distribution center from where drones will be able to deliver parcels to special events like sports matches or pop concerts. These airships operate at an altitude of almost 9 miles , enabling drones to take a "freefall" with low energy expenditure as they deliver parcels to the required spots.[33]

Consumers are ready for it. Around 80 percent of American consumers would prefer to shop at a retailer who can offer drone delivery within the hour, and close to 77 percent would happily pay extra for the privilege.[34]

Skeptics, however, have grave doubts about drone delivery ever truly taking hold. In developed countries, there are very few areas that are unreachable by car. The vast majority of people live in urban areas: how does a drone deliver a parcel on the third floor of an old apartment building? Air infrastructure, or the lack thereof, is simply an accident waiting to happen, so they say. For the moment, the cost of drones and of the energy expenditure to operate them cannot be recouped by the benefits of drone delivery.[35]

Yet, a group of more than 25 companies — including BestBuy, Google and Walmart — have made a joint application to the US Federal Aviation Administration for permission to carry out drone deliveries. Amazon has even submitted a plan for separate designated flight paths for drones and has new patents pending for special delivery drones.[36]

Ultimately, after all the obstacles have been scaled and the cost of drone deliveries has gradually diminished, the future will tell us that drone delivery is a viable option.[37]

In-store distribution center

It could hardly be a more obvious solution: using physical stores to solve last-mile dilemmas. Why should a washing machine ordered online need to come from some far-off distribution center if there is a nearby store in town that has it in stock and can deliver it without incident? There are huge advantages to having it delivered by a local courier or the store's service staff: lower costs, better and faster service, and a more sustainable endeavor.

In the United States, it's becoming more prevalent to make brick stores the point from where customer deliveries are made. If you order at a *brick & click*, the web store simply checks to see which physical store has the item in stock. They then make sure it is sent to the customer as soon as possible by using a local courier (in a car or on a bike).[38]

Not a new concept, then. Many traditional physical stores do find it surprisingly hard to execute, particularly when large numbers of goods are being ordered. Most brick & click stores simply do not have integrated delivery at their disposal. At present, physical stores and web stores do not share the same IT system, resulting in separate logistics paths for online and offline sales. Therefore, online customers have no real-time information about what is in stock at the brick stores.

A separate problem is how to deliver items ordered online from stores on busy shopping streets. These stores are neither equipped to deal with endless coming and going of delivery trucks nor for a flurry of couriers on (motor) bikes.

A concept successfully implemented by brick & click stores in their delivery options is the in-store pickup of items ordered online. The benefits scarcely need mentioning: there is no additional shipping fee thanks to savings on fulfillment and logistics, and when customers come to pick up their order, it means an extra visit to the store. The English department store John Lewis happily noticed that one in three customers picking up online items made additional purchases.

Retailers frequently note around 30 percent of goods ordered online being picked up in-store. The variations on the *click & collect* theme are nearly infinite. For example, at Belgian supermarket Colruyt, you can reserve non-food items online, come and look at them in-store and then decide on the spot whether or not to purchase them.

Returns

For years, returns have been an inextricable part of "mail order" retail. The old-school mail order companies and newer web stores are well-versed in this process and have fully integrated return shipments into their business model. Traditional retailers who, until recently, only operated physical stores, find the large volume of returns to be traumatic. They are not equipped for having items sent back, leading some retailers to even set a limit on returns.

Onlife consumers have zero qualms in sending back items without specifying the reason why. A store with a sound return policy might even become more attractive for both repeat visits and repeat purchases.

The flow of returns to (web) stores encompasses a wide range, depending largely on the product segment involved. Fashion retail has a far higher number of returns (between 30 and 40 percent) than other sectors (an average of 12.5 percent). While some companies may have implemented returns as part of their service (Amazon, Zalando), they still remain a drain on the budget for (web) stores everywhere. Retailers are very motivated to minimize the number of returns and are happy to report they are succeeding at doing so. Large fashion (web) stores have reported a gradual decrease (roughly 1 percent annually) of returns, thanks to improved product photography and videos. Automatic sizing advice can help customers order the correct size. When a customer has ordered three different sizes of jeans – for the third time – and returned the two larger sizes on the two previous occasions, the store can gently point this out during ordering.[39] Suggesting which size would suit best (based on previously-entered measurements by the consumer) is another way to reduce returns. Digital dressing rooms, body scans and augmented and virtual reality technology all help, too. English fashion titan ASOS has implemented 2D-technology, which involves consumers making a 2D outline of an item of clothing from their own closet. This outline is then matched to clothes on the website. ASOS has stated that the number of returns based on fit has been cut in half.

A last resort in the attempt to reduce the number of returns is to slightly complicate the return process. Jet.com, the relatively new US online department store (acquired by Walmart), has taken a kinder approach to this idea by offering customers the option of cancelling their right of free returns in exchange for a small discount on their purchase.

And finally: the last *green* mile

Gradually, over the next few years, we can expect logistics procedures to be made more sustainable. Apart from catering to consumer demands for sustainability, it's a necessary business decision in order to cut costs. It is precisely in the logistics innovations and increased last mile efficiency that a happy union can (often) be found between cost reduction and protecting the environment.

A growing group of onlife consumers is prepared to adapt their customer journey according to changing ecological circumstances. Mindful of resource scarcity, they realize we must reduce the mountain of waste we have created. For instance, consumers will start questioning the need for buying a washing machine produced abroad. How "green" is it, after all, to have this item shipped from somewhere far away, simply to save 20 dollars? Retailers (or third parties) who manage to make goods more sustainable all over the world are the ones who will earn the favor of onlife consumers.

SUSTAINABILITY AND ITS EFFECTS ON DELIVERY

DESTEP[40]	Our consumer behavior becomes more sustainable	Consequences for delivery
Demographic	– More single-person households – More double-income families – More over-65s – Urban population growth	– More attention for urban circumstances: electronic cars, efficient deliveries
Economic	– From linear to circular – Sharing economy – Consuming less – Re-using – Returns – Increase of second-hand possessions	– Fewer returns – Returns may be used to fulfill new orders directly – "End-of-life" returns become part of delivery – More transport movements on average, according to product lifespan

DESTEP[40]	Our consumer behavior becomes more sustainable	Consequences for delivery
Socio-cultural	– Boundaries between private and work life blurring – More working from home – More personal matters sorted out at work	– Increased number of delivery and pickup locations – Flexibility overrules accuracy of deliveries – Home deliveries remain a valuable commodity
Technical	– Increased transparency of the value chain – Improved technical knowledge regarding data processing, planning, etc.	– Actual transport and ecological costs become visible – Transparency becomes a prerequisite – Improved route efficiency
Ecological	– Improved resource collection – Increased product lifespan	– Delivery costs for products will increase – Server park energy costs will become transparent – Increased logistics of returns – Increase of spare-part deliveries
Political	– Ecological developments the driving force for legislation and regulation	– European regulation will require consumer prices to incorporate the environmental costs of goods and services

Last mile effects

In recent years, onlife shoppers have adopted a mentality of *I Want What I Want When I Want It,* and powerful companies have happily played to that mentality.[41] The new normal is now: order at any time of day or night, and decide when and how to receive delivery.

In the future, customer demands are bound to be the driving force behind new concepts of delivery and pick up. The various parties in the retail chain – ranging from vendors to national and international mail and parcel delivery carriers – are being forced into tough decisions. Do they still want to operate independently, or are they going to choose to work together? Political forces may well compel them to increased cooperation. The growing volume of traffic in residential areas and inner cities, as well as considerations of environment and efficiency, may leave them no other option.

In my mind's eye, I can see it happening: independent transport workers — adorned with logos of several different logistics service providers — who pick up parcels from every conceivable web store at dedicated distribution points on the outskirts of cities. They then deposit all the parcels to (un)manned pickup points in residential or inner-city areas, or they might just do their rounds in your very street or neighborhood.

I fully expect governments to start using incentives to increase the attention for sustainable delivery. In the future, new types of delivery — which consolidate the flow of distribution, reduce environmental impact and use local communities more efficiently — will prove to be crucial in a lasting and sustainable means of customer service. Local initiatives, including deliveries on bikes or electronic vehicles by people you know and pickup points in neighborhood stores and residential areas: these are all solutions which cater to sustainable delivery and, in effect, color the last mile green.

> "We are a service company that just happens to sell shoes."

**TONY HSIEH,
CEO OF ZAPPOS**

11

Customer care: customer service becomes customer intimacy

Customer care encapsulates sincere interest in the customer and commitment to the care he deserves. It's so much more than basic (aftersales) service or simply responding to customer queries. Instead, it's ensuring the very essence of quality throughout every step of the customer journey.

Customer care is step 5 of this journey, after orientation, selection, payment and delivery. The reason why I eschew the term *customer service* is that it brings to mind being put on hold endlessly when calling a helpdesk or of in-store customer service desks cleverly tucked away.

First, I will use this chapter to discuss the evolution from customer service to customer care, taking into account the influence of the Internet. As we will see, some retailers have plunged themselves into (almost) "obsessive customer care" by integrating ultimate care with customer service on every level and in every aspect of (web) stores.

In the second part of the chapter, I look to a possible future of ultimate care based on innovations like robotization, artificial intelligence, digital personal assistants, chatbots and robot advisers. Will they replace the human touch, or will real people always matter to customer care?

Finally, I will turn to *customer intimacy*, aimed at bringing back human dimensions to retail and helping customers feel properly recognized by giving them personal attention. Truly a challenge occupying the mind of many a retailer.

Customer service evolution

Scaling up played a large part in losing sight of consumers as individuals in the twentieth century. Similarly, the rise of in-store self-service reduced customers, by and large, to mere statistics. For many retailers, customer service and the handling of complaints became an annoying debit line on their budget.

Around the turn of the century, customers with issues or questions became piece goods, a sum per completed phone call, with a premium awarded for processing *calls* promptly. Staffers working in the customer service or claims department were judged on the speed and efficiency with which they handled the issues before them. Automated helpdesk systems would triage calls from customers with complaints, problems or questions towards primary or secondary service desks. Digital screens would display the number of callers waiting and the length of each call in minutes. Retailers tended to strongly encourage keeping customer contact to a minimum and would dictate the terms in which customers could use their services.

Transparency

As the twentieth century neared its end, the rise of the Internet created an unprecedented degree of transparency into all the steps of the customer journey. All the information you could possibly want about every single product or service was suddenly available online 24/7 at the click of a mouse. Comparing prices became easy as pie, thanks to search engines, marketplaces and comparison websites. Even the level of service and other aspects of customer care could be compared between stores.

From day one of online shopping, excellent service was the best way to win and retain customer confidence. More than ever before, customer service has since grown into a serious deciding factor for consumers as they deliberate where, when and how to buy. Excellent (customer) service is imperative; this is now an undisputed fact.

Physical stores, too, realize their sales staff needs to deal with customers who come into the store well-informed. They've done their research and fully expect the salesperson to know their stuff as well. In-store, onlife consumers want to engage in conversation about the goods and services they are keen to purchase.

At call centers, staffers have noted an increase in articulate customers who just refuse to back down. Social media provides channels where complaints are visible for all the world to see — unlike phone calls — and pose a possible threat to a retailer's reputation.

The role and purpose of customer service has been altered profoundly by all these circumstances. Gradually, businesses have come to understand that this type of service is much more than a debit line; it has many opportunities to offer as well.

Reviews

After the turn of the century, customer contributions to website and web store content became popular. Customers would write reviews of goods and services on web stores or describe their experiences on forums. In 2000, TripAdvisor was one of the first to launch a new service model for the travel and hotel business built on free contributions from customers.

Initially, businesses were extremely wary of displaying (negative) customer experiences. This particular genie refused to get back into the bottle, though. Onlife consumers are inspired en masse by other people's experiences. Years ago, when I was on the lookout for a baby stroller, I stumbled upon a review by a NASA engineer. He gave a detailed description of all the technology and materials used for that particular stroller. He said that he believed this was the best and safest stroller in the United States. That was all I needed to know before I bought it: I felt I could trust the verdict of this experienced and independent user.

NPS

Since 2005, the Net Promoter Score (NPS) has become a popular management tool that helps you understand the reputation of your company. Large web stores, in particular, often ask customers to share their experiences of all the separate steps of the customer journey. This gives the retailer an idea of how many customers are satisfied enough to recommend the web store to family and friends. The NPS is an especially useful way for web stores to stand out in a competitive online market, thanks to the information it produces regarding customer satisfaction and company reputation. Asking customers to review their purchases is the new normal. On the whole, retailers have relinquished their fear of bad reviews because they know reviews will only be taken seriously by the consumer if there are negative ones, too. Many a retailer has now grasped that NPS scores and direct consumer recommenda-tions send a far more powerful message than a lot of expensive advertising could ever do.

Social media

The immense boom of social media in the everyday life of the onlife consumer has made customer responses even more important. A new element has been thrown into the mix, though. Not only does the quality of the review count, but also the speed and manner in which retailers respond to complaints, questions or problems.

Consumers who live the onlife way fully expect businesses to do the same. For them, it's evident that a business open 24/7 ought to provide service during those same hours. They also expect to be able to choose the channel on which they wish to communicate, be that Facebook, Twitter, WhatsApp, WeChat, email or phone. Which one they choose might depend on the product or service, the time of day, or even their current mood. Sometimes human contact is preferable, or even necessary, and sometimes it is not. The onlife consumer is certainly not one to accept being put on hold endlessly.

OBSESSIVE CUSTOMER SATISFACTION FOCUS

At online footwear store Zappos, acquired by Amazon in 2009, there is a self-confessed obsession with customer satisfaction. They even have an actual Chief Customer Satisfaction Officer, and they always save a seat for "the customer" at important meetings (as Amazon also does, by the way). Zappos was one of the first stores to keep track of its NPS scores.

Zappos is not interested in "satisfied" customers; they want custom-ers to be thrilled, ecstatic, and over the moon to the point of acting as ambassadors and convincing others to buy there, too. This is not a selfless motivation for Zappos. When I visited Zappos in 2018 I was inspired by the way employees share a profound belief that ecstatically happy consumers will generate more revenue and, obviously, more new customers

On July 11th, 2016, Steven Weinstein, a Zappos customer loyalty team member, received a call. It would prove to be no run-of-the-mill call. The customer was having some difficulty placing an order, and Weinstein managed to fix this right away. However, this was not the end of the call – Weinstein and the customer fell into a conversation for an amazing 10 hours and 43 minutes.[1] Even for Zappos, this is rather excessive, though not completely unheard of. In a blatant defiance of general customer service practice, Zappos staffers are allowed to stay on the phone for as long as they want. Building relationships is considered far more important than scoring *sales*. Whenever a lengthy call happens to go on during a busy time, it is not cut short; instead, people from other departments jump in to help customer service.

Zappos is well aware that the personal touch can make the customer happier and produce a substantial higher number of (follow-up) sales. The company trains its staff to make at least two attempts at something personal in the conversation, perhaps by referring to the dog they hear barking in the background or what the weather is like in the area where the customer lives. They call this practice *Personal Emotional Connection (PEC)*. One of the mottos of Tony Hsieh, founder and CEO of Zappos, is *"to create a little fun and weirdness."*[2] If you find the perfect blend of weirdness and fun, you just might end up with a ten-hour marathon phone call.

Empathy

Creating a wealth of exceptionally happy customers takes hard work: not just financial investments, but also perseverance and patience. Many businesses find they need to reinvent their manner of interacting with customers. A prerequisite for the shift from customer service to customer care is having empathy for your customers and imbuing the whole company with that empathy.

The key step in making customers into ambassadors might well be asking them about their experiences along every stage of the customer journey, from orientation to selection and payment to delivery, and dealing with queries and complaints. Every single interaction with customers is an opportunity to build on customer happiness and satisfaction.

Understanding the viewing/choosing/buying behavior of customers is what helps retailers make their products more personally relevant without harming the privacy of the customer. The retailer might suggest a purchase based on the products other consumers chose to complement. They can also glean information from knowing in which stage of the customer journey someone is and which device the customer is using at any given moment.

Consumers who have given their permission outright for their personal data to be used should expect to receive personal and bespoke offers in years to come. Already, users of Amazon, Apple (iTunes), Booking.com, Facebook, Instagram, Netflix, Pinterest, Twitter, Snapchat and YouTube have seen their personal pages become more relevant. Many traditional retailers still fail to use the loads of behavioral data that they have. At present, only a few large traditional retailers and supermarkets use previous purchases and viewed products to suggest offers to customers. Most retailers, however, find it a struggle to improve service and customer care based on data.

Customer care within the smart, sharing, circular and platform economy

In the future, the growing opportunities afforded by technology in the smart economy will present the first ever possibility of one-to-one customer care. Big data and digitization are going to provide more opportunities than ever before for distilling relevant patterns from the huge amounts of data. The Internet of Things (IoT) is set to both make this revolution possible and nourish it. It's an almost inconceivable source of countless little chunks of data, all of which end up producing valuable understanding, patterns and trends.

The very same technology used to make personalized recommendations and special offers can, in fact, be used to predict which items a customer is going to buy. As a result, the whole buying process of the company can be turned upside down, making it more tailored to consumer needs.

AMAZON'S ANTICIPATORY SHIPPING PATENT

It was Amazon that already patented "anticipatory shipping" in 2013: predicting the demand of users for the purpose of sending products before being purchased. Amazon may box and ship products it expects customers in a specific area will want. It works by predicting what customers will buy before they actually buy it and shipping the products to nearby hubs or trucks until an order arrives or by sending products to the homes of Prime members even before the sale has been made. Pure genius[3] or a dubious patent?[4]

What is it going to mean when we're connected to Internet 24/7 through all manner of new gadgets and devices? What are the consequences for the customer journey in general and for customer care in particular?

The sharing economy and the circular economy pose similar questions. How will customer care be affected when goods are being shared with other people, or when step 5 of the customer journey is step 1 at the same time? What happens when a product is no longer matched to just the one user, but instead is being lent or rented out (and coming back to the retailer) or being swapped or resold (moving on to yet another consumer)? How can you tell that the item has been used properly during its life cycle? How can you determine the value of second- or third-hand goods? How do you best coordinate maintenance services and the most suitable insurance? How do you instruct all those first-time users, offer them the help they need and give them relevant tips & tricks? It's not far-fetched to wonder how a retailer could ever pull it off, coping with all these different opportunities and threats to customer care.

In the platform economy, the large technology firms and global shopping ecosystems are the places onlife consumers feel most at home. The investments made by these giants in new applications for customer care run into the hundreds of millions of dollars, euros and yuans. Small retailers face a very real challenge of keeping up. They can opt to join the infrastructure of the shopping ecosystems for customer care services. Alternatively, they might go for distinguishing themselves by their small scale, local products and friendly, old-fashioned service (see Chapter 5).

Artificial intelligence in customer care

Over the next few decades, virtual assistants, digital PAs, chatbots and robot advisers are going to help provide excellent customer care to consumers. One way or another, robotization and AI are bound to affect us all.

SANNE, OUR VIRTUAL ASSISTANT IN MACROPOLIS

In the late 1990s, the most famous virtual assistant was the unparalleled Miss Boo at the hip and trendy online fashion store Boo.com.[5] The company had invested 70 million dollars in an avatar with whom customers could have a friendly chat. In our web department store Macropolis, we experimented with a virtual assistant called Sanne. She could answer simple questions and (occasionally) offer more help than that. Sanne, just like Miss Boo, proved to be a failure though. Often slow, she halted and malfunctioned a lot or sometimes just stayed mute. Nobody wanted a slow and halting performance out of their assistant. Sadly, Miss Boo didn't make it either. She was one of the more expensive casualties of the Internet bubble bursting. Miss Boo, once worth 70 million, was sold for 250,000 dollars.

Now, 20 years down the line, there are more successful tales to be told of virtual assistants and chatbots. International retailers such as Walmart (Walmart Simple Text), Tesco (Rachel), Toys"R"Us (Emma) and H&M (Kik) all have them. These are the precursors of the virtual assistants that will greet us on our smartphones in years to come whenever we walk into a store.[6]

Virtual assistants

Virtual (personal) assistants who are able to answer simple questions or resolve easy problems will be the first points of contact in customer care. Large tech companies, web stores, insurance companies, banks and telecom companies are already busy experimenting with virtual assistants. Consumers are finding this means they get served more quickly.

The next generation of virtual assistants will be able to give sound advice and make useful suggestions to customers. Any complaint will receive personal attention, and consumers need not worry — there is always the option of switching to a human member of staff.[7]

Robot advisers and personal assistants (PAs)

Soon, we can expect to see more advanced robot advisers sending us computerized advice by email, text message or WhatsApp. The voice response systems on our smartphones are improving, too: Apple Siri, Google Assistant, IBM Watson, Microsoft Cortana and Samsung Bixby are personal assistants currently in effect. We should expect developments in this field to speed up enormously, giving the world of customer care an extreme makeover in the process.

Take Amelia, an artificial intelligence-based digital assistant who understands to whom she is speaking and is capable of actually having a conversation. She can even gauge someone's mood and adjust her response accordingly. It's expected that Amelia and other digital assistants will mature into full-blown digital staffers who will make their marks on the retail sector.[8]

Facebook is also experimenting with a digital PA. A tiny button on the Messenger app allows you to send a message to M. Whether it's scheduling an optician's appointment, booking a trip, suggesting options for a weekend mini-break or giving you ideas for new garden furniture, M will be able to do it all. Facebook has decided to make M a hybrid of artificial intelligence working together — for now, at least — with human staffers.[9] The knowledge about people's behavior that Facebook has gleaned from its own platform is the foundation for M.[10]

With Amazon Echo, Amazon managed to successfully introduce a physical interactive voice response system. It can not only play music or read the news aloud, but the smart home speaker also answers questions, among many other things. With the introduction of Amazon Echo Look and Amazon Echo Show, the company is focusing on new domotics services aimed at its Amazon Prime members, with an incredible number of potential customer care opportunities.

Amazon Echo Look is a smart voice-operated camera that can help you to decide on outfit options using a video app.[11] Amazon Echo Show is a voice-operated screen, the size of a tablet, which you can use for Skype or FaceTime. Imagine how convenient it would be if you were going over recipes in the kitchen with your partner and wanted to order the items on Amazon at the same time. Consumers see having an Amazon Echo device as a reason to subscribe to Amazon Prime.

Amazon's domotics features are a means for the company to consolidate the relationship with these consumers through customer care at every stage of the customer journey. The Echo might not be able to vacuum your room, but in the future they might well be able to tell robots to carry out household chores for you.[12]

ECHO AND HOME HEAR ALL

What happens to all the data Amazon collects with Echo and Google with its equivalent Home? Well, it remains available to Amazon and Google. Amazon has not been secretive about recording parts of in-home conversations. These are not just the questions directed at the machine, but background noises, too. Echo and Home can be operated with one button and activated by saying the name "Alexa" or "OK Google" out loud. A small light lets you know that the system is recording sound, though you can always erase the recording afterwards.

It is not really clear whether the shopping list applications of Amazon and Google are used for advertising purposes or for drawing up personalized wish lists or recommendations.[13] Still, it would hardly be surprising if Amazon and Google did indeed use all the possible available data to improve its products and, most importantly, its customer services.[14]

Personal contact

Are all these far-reaching developments in technology going to be just as beneficial to consumers? Can (web) stores do without the human touch? Or is human, personal attention the way forward if they want to set themselves apart in this competitive market? Onlife consumers can be expected to make split-second decisions in the future: which kind of customer care is going to be the most effective for me at this point in time?

There are some who remain unconvinced that consumers are going to respond well to innovations like robotization. Research has shown that many people do not regard artificial intelligence as the most important innovation around, whereas the large technology companies are hurling themselves at it as if there were no tomorrow.[15] Time will tell if AI can live up to all that it promises to be.

Virtual PAs, digital assistants, chatbots and robot advisers might become smarter and smarter in the future, thanks to self-teaching algorithms and deep learning techniques. Still, many consumers feel nothing can beat personal, human attention. In the future, chatbots may however become almost indistinguishable from actual humans, though. The personal health coach Lark, operating through an app, is a prime example.[16] If a customer feels like it, he can always switch over from a chatbot to a human member of staff. Consumers ultimately expect customer care to provide them with nothing more — or less — than good answers, relevant solutions, a sense of being taken seriously and a friendly chat.[17] For the moment, human staffers can use their unfeigned interest and personal attention to set themselves apart from digital assistants, virtual PAs and robot advisers.

Customer intimacy

Over the past 20 years, Internet and digitization have radically altered the interaction between suppliers and recipients of customer service.[18] The large tech platforms and shopping ecosystems can truly make the customer the center of attention every step of the customer journey, thanks to new technological opportunities. In the past, the stores themselves were all that mattered. Then, the goods and services they sold were at the center of attention. But now, it's the interaction between people and businesses that matter. Shopping platforms understand that they are not about stores or selling products and services. Platforms are truly about selling core interaction between people.[19] It fundamentally changes the rules of engagement for customer care, as the rules have to be fundamentally rewritten. Now, the synergy of technology and the human touch produce exactly the added value that onlife consumers of today insist upon.

Service is no longer a one-way street from the retailers ("push"); it is now an interactive process among customers and between customers and retailers engaging in a mutually beneficial conversation ("pull and push"). More than ever before, customers are now in charge, partly because of their having so much more relevant information on the goods, services and companies they plan to use.

In the future, customer care can only become even more multidimensional. Based on personal customer data, retailers will be able to provide customer intimacy as well. A sense of confidentiality in the customer-retailer relationship will give people a warm and fuzzy feeling, similar to the one you experience with close friends and family. A retailer who succeeds in creating customer intimacy can be sure of very happy customers.

The "cold" integration of technology and systems is but one condition for customer care; customer intimacy, however, calls for a wholly different and more customer-focused mindset. Every single aspect of the retail operation needs to live and breathe that mindset. The essence of customer care today — and tomorrow — is an authentic adoption of the perspective of an individual consumer.

Employees working in this field can no longer be "constrained" in the multi-level front and back office scripts for scaling up protocols. The customer care worker is a person of flesh and blood, with a proper mandate for real interaction with customers (someone who might send an email later in the day following a live chat to check if the situation is resolved) and a budget to help solve problems there and then. This degree of freedom makes the job more interesting and more fun, with happy employees producing happy customers, which in turn leads to better NPS scores. The human touch is what can lift the relationship between the retailer and the customer to a higher level. Onlife consumers want to sense that someone actually cares about them, is willing to help them and will even take care of them.

New generations of powerful onlife consumers will determine how, where and when they want to have service. They've come to expect an integrated customer care setup, available seamlessly on a full range of channels, at all times of day and on all possible applications. Retailers need to wake up to the fact that customer care is not at all separate from how they do business, but rather the very essence of the service they provide. Flexibility is the key to adapting their organization, products and services accordingly.

"The customer is always right 3.0" requires immense effort from businesses. Not only do they need to keep up with the lives of on-life consumers, but they need to proactively offer them onlife experiences as well. Organizations will need to adapt faster than ever before, improve at the same pace, and measure facts every hour before learning from them and adapting to these lessons. Businesses will have to work hard at earning customer intimacy.

"It is not the strongest of the species that survives, nor the most intelligent, but the one most adaptable to change."

CHARLES DARWIN,
AUTHOR OF *ON THE ORIGIN OF SPECIES*

12

New business models

The retail world was always reasonably easy to understand. All the players knew their parts. Buyers would decide, four times a year, what outfits people were going to wear; at travel agencies, the holiday brochures were neatly lined up according to season; and insurance companies would regularly draw up new policies, rarely straying from the familiar.

Internet and digitization have turned this upside down. An unprecedented transformation has taken place — laying the groundwork for a data-driven smart economy, creating conditions for the sharing and circular economies, and opening up the glocal platform economy. Retailers are finding themselves forced into a search for new business models, thanks to these developments combined with the power of the onlife consumer and a customer journey made new.

Change begins

From the mid-1990s onwards, the first online stores, department stores, travel agencies and insurance companies started to use digital ways of reaching consumers. These shops-on-the-internet did not use new business models; they were basically digital variations on old revenue models: individual sales of goods and services, advertising revenue and subscriptions. Individual sales online are not different from offline: the profit margin counts. Creating a high turnover of goods is the path to success, with large-scale sales always having benefits. Using online platforms, marketplaces, and search engines is really not that different from the existing business models of advertising and middlemen. Essentially, they're referrals to someone else's goods and services. Subscriptions, too, remain unchanged: a customers pays a lump sum (even if the payments are spread out over months) in exchange for certain services. Even Amazon loyalty program Prime is nothing more than a subscription.

Same old, same old. The digital age is just that – or is it? New business models and revenue models have put the retail sector on edge. Changes in consumer behavior have compelled retailers to make tough decisions. Most retailers cannot be everything to everyone anymore. Only the happy few global businesses can pull that off.

In this chapter, I will discuss four generic revenue models that are set to become the benchmark for several different segments of the market. I plan to focus solely on the business models aimed at consumers, leaving the B2B market aside, despite the many similarities between the markets. The four business models are shown in the following table. I plan to clarify each of them in the next section.

CHARACTERISTICS OF THE FOUR REVENUE MODELS OF THE FUTURE[1]

	Own brand?	Own supply?	Does the consumer become the owner?	Width or depth of selection?	Onlife consumer advantages
Platform/ Market-place	No	No	No	Both	– Convenience – Everything in one place – Unique selection
Department store	Some-times	Yes	Yes	Wide	– Security – Reliability
Specialist	No	Yes	Yes	Deep	– Specialist advice – Unique or exclusive selection
Brand	Yes	Yes	Yes	Deep	– Security – Specific selection

Platforms and marketplaces

All over the world, a town or village's marketplace has always been the place where supply and demand are brought together. Physical department stores and shopping malls are basically no different. The new business model of platforms and marketplaces is based on that very principle: providing somewhere for consumers to buy goods and services from a variety of retailers and to meet each other.

Over the past two decades, this online phenomenon has flourished at warp speed, particularly in the last few years. The strength of platforms is that it connects the consumer to an almost infinite supply, be it on a regional, national or even global scale. Marketplaces are most often one-way-platforms. They attract, match and connect those looking to provide a product or service (producers) with those looking to buy that product or service (users).[2] Marketplaces are the new middlemen between sellers (retail), brands and buyers. In so-called two-way-platforms, however, it's not necessarily about the goods being moved or the services being sold. On these two-way-platforms, it's all about the interaction between consumers. What really matters on these platforms are the consumer encounters. This *core interaction* between consumers is an essential way to build a foundation from which platforms can sell goods and services.

In China, over half of online sales occur on platforms and marketplaces, as well as one-third of sales in the United States. In Europe, there are now over 300 online platforms and marketplaces operating.[3] Amazon Marketplace, eBay and Alibaba's Taobao, TMall Global and AliExpress are the most well-known global platforms. In Southeast Asia, Rakuten (Japan) is a key player, with Zalando (Germany), PriceMinister (France) and Allegro (Poland) all playing important parts in Europe.

MACROPOLIS BUSINESS MODEL

In late 2000, our Macropolis online shopping portal is ranked fourth on the list of most-visited Dutch web stores. Amazon.com is ranked number 5. Why shouldn't we attempt to expand the success of the retail portal into a much wider search engine?

KPN, the Dutch national telecom company, suggested to transform the site into a search engine, and then pay kick-back fees to Macropolis for the phone revenue it produces. We decided to reject this proposal, because we wanted to stay independent, smoothly missing out on the millions of dollars that an IPO might have yielded.

We kept looking for the right business model, and considered the option to display ads above the search results, for which we would charge (web) stores an advertising fee. At the time, such *sponsored links*, made popular by Google, were unheard of. We got cold feet, in the end, because of our concern that the search engine would no longer generate a fair result for consumers.

The Internet bubble bursted shortly after, and thankfully we were able to find a buyer for Macropolis just in time, the AEX-listed company Newconomy. I felt it was time for a change after all this and started Thuiswinkel.org in 2000, a new Dutch professional organization for (web) stores. Eighteen months later, Macropolis goes belly-up in the wake of the Internet bubble burst.

Commission

The business model of platforms and marketplaces has been shifting in recent years from advertising revenue (fixed sums based on the number of referrals) to sales commission. On eBay and Amazon, commissions range from 8 to 25 percent, depending on the kind of product, with most commission percentages between 10 and 15 percent. Alibaba makes money from merchants on TMall, collecting a percentage of the transaction value that varies by product category, typically ranging from 0.4% to 5%. It also charges upfront service fee, fees for online marketing service, third-party affiliates and storefront software.4 This can create a substantial revenue, not least because there is such a high margin, almost 100 percent, on commission. After all, platforms need hardly lift a finger to add an item or service to their range. In fact, the retailer selling is usually the one doing the work (see Chapter 3).

Smooth customer journey

In the platform and market place business models, the individual steps in the customer journey are carried out by different parties. Orientation, selection and payment most often take place on the platform or marketplace, whereas the individual retailer takes care of delivery using their own trusted delivery service. Consumers have trouble grasping this setup and are unsure to whom they should turn when things go wrong, for it is often unclear who is responsible for what. For consumers, the customer journey on platforms and marketplaces tends to feel disjointed and unnatural.

For large platforms and marketplaces this is one of the reasons to provide all kinds of services to the retailers who are selling on their website. Fulfillment services (storage, order picking, shipment) can be the way for them to build a better customer experience. Of course, they charge for these services, but a retailer and brand manufacturer is more than happy to pay this fee. Anything goes in the race to benefit from the immense reach amongst platform and marketplace customers. Besides, they've often negotiated competitive bulk rates with parcel delivery businesses, cutting costs significantly in the process. Small retailers find themselves persuaded by the low shipping fees and give into the temptation of embracing the platform and marketplaces as a new distribution channel. Platforms and marketplaces find two positive sides to this coin. Not only do they make money off providing these services, but they also create a seamless and annoyance-free customer journey for repeat customers.

Vulnerability

Outsourcing all the primary management processes of businesses to platforms and marketplaces increases the vulnerability of retailers and becomes a real threat (see Chapter 5). It is an important reason why well-known brick & click stores, (web) stores with their own distribution centers and brand manufacturers are opting for a presence on more than one platform at a time.

Small-scale retailers with low brand recognition or an unfamiliar name do not have that option. For small(er) brick stores and stores that only operate online, platforms and marketplaces are the only hope of reaching a global audience. In the United States, it's not unheard of for retailers to make over half of their online turnover through Amazon. In China small-scale retailers are almost fully dependent on the marketplaces of Alibaba. As a result, web stores that only sell online are fast becoming a kind of virtual buying organization.

Own marketplace

The traditional retail titans of days gone by are desperately trying to catch up with this platform and marketplace trend. Hopefully, they go about opening their own online one-way-marketplaces and shopping portals, slightly desperate to make up for lost time. This is not as easy as it looks. eBay provides the facilities for over 25 million sellers (businesses and individuals), Amazon Marketplace does the same for 2,5 million, and Tmall Global has over 70,000 vendors. Estimates show that eBay and Amazon take 90 percent of all marketplace revenue. Other retailers — such as ASOS, Best Buy, Barnes & Noble, Fnac, Otto, Sears, Staples, Tesco and Walmart — who often have "only" a few dozen millions of items being sold through mere hundreds of vendors still have a very long way ahead.

Traditional retailers with a lot of square footage in-store need not lose heart yet. The way forward involves joining forces with other stores to complement what they can offer on their own marketplace. By doing so, they can confidently promise consumers a comprehensive range of goods. Offering fulfillment programs to participating retailers is another option.[5] Thanks to bypassing the need to invest in new products, not to mention avoiding the risks of storage and write-offs, they face a huge *return-on-investment* (ROI).

Specialist platforms and marketplaces

Over the next decade, niche platforms and marketplaces are going to pop up left, right and center. Built around a community or theme, these platforms will offer the exceptional and wonderful. Unlike generic platforms, they can realize higher commission percentages and profit margins. With no need to purchase goods in advance — thus avoiding the perils of supplies and financing purchases — they can basically present consumers with an infinite range of items, a selection both deep and wide to choose from. Of course, specialist one-way-marketplaces need to offer sufficient economy of scale, an appealing blend of retailers and brands, and most importantly, acceptable prices. In a niche market, the target audience is by no means infinite.

Two-way-platforms are not just about mediating between supply and demand, but also about the actual people who are buying and selling. Fast-growing Etsy, the online niche platform for hand-made goods, is a well-known example of a specialist two-way-plat-form. You can sell your own handmade, knitted or crafted items on Etsy. It's also one of the most successful platforms in the shar-ing economy. There are others following their lead: Zalando has decided it wants to become a specialist fashion platform[6], and in England, a niche has been carved out by Farfetch, offering a home to independent designer boutiques.

Niche platforms and marketplaces are popping up all over the world, ranging from Swedish design, ecologically friendly items or French wines to antique furniture, gourmet food or Eastern delica-cies. The platform model is appealing to startups and established retailers alike, as they are equally keen to find new and specific groups of onlife consumers. When they succeed in reaching these groups, they can charge higher commission fees than eBay, Ama-zon and Alibaba.

The idealist shoe retailer TOMS and travel organizer trip.me are both examples of community platforms. In 2013, TOMS already set up its very own community marketplace themed around "so-cially conscious business." Only other businesses that fit the bill are allowed onto the TOMS Marketplace, which now has a selec-tion of clothing, interior design, jewelry and travel numbering in the thousands. Trip.me is a community marketplace for travelers to reach out to local guides and tour operators to craft their very own travel itinerary: a one-of-a-kind trip.

Department stores

The department store business model, otherwise known as "ge-neric reseller", is similar to a marketplace in that it offers a wide selection of goods and services. Generic resellers are mostly estab-lished department stores, chain stores, travel organizations and (financial) service providers. They are often independent retailers who are part of a chain or franchisers operating under the wings of the generic reseller's brand.

At present, the generic reseller business model operates on the benefits of (large) scale. As a result, goods and services can be pur-chased by the retailer at a competitive price, which is then passed on to the consumer. In onlife retail, however, other things matter too: consumer experience, new services and excellent customer care.

In exchange for supplying their personal data, the onlife consumer expects a personalized selection and services tailored to their needs.[7] Gradually, the traditional generic reseller business model is inching away from "buying and selling" to providing consumers with services that truly add value.

Own brands

For now, most physical department stores have a fairly wide selection, though not wide enough for them to compete with (specialist) marketplaces in the long run. Price is another area they'll find it hard to keep up with marketplaces. For many department stores, offering their own brands is bound to be the best option to vanquish the competition, in both pricing and selection of range. The number of generic resellers carrying their own brands is set to increase as a result. After all, why bother selling the goods of another brand if you could just as easily build up and sell your own brands — sometimes even through co-creation with beloved customers? Generic resellers, online and offline, will be able to control the quality and the price of goods if they do this.[8]

New services

Another way for department stores to add value is to provide the facilities for shop-in-shops, both online and offline. In effect, they become "curators". The physical department store then takes on the added role of pickup and drop-off point for goods ordered online, as well as a potential post office, financial service hub or travel agency.

Department stores, in particular, will find new technology like VR, AR and holograms of interest. These can deepen the in-store experience — even if only in temporary hubs, shop-in-shops or pop-up stores — for the onlife consumer. The store loses some of its purpose as a point of sale and instead becomes an *experience center* and/or *service center*. Technology is then used to spike the imagination of the consumer and show the allure of a trip or a new home furnishing design.

Unique combinations in the world of travel

Generic resellers in the travel business have successfully adopted the content-is-king mantra, and they're among the first to grasp the true value of big data. Transforming themselves into content owners of fully designed trips is now their middle name. They set their minds to buying airline seats and hotel rooms before using their savvy to build one-off selections for consumers. These bespoke packages are then marketed under their own brands with an improved profit margin.

TRAVEL COMPETITION

Generic travel resellers need to face off the global shopping platforms of Google (Hotel Finder, Flights), Booking.com, Expedia and TripAdvisor. An almost inconceivable level of convenience is offered to onlife consumers with booking processes that seem to become more efficient by the minute. Customers can receive support in every aspect of their planned trip, and the ecosystems are always service- and customer-oriented instead of product-minded. Furthermore, they're the first ones to embrace innovations like voice recognition, VR and AR, and they make onlife travel consumers dynamic offers based on personal preferences.[9]

For generic resellers, presenting customers with an integrated proposition is the surest path to survival — a seamless customer journey through manifold channels, ranging from physical store to web store and from smartphone to social media. Experience is the byword for being inimitable in every step of the customer journey.

Specialist

In the next decade, specialist resellers will undergo a renaissance, with online niche players making up the greatest part — their deep and almost infinite selection is unparalleled. There are hundreds of thousands — or possibly even millions — of small web stores vying for every conceivable niche of the online market. In many countries, more are appearing than going bust — making a contrast with the physical shopping streets where stores are closing down, leaving empty storefronts in their wake.

To be fair, a lot of these specialist web stores have business models that are not viable. There are countless startup retailers, and often the web store may actually belong to a physical store. The sheer number of web stores run by happy-go-lucky amateurs is mind-boggling. Because they barely — if at all — calculate costs for staff, office or storage space in their prices, they can stay ahead of the curve.

Certainly, there are some gems in their midst, disrupting the market with exceptional goods and services frequently matched with some special kind of service or proposition. These are the businesses from whom we should expect to see great things in the future. However, successful new specialist resellers are notorious for having short lifespans. When they succeed, they often inspire copycat businesses, or otherwise generic resellers or brands decide to acquire them. More often than not, though, these web stores have a tendency to disappear after a few years of fruitlessly trying to break even.

The big league chooses bricks & clicks

Specialist resellers might also be national, regional or global market players, such as Nike, Zara or Media Markt. They have found unique product-market combinations that have a particular appeal to the consumer. These resellers focus on bespoke service, convenience and an absolutely stellar reputation as the defining factors of their success.

Some successful online resellers have made the move to physical stores, surprising as it may sound. They open up service and experience centers — places to serve their loyal customers and provide the personal touch. In the next few years, Amazon is planning to open more bookstores, pop-up stores and — through the acquisition of Whole Foods — supermarkets (see Chapter 5). In China Alibaba, JD.com and Tencent/WeChat are moving from online to offline as part of the Chinese online to offline (O2O) trend (see Chapter 1).

A new development is that large specialist stores are exchanging their outlying locations for inner-city stores. Swedish furniture department store IKEA is opening local "city stores", with hardware & DIY stores in various countries following suit. The idea is to have smaller stores closer to where consumers live.

Local and regional specialist resellers, too, can find a home on main street. Their artisanal goods and personal services are often infused with consumer confidence and goodwill.

There is not a single established specialist reseller who will manage to succeed in the future without an omnichannel proposition. Some of them have, in fact, already become global resellers, using a full range of channels to reach their customers (H&M, Zara). Their stores have frequently been turned into miniature distribution centers. From there, they deal with the fulfillment of items purchased online, swiftly moving towards the realization of same-day delivery.

Specialist travel advice

The specialist travel reseller has a particularly good position from which to relieve its customers of all their worries. Be it in their physical store or in the consumer's home, they can use VR and AR to conjure up all sorts of trips. Onlife travel advisers will be available at any time of day, anywhere you want. They can even "guide" onlife travelers during their trip, thanks to proactive notifications and useful, relevant updates. More than ever before, travelers are willing to pay extra for specialist advice and extra services.

In addition to the global specialist online travel resellers (Booking.com, Airbnb), community travel agencies are becoming more popular, too. They serve travelers in a community with a common preference for a certain city, boutique hotel, etcetera. Agencies providing this kind of service can match dynamic content to the personal preferences and reviews of a specially-selected group of like-minded onlife travelers.[10] They can then reach out to specific target audiences (global, national, regional) and offer them exceptional and full-service travel experiences — with an appropriate commission and profit margin, of course.

Financial services

The travel business is facing challenges, but the financial service sector is even in deeper trouble. Unless these intermediaries succeed in creating highly specialist knowledge in areas relevant to consumers, they're going to find themselves bypassed and left behind at an alarming rate. Until now, simple financial products were the ones sold online. We can expect this to change in the short term: products of increasing complexity are set to be acquired online, including mortgages, stock trades and wills. Excellence is the prerequisite in every realm of business nowadays, but nowhere is it more essential than in financial services. Only if they have a point person of their own, convenience, personally-tailored advice and outstanding levels of service will onlife consumers be prepared to pay extra for services like these.

Brand

There's long been a reticence among brands towards selling to consumers directly. It was something of an unwritten rule that manufacturers produced goods for retailers to sell. The Internet has created a startling level of tension in the traditional chain of manufacturer-wholesaler-retailer. Brand manufacturers no longer have the luxury of ignoring the online sales channel and its ever-growing appeal.[11]

For the longest time, traditional retail attempted to prevent brand manufacturers from selling directly or even supplying web stores with their goods. The result was selective distribution, with web stores unable to purchase items or only at a much higher price than physical stores. Through parallel imports from abroad, web stores would manage to bypass this practice.[12] Some traditional manufacturers are fiercely trying to constrain web stores by prohibiting the sales of their brands on, for example, platforms and marketplaces.[13] They hope this will give them more influence and control over their goods and marketing propositions.

LEVEL PLAYING FIELD

In 2009, German fashion designer Karl Lagerfeld succeeded in forcing the European Parliament to insist luxury brands – such as Chanel and Louis Vuitton – could only be sold in online stores on the proviso that the store also had a physical branch and fixed prices.[14] These stores were carrying the cost of a retail building, inventory, supplies, and specially-trained staff to sell the luxury brands.

Other sectors have adopted the *level playing field* argument as a way to sabotage the online sales channel and insist on fixed prices (which is, in fact, a prohibited practice in most countries) in order to protect their market.[15] This can only be seen as rearguard action.

It was not until 2012 that Karl Lagerfeld stopped prohibiting online sales through web stores without a physical store. Prada, Burberry and other *high-end fashion labels* are now fully available online through Amazon, NET-A-PORTER, Zalando and TMall. In fact, in 2015 Lagerfeld went on to open his very own web store: KARL.com.

Direct customer relationship

Most of the global brand manufacturers have started to succeed in the direct sales of their brands to consumers. More than ever before, brand items are being sold in their own online stores with higher margins than their physical stores could yield.[16] This is an unstoppable trend: brands are extraordinarily well-equipped to cater to consumer experiences.

Over half of consumers now start their search for a specific item or a particular service by a brand on the website of that same brand manufacturer.[17] Manufacturers then have all the opportunity they need to build a direct customer relationship. Using the online sales channel, they are able to blend a full brand experience with custom-built personalized services. This takes precedence over the simple sales of goods or services, which is the practice of generic and specialist resellers. Why should they refrain from constructing their own customer relationships and maintaining these? Why should they give up any margin whatsoever to generic or specialist resellers?

Over the next decade, we can expect to see the majority of global and national brand manufacturers come around and start selling directly to onlife consumers. Over half of all leading non-food brands sell goods directly to their customers. In the service sector (travel, insurance, etc.), we should see this percentage rise to well above 90 percent in the next decade.

Manufacturers of supermarket items are going to make the switch, too. After years of coping with the pressure from the retail chains, the manufacturers have started to fight back. They are now openly flouting the power of the retailers by selling their goods through social media, marketplaces, platforms and their own (web) stores. If it benefits them, they sometimes even sell products of competitors in order to keep selling directly to the consumer without an intermediary. Procter & Gamble already opened its own e-commerce platform back in 2010.[18] The platform not only has a P&G store that has free delivery when you order enough, but customers can also take out a subscription for Tide detergent pods or Gillette Shave Club razors. The corporation felt compelled to take this step when it realized market share was seeping away to online competitors like the Dollar Shave Club and Amazon Shave Club. Unilever, who acquired the highly successful Dollar Shave Club in 2016, has been pairing free product trials with e-commerce for ages.[19] Heineken has launched an online beer store called Beerwulf.com, and Philips has its own web store to respond to the trend of consumers buying straight from the source. Philips has since been gleaned more understanding of consumer needs and wishes.[20]

SIX REASONS TO SELL DIRECTLY
Manufacturers of non-food items have the following reasons to pursue the option of selling directly:[21]

1. Better understanding of the customer: Klöber.com, supplier of office chairs, helps online customers choose between chairs with a "chair configurator." This way, the company can gather information on consumer needs and behavior patterns.
2. Strengthening the brand identity, consumer commitment and brand image: fashion brand Burberry uses the web store to boost its identity, using rich visuals, videos and narratives.
3. Possible realization of innovations: using the motto *Design your own,* sports brand Reebok offers consumers unique uses and encourages interaction with the customer, something that generic web stores do not offer.
4. Adding new items: toy manufacturer LEGO offers consumers the chance to design new blocks online, which might then be ordered by other customers, too.
5. A chance to improve service levels and provide information on the company and its products: Dorel, the proprietor of baby brand Maxi-Cosi, is keen to provide services for both its generic and specialist

resellers by allowing customers to purchase spare parts directly from the manufacturer.

6. Creating new turnover paths with higher margins while capitalizing on brand experience: cosmetics brand Nivea has begun selling directly to consumers in the UK on shop.nivea.co.uk. The brand is focusing on online budget propositions such as "3-for-2" and "big value bundles," which are combinations on several items together sold at bargain prices.

The three options for manufacturing brands

There seem to be polar opposites available to brand manufacturers: either opting for their own e-commerce platforms or deepening their current relationships with retailers. Brands that choose the former have managed to leave behind any reservations they had. Business sectors such as consumer electronics, hardware, household appliances, software, games and airline tickets show a propensity to lead brands towards controlling the full sales cycle. They want to know their *own* customers, provide them with every service imaginable and properly involve them in the brand.

Other kinds of manufacturers – high-end brands in particular, including fashion, jewelry, fragrance, bags & accessories, cars, and so on – prefer expanding on their existing relationships with (online) retailers. They often go for shop-in-shops, online or offline. Their own websites are primarily a source of information for consumers and a place to experience the brand. The official website often has a purchasing option, though the prices tend to be steep here: the full brand experience is worth the extra money.[22]

Some brand manufacturers – and their number is growing rapidly – manage to blend the two options and then add the sales of brand items through marketplaces and platforms. They differentiate their selection and service level according to the sales channel by, for example, stocking retailers with trend items and locally-preferred styles. The online prices are the same as the ones in-store. At the same time, they offer their goods and services to consumers directly through (online) department stores and (web) stores. More and more brands are appearing on platforms and marketplaces – in addition to the channels mentioned above – where they anticipate consumer behavioral changes. Standardized product information helps to ease any difficulties in this omni-channel approach. In the end, manufacturers realize that it's up to the consumer to decide where, when and how they will make their purchases.[23]

Experience

New technology is bound to help brands create an amazing brand experience, with personalized digital services playing a large part. Social media can check whether a brand is living up to expectations. The days of overly-positive stories packaged in clever marketing campaigns are long gone. In a transparent digital world, brand manufacturers are going to be judged by their actions, not their words.

In years to come, new and current brands will enter the market with new concepts that fully tap into the power of the Internet. When the brand experience and personalized (digital) service are at their very best, consumers with a lot of brand awareness are perfectly happy to pay extra and become loyal, trusted customers. When brand manufacturers align with generic and specialist resellers, then everyone gets to do what they do best: the brand can sell directly to the consumer, with the generic or specialist reseller providing the customer service and — if needed — maintenance.

The center cannot hold

In the world of retail, "the center cannot hold" has become a popular adage. In a nutshell, this means the mid-market segment is going to disappear — in every single sector, no less. Some economists even go so far as to say that resellers everywhere are on the shortlist to become obsolete. Author and trend watcher Farid Tabarki has stated that in a "fluid society," there is, in fact, no room at all for the middle or center.[24]

Mid-market retailers are indeed in dire straits, feeling the pressure of changing sales circumstances in inner cities and popular shopping streets. Still, they find it very hard to relinquish the business models that for decades were always profitable to them. Most resellers are aware that it's crunch time: they have to adapt their strategy if they want to retain customers for the long-term and gain the favor of the onlife consumer.

What is the way forward? Should they cling to traditional business models, desperately ignoring the shrinking profit margins, or should they step into the unknown and face the adventure of omnichannel business and the investments it requires? Many retailers, particularly older ones and established businesses, feel this is a diabolical dilemma.

Unapologetically physical

Traditional retailers might have a few more years in them if they unapologetically embrace the physical distribution channel. There are plenty of stores who see the appeal of this option, not least because they need not invest in a web store. The website, then, is little more than a contemporary digital version of the company brochure or weekly flyer.

Discount stores such as Action and Primark have a rationale for choosing this path. They invest all their money, time and energy into a fast turnaround of their selection, opening new brick stores and training their sales staff — after all, they are the ones who will be making the difference to the consumer.

Smaller physical stores who cannot (or do not want to) keep up with this frenetic pace might decide to bide their time and pamper their customers with as much care and attention as they possibly can. They are letting the digital maelstrom pass them by — in effect, these entrepreneurs end up needing to "roll up their sleeves", words uttered to me by an owner of footwear stores. Instead of (remotely) managing one or more stores, they find themselves serving customers in-store once again. It is their only option.

Hundreds of thousands of web stores are facing tough times, too. As a rule, these entrepreneurs have other sources of income besides their web store revenue. For others, the operational costs of the web store are spread out evenly over their other business ventures. Both are ways to avoid going under. These retailers will be presented with two options in years to come: either carry on as they are for as long as they can cope, or do some serious investing — provided they can even afford to do so — and scale up to the next level in the hope of ensuring their survival.

Alliances

Retailers have another option to help them navigate out of this conundrum: building alliances.[25] By exploring creative collaborations, organizing buying groups or cooperatives, working together in strategic retail alliances or finding an online (niche) platform to participate in, (online) retailers can create a win-win proposition. Physical stores like bookstores, coffee shops or local specialty shops (produce stores, organic food shops, florists, art galleries and the like) can merge in cooperatives where professional staffers work alongside volunteers.

Online retailers might embrace the platform or marketplace model. Resellers can strengthen their position by selling items from manufacturers without needing to buy these themselves in advance. This can be an effective business model for resellers and suppliers. Instead of spending all their money on a fully supplied storeroom with items that might end up unsold, they can focus on developing smart algorithms to offer onlife consumers personalized matches. In turn, the manufacturers can benefit from the wide reach of the web store. It's particularly hard for them to make themselves searchable online for consumers. Any added site traffic and extra sales through web stores are bound to be much appreciated.

Working together in alliances is an excellent opportunity for retailers and suppliers to provide the very best services they can to specific groups of customers. By choosing their target audiences wisely and tweaking their market positions, selection of goods and price policies, optimum customer care is suddenly within reach. After all, as I stated earlier, retailers can no longer manage to be everything to everyone. They can, however, set themselves apart by being exceptionally relevant to certain groups of consumers. By fulfilling their *customer promise*, current customers are retained and new ones are won over.

New opportunities

It was in 1997 that Harvard professor Clayton Christensen pointed out that established businesses tend to respond to disruptive innovation only when it is already too late.[26] Retailers need to re-engineer their trade, reinvent it once and again, and dare to be vulnerable and dive into new business models with reckless abandon.[27] "You have to become your own fiercest competitor and disrupt or destroy your own business before competition does," says Indian author and consultant Rajesh Srivastava.[28]

It's a do-or-die time for retailers now. Old business models will be given their umpteenth new coat of paint, though there will (happily) actually be new business models too in the years ahead. New business generations will want to embrace the mid-market segment and seize its opportunities, and some of them might just succeed. Stores selling their own brands have a fair shot at success. Innovative entrepreneurs can best serve the onlife consumer by giving current business models a good old shake-up through adopting new models and mixing the two together in a wonderfully vibrant cocktail of cutting-edge technology and applications. In a changing world, it's time to change.[29] The sky is the limit.

"There has never been a better time to be a worker with special skills or the right education, because these people can use technology to create and capture value. However, there's never been a worse time to be a worker with only 'ordinary' skills and abilities to offer, because computers, robots and other digital technologies are acquiring these skills at an extraordinary rate."

ANDREW MCAFEE AND ERIC BRYNJOLFSSON,
AUTHORS OF *THE SECOND MACHINE AGE*

13

Work and study in onlife retail

Businesses and staffers are both reeling from the immense consequences of Internet and digitization. Gradually, computers are replacing people, entire businesses and even whole sectors. CEOs and other executives in retail are up against huge challenges, compelling them to choose their strategies wisely. As onlification ripples through society, it requires new kinds of organizations and a new perspective on the job market and education. Employees are expected to meet society's need for new expertise, and entrepreneurs need to show a leadership style to match.

In the first part of this chapter, I will discuss the rapidly evolving job market, where old jobs are being exchanged for entirely new professions. I will delve into the effects and impacts of robotization on the retail business.

In the second part of the chapter, I turn to two opposite forces: analogue bureaucracies and digital network organizations. Neither one is inherently superior, though the latter is likely to be a better fit for a society in transition and for new generations of staffers.

Those very staffers are the focus of part three of this chapter, thanks to the *War on Talent* spreading like wildfire. What is the best way for education and retail to join forces and ensure talented young people grow up to be fully fledged e-business professionals who can boost the competition between national economies?

The retail job market

In developed countries, the job market is on the verge of an unprecedented transformation. In 1983, American economist Wassily Leontief predicted that technology would cause changes to occur at such a rapid pace that many employees would be left behind empty-handed. He believed this would lead to jobs being lost at an annual rate ranging from 5 to 10 million.[1] Labor economists have not been able to agree on the number of jobs that will be lost through digitization of society in the years and decades to come. According to researcher Nesta 20 percent of jobs in the United States and the United Kingdom risk disappearing by 2030.[2] According to McKinsey, some 60 percent of human work will be taken over by robots in 2055, which means this is still decades away.[3] In the fastest scenario by McKinsey, technology will go through its greatest development between 2025 and 2030, though the actual large-scale adoption of these new working methods is more likely to take place between 2030 and 2050.[4]

According to the World Economic Forum, 7.1 million jobs in the 15 key economies are set to disappear by 2020, a figure equivalent with 65 percent of the global labor force.[5] In *Rise of the Robots,* Martin Ford warns us that routine jobs are in great peril of being wiped out, particularly in offices, stores and supermarkets, travel agencies and banks.[6]

These are all predictions to be taken seriously. One way or another, millions of jobs are going to be annihilated over the next decade by digitization and automation. Photography mogul Kodak was one of the first casualties. In 1988, the company had 145,300 employees, and, in fact, the organization would be one of inventors of digital photography. The concept of digital photography, however, was not taken seriously by top management. As a result, they were sadly not able to keep up with innovation and developments. In 2012, Kodak went bankrupt. It would end up being one of the most renowned victims of the digital revolution — together with Finnish brand Nokia and Japanese Motorola (both of which were in the cell phone business). Bizarrely, and yet perfectly typical, Facebook would acquire Instagram, the immensely popular free online photo service, in the very same year that Kodak shut down. The social media giant paid 1 billion dollars for Instagram, which had only 13 members of staff at that time.

Internet and digitization has substantial effects on retail, too. According to Deloitte, the impact of robotization and changes in consumer behavior will translate into a serious reduction in jobs in the next two decades. McKinsey estimates that 47 percent of the work done by a store assistant could be automated or done by robots.[7] In the UK, nearly 60 percent of retail jobs, roughly 2 million jobs, are under pressure.[8] The British Retail Consortium has calculated that there will be 30 percent (900,000) fewer jobs in retail by 2025.[9]

Fewer stores, travel agencies and bank offices means less physical bustle and business with less need for managers, store clerks, cashiers and so on. Supermarkets are slowly bidding farewell to checkout staff: the self-scanner is gradually becoming more popular. Mobile and online banking is the cause of bank branch offices closing down. The online research, selection and closing of insurance policies means redundancies at insurance companies. Post offices are being shut down as a result of the sheer volume of email traffic. Telecom companies are even now in the midst of preparing for the next round of lay-offs. They were late in catching on to the speed at which people have adopted messaging through WhatsApp, Snapchat, Skype, and the like. At banks and call centers, smart and clever software, chatbots and robot advisers are fast replacing bank clerks and call center staffers on account of being cheaper, more effective and available 24/7. Distribution and fulfillment centers, too, are phasing out human workers and using robots instead. After all, they get the job done without complaint and are unlikely to ask for a raise.

GROWTH OF RETAIL IS SHIFTING RETAIL JOBS

Online shopping is accounting for a significant growing part of all retail sales. But what is the true effect on the retail workforce? The hundreds of thousands of jobs created by new online firms have not absorbed the millions of job losses of traditional retailers. The Bureaus of Labor Statistics and Census Bureaus all over the world are struggling in their calculations of job numbers. The problem is that the way jobs are calculated do not accurately reflect the shifts taking place in the retail sector. Most systems only count employees who work in stores as "retail". Retail company employees who work in retail warehouses, distribution centers, call centers, regional centers and headquarters are often classified in other sectors.

ROBOT TAX OR EMPLOYEE BENEFITS AND RIGHTS FOR ROBOTS
Governments ought to levy taxes on income generated by robots. In doing so, they will ensure the speed of automation is spread out and that other types of work can be developed for people. At least, this is what Microsoft top executive Bill Gates recommends. If work done by a person in a storeroom is taken over by a robot worth an annual income of $50,000, then you should expect the robot to be taxed for income taxes and social security. Gates believes that governments should be trailblazing a reshuffling of jobs in order to benefit care for the elderly and coaching of young people in schools.[10]

In 2017, the European Union discussed the future civil rights and responsibilities of robots. Topics included when a robot should be held accountable for a particular act and when its maker or user should be. Some people believe it's but a matter of time before robots are given employee-type rights. A collective agreement on employee robot benefits seems obvious: including a suitable salary or the right to change jobs. The European Commission, for example, intends to look into the concept of an "electronic personality" in order to award robots legal standing.[11]

New jobs
Apart from the predicted job losses, there are also millions of jobs to be created in the years to come. That very same World Economic Forum has stated that there will be around 2.1 million jobs added in the 15 top world economies.[12] In China, the digital sector is in the process of creating millions of new jobs, such as so-called cyber anchors. These help people by live-streaming advice to people on all kinds of topics. "Purchasing agents" are another, and they help Chinese people make overseas purchases.[13] Retail and e-commerce in particular are going to need a multitude of new talent the world over, mainly in tech, distribution, fulfillment and commercial fields. Retailers will be seeking algorithm developers, web developers, software programmers, process operators, front-end developers, *affiliate* marketers, social media specialists, web and data analysts, SEO and SEA specialists, artificial intelligence officers, 3D printing engineers and cybersecurity experts, to name but a few of the experts from all sorts of fields.

Harvard economist Kenneth Rogoff believes technology developments are, in fact, not threatening at all to employees in the long-term. In the past, technological breakthrough has always created an influx of new jobs. This revolution will not differ from previous industrial revolutions, where people were always able to find new jobs. Unfortunately, there is always a painful transitional period when society is in turmoil and people are out of work. From the perspective of progress, a temporary loss of jobs is to be expected and is by no means a new occurrence. Not that the workers in stores, distribution centers or offices of (web) stores will find much solace in that.

THE STRANGE EVENTFUL HISTORY OF JOBS

Old job	New job
Mail men	Parcel deliverers
Bank clerks	Algorithmists
Salesperson	Product curator
Data entry workers	Data analysts
Copywriters	Robotic authors
Cashiers	Scanners
Shelf stackers	Robots
Customer service staffers	Robot advisers
Parcel depot manager	Hub entrepreneur
Street salespeople	Email marketers
Telephonist	Live-streaming advisers
Regional managers	Community managers
Insurance acceptance clerks	Social media specialists
Claims handlers	Web developers
Couriers	Drones
Translators	Google Translate

Store floor opportunities

The opportunities for in-store staff who understand a new generation of onlife shoppers are endless. Actively coaching customers in using virtual or augmented reality, or other technological innovations, is one way for physical stores to distinguish themselves. These services all require different expertise and skills on the part of retail workers. This also applies to consumers who want to take their onlife shopping experience into the store. Onlife in-store concepts all need retail staffers who know how to find and compare information swiftly and smoothly and possess fluency in the use of the appropriate devices.

Expertise, strong people skills and excellent communication are essential for working in stores — just as they have always been. The skills for advising on a beautiful cut of meat or suggesting which color shirt would suit someone, these are skills that still add value. It might prove that Moravec's paradox — which states that the things humans find hard, are often easy for machines, and vice versa — can also be applied to retail.

Old-school and new-style retailers

If the required skillset for workers on the shop floor changes, then businesses need to restructure their organizations. For many retail and service organizations, a centralistic hierarchy of top-down is still the way to go. I like to call these kind of organizations *analogue bureaucracies*. They are run by an excessive number of managers: at company HQ, regional offices, company hierarchy and individual branch offices. In every level of the organization, employees are judged solely on their efficiency and efficacy, and they're spread out over neatly separated silos. Changes in the market and the developments in technology will compel these organizations to rethink their structure, turning themselves into digital network organizations instead. These are decentralized organizations that tend to favor a bottom-up decision-making process. Employees fit into a so-called flat structure, operating in multi-disciplinary teams to work on improving products and services.

Analogue bureaucracies and digital network organizations are, of course, two extremes in a wider spectrum of methods for organizing retail businesses today. Digital network organizations are not necessarily better than analogue bureaucracies. The latter can result in lovely stores with a lavish selection of goods and highly-skilled staff. Digital network organizations do, however, have an edge due to their knack for successfully transitioning into onlife retail. And maybe more important yet: they can also be a better match for the talent and wishes of new generations of onlife employees.

A DIGITAL BOARDROOM BUDDY

Vision is something sorely lacking from many retail executives and shareholders, as are the digital expertise and modern leadership skills needed to navigate the right course for their organizations. I often speak with board members of a certain age who freely admit that their (grand)children are their path to knowing about developments in technology and society. Imagine what a fresh perspective could be offered by having the consumer's perspective regularly taken into account in boardrooms.

From the very beginning in 1995, Jeff Bezos of Amazon always saved an empty seat at board meetings for "the customer." He felt this was the ultimate statement that the consumer be taken seriously in every single company decision. Other organizations would be wise to follow Amazon's example. Involving millennials is probably the most important step of all! What a bold move it would be if executives and supervisory board members were matched to a younger "digital buddy" for all things tech-related.

Analogue bureaucratic businesses

These organizations — centralistic hierarchies — are the real reason why so many retailers are completely out of touch with their customers and even their staffers. Grassroots ideas are quashed before they get off the ground, and it can take forever to reach any kind of decision. In-company buyers often have a free rein but fail to address the diversity of all the separate sales channels. For innovative employees, the pyramid structure can feel constricting and stifling. More conventionally minded workers find it convenient to hide behind their managers.

The thing is, ideas for new products and activities tend to germinate down where the worker bees are. I firmly believe that every workplace has good ideas floating around. Too often, though, they are crushed by company hierarchy. Psychologist Daniel Kahneman has stated that risk-averse behavior leads people straight to medi-ocrity. In this kind of atmosphere, people are inclined to steer clear of risks and choose safety over opportunity every time.[14]

On the other hand, people do want to matter, feel noticed and make a difference. Everyone has ideas. Everyone. Organizations, then, need to find a way to encourage their staff so that they feel comfortable throwing caution to the wind. Being co-foremen is the way forward for managers. They can be essential links between ex-ecutives, teams and the customer. Give-instead-of-take is essential for this type of manager, who is more like a mentor or a coach.[15]

FLIP THE SYSTEM

In a digital network organization, the boardroom is not the top of the hierarchy; instead, the customers and employees are. The motto is *flip the system.*

Analogue bureaucracies	Digital network organizations
Shareholders	Customers
CEO and Board of directors	Employees
Upper management (head office)	Agile coach, mentor,
Middle management (regional office)	product owner
Lower management (branch offices)	CEO and Board of
Workers in stores	directors
Customers	Stakeholders

Digital network organizations

The difference between digital network organizations and ana-logue bureaucracies is that the former follow a bottom-up flexible strategy. Small agile teams operate within a greater framework of company targets, with each team responsible for a specific prod-uct or service. Digital aids are used all the time — they provide the facilities with internal and outbound company procedures — and help achieve the set goals and targets. At the top of their game, such teams are fully committed to working together on short-term projects and have an unfailing drive for improvement. Companies need to have *agility* in their organization to make this work. Em-ployees, in turn, need the ability to reinvent themselves and improvise. New technology provides the conditions for a network of people and procedure, making it possible to have synergy and, in effect, turn the organization into more than the sum of its parts.[16]

Startups

There are digital network organizations of every type and dimension in every conceivable area of business. However, there is still but a handful of retailers who manage to immerse themselves fully in a transformative state — which is one of the key characteristics of a digital network organization. More often than not, the ones that do are startups, and it's part of their nature to do so. They set up new niche websites, program apps no one can do without, create (sharing) platforms and coin all manner of new ideas for retail services. In the genes of the founders is a propensity for associating with young multi-talents in order to get their business up and running. The very instant the business begins to transcend the startup phase, they find themselves facing exactly the same issues as any other organization when it grows. How should the organization be structured? In other words, they are forced to consider how to deal with their employees, and they ultimately do not always go for the modern way of doing things.

Gradual change

Large retail businesses often decide to make a gradual transformation towards digital network organizations. They are fully aware that it is possible to give responsibilities back to their staffers, though it can be difficult to match the immensity of the company to the preferred smaller scale of teams operating on their own. They wish to make themselves over into online and digital, into decentralized and bottom-up, but how to go about building a business that is perpetually in flux is another question altogether.

Some retailers decide to restructure their organization extensively. They simply decide to introduce multidisciplinary, project-based working methods — in project teams or development teams — and these become miniature societies or startups within the company. From there, the digital network organization can slowly take hold. The ING (Direct) Bank has started to move, in stages, from an old-school bank to a network organization consisting of flexible *agile* teams. Their aim is to be an agile IT business, able to adapt and meet customer wishes as they change, both virtually and physically. Working with *squads and tribes* — self-guided teams which decide their own agenda and initiatives according to their interaction with the customer — is how ING finds space to respond to new circumstances in the market in a decentralized and bottom-up fashion. Sports retailer Decathlon started to throw overboard all of its management layers in support of what has been called the *corporate liberation movement*: the philosophy of creating a workplace based on respect and freedom, rather than distrust and control.[17]

Various other traditional service providers and retail companies have set up startups of their own, operating separately from the conventional business. These so-called *greenfield* operations are supposed to come up with much-needed innovations. In the United States, Walmart set up its own tech firm in an attempt to keep up with Amazon. WalmartLabs was not housed at the Bentonville, Arkansas HQ, but in Silicon Valley instead. Thousands of graduate-level "techies" are pushing the boundaries in retail commerce innovation.[18] In Germany, MediaMarkt and Saturn set up a separate company for coordinating and managing all the e-business activities.

In an attempt to adjust and connect to market changes, these businesses try to create agility and speed without needing to carry the load of the mother company. It is too soon to tell if this is, in fact, "too little, too late", as some critical observers have deemed it. The danger of the new business cannibalizing the old company is irrelevant, or so experts would have us believe. Steve Muylle, Professor at Vlerick Business School in Belgium, says: "It is better to shoot yourself in the foot than be shot in the head."[19]

Some retailers acquire young startups instead, hopeful that their young staffers and the culture of openness and innovation will rub off on them. They use the startup as a kind of sounding board or role model for their own rusty and dated organization. Startups and established traditional companies can both benefit from this kind of thinking. Learning from each other, offering inspiration and coming up with startling combinations is all part of the game.

Other traditional retailers have bought established web stores in hopes of gaining innovation and speed. Walmart acquired American marketplace Jet.com (with its Smart Cart algorithms), online fashion retailer Bonobos and online outdoor retailer Moosejaw all for that very reason: to acquire technology, talent and customers.

WHAT DOES THE MILLENNIAL WANT AT WORK?

By the year 2025, millennials – everyone born after 1980 – will hold over three-quarters of all jobs globally.[20] What is the "me-and-selfie generation" motivated by? Challenges and opportunities are apparently at the top of their work wish lists, research has found. They also enjoy working for appealing brands, and they like inspirational places to work. This is the first ever generation to be vocal in its desire for new working methods. They prefer cooperation to competition and are keen to harness their digital talents and expertise to achieve innovation, though they do not want to sacrifice too much of their work-life balance. Committing to one single employer for life is an outdated concept to them; they would rather shape their career in a more flexible mold. No one has a better sense than millennials of how to deal with the deluge of information, emails and messages they're inundated by every single day. They have no trouble deciding what matters to them and what truly counts, both at work and at home.

Interestingly enough, nearly two-thirds of millennials have stated they would like to make the world a better place.[21] They would even be prepared to forgo a substantial paycheck or even a stipend for interns if it meant working for a stimulating startup or web store.[22]

Physical network organizations

The physical shopping stores are falling in love with the idea of self-steering, too. And why shouldn't they, indeed? Store assistants have the very best sense of what is needed to run their store, and at chain stores, new technology manages to provide contemporary methods for self-organization and self-management.

Store assistants have no need for managers who order them about; they cope perfectly well with a coach who offers the necessary support for independent teams. How to best work together, reach decisions, deal with problems and conflict, and how and when to give a discount — these are all questions they can be trained to answer. If they have the proper digital technology at their fingertips, their actions at work can be fully transparent for their co-workers and the head office.

In fact, self-steering is not really a new idea on the store floor. Back in the 1950s, sales assistants had a significant degree of autonomy. Every village store and neighborhood shop was in fact a small community where all the required roles and jobs (employee schedule, buying, storeroom management, balancing the cash register, doing the books and stocktaking) were assigned to different staffers according to their talents and expertise.

HOLACRACY AT ZAPPOS

The very pinnacle of digital network organizations is holacracy. This new way of structuring and governing organizations is focused on self-organization and developing a body of collective knowledge and creativity. Zappos – owned by Amazon – presented this new form of organization in 2013, which is how the company hopes to safeguard its core value of *delivering happiness.* It's not selling shoes that matters, but "making customers happy with shoes."

Without any management levels and by using self-steering teams, the over 1,500 staffers at Zappos manage to constantly improve their innovative ability and degree of productivity. To a certain extent, they are treated as entrepreneurs, given all the freedom and responsibility they need to make customers happy.[23]

To provide a conduit for self-steering, procedures and communication, Zappos uses a web app called GlassFrog. This clearly shows who is responsible for what, which results have been reached so far and what people are busy working on.

Human capital

Every single digital network company will feel challenged by putting onlife workers first. New technology and resources can help employees reach their full potential according to the individual's own particular blend of talent, idiosyncrasies and flaws. The basic idea is that blending people and digitization always produces more than the sum of their parts. Ask not what employees cost, or what their use is for the company, but ask instead what they can do for the organization in its entirety. In a digital network organization, maximizing productivity and efficiency is not what matters most, instead finding ways to fulfill the potential of their staff is what truly counts.

War on talent

In recent years, I have visited the campuses of Alibaba, Apple, Facebook and Google, amongst others. It was there that I experienced how they get new generations of staffers to commit to their organizations. They throw the relaxed, laid-back *California way of life* into the mix, blending it with an improbably high turnover of projects and solid-as-a-rock deadlines. All around you, there is the adrenaline of young people from all over the world who want to bring their ambition, courage and determination to the future of tech. *Getting things done* matters more than *getting things done right.* Everyone knows it is okay to fail at work. I saw posters on the Facebook campus with the phrase "Fail hard".

Top talent the world over knows where *the places to be* are: campuses in Hangzhou (Alibaba), Menlo Park (Facebook) and Mountain View (Google). Right now, over 60 percent of all working graduates in Silicon Valley are from other countries.[24] The War on Talent has started here, well before it begins to spread to the rest of the world.

The global shopping platforms are the ones who succeed in enticing the best talent of the world to join them. From the middle of 2016, the Alibaba Global Leadership Academy (AGLA) has been offering a 16-month training program at the Hangzhou Alibaba campus aimed at top talent a few years into their career. The training program has a guaranteed job in the United States or Europe at its completion.[25]

As the number of digital network organizations continues to grow, so too does the need for the right kind of people to increase on an exponential scale. Initially, multinationals will be the ones fighting over the smartest graduates, snapping them up as soon as they finish their degree. Next, traditional retailers and service providers will gradually step into the fray. For now, their public image says they only offer unskilled and low-paid positions. By setting up their own academies and increasing salary levels, large retailers like Walmart are trying to turn this around and become known as new and appealing places to work.[26]

Education system

It is hugely telling that the large tech firms are setting up their own institutes for education. A great many traditional education institutions around the globe have completely lost touch with the world around them. I was trained as an education scientist before I obtained my MBA and am well aware that education can be a monster with a thousand heads. They can be prone to introspection, hugely fond of established methods and deeply entrenched in structure and hierarchy. As a result, students and schoolchildren still have to be the round pegs in a square hole — conforming to the status quo of classes, fields of interest and levels — rather than have the system of education shape itself according to the onlife world of experience, learning and the life of the students.

Many schools and colleges for vocational and tertiary education are in the process of teaching people skills for retail jobs that will soon become extinct. Class schedules and curricula are gone through by rote and in manner of a factory production line — not to mention, the host of teaching examples and case studies that date back to the pre-digital age. Every year, around June, a new batch of graduates falls off the assembly line.[27]

This is by no means the first time technology and education are out of sync. Two Harvard professors, Claudia Goldin and Lawrence Katz, have determined that the education system has failed to keep up with ongoing developments in technology for the last three decades at least.[28]

In the future, retail will need professionals with a broad education in *e-business and digital commerce.* They will need to have specialist expertise and *skills* in their chosen fields, be that e-business, e-data, e-marketing, e-fulfillment, e-ICT and so on. This will not be enough to satisfy the requirements of the market, however. Workers need to be fluent in the generic procedures of the retail value chain as well. After all, they will soon be expected to confer with others in multi-disciplinary teams and must understand what others are talking about. *Soft skills,* in particular, are going to become essential in the retail jobs of the future, from the shop floor all the way to a web store back office. Communication skills and social ability are going to be game changers, not least because those are the skills in which humans excel compared to robots and machines.

T-shaped retail education

Vocational courses and university degrees need to find ways to implement the new *T-shaped* programs in order to meet the demands of the retail market. These courses still need to be developed at present and should pair specialist knowledge (the vertical bar of the T) to general knowledge (the horizontal bar of the T). Students ought to practice working in multi-disciplinary teams and experiment with topical e-cases from the business world. New project methodologies, such as scrum, should also be learned and practiced at length. Personal development coaching and fine tuning social skills should also be part of the student learning experience. These aspects of education are often cut from the curriculum to save time or money. They are, however, an essential condition for talented young people to excel in new retail professions.

THE LINK BETWEEN BUSINESS AND EDUCATION

T-shaped courses offer excellent opportunities for change – from within, no less – to the education system in countries the world over. As the new world order takes over from the old, it's a time of transition in which the divide between business and education can be closed. In order to accomplish this feat, it is essential that business, education and unions truly cooperate:

- Digital skills need to become a core part of the curriculum in business and technology courses. A digital curriculum needs to be updated every single year. Flexibility and agility are, then, essential to the education programs, as are sufficient resources for updates and a close, coordinated method of cooperating with the business world.
- In addition to digital theory, digital practical skills must become vital to higher education. Business experts will need to share their practical knowledge consistently. Educators and businesses should cooperate to produce case studies using (central) practice labs or simulation games.

- The turmoil and transition surrounding retail call for agile, flexible and incremental innovation in multi-disciplinary teams with responsibility and accountability for the final product. Agile work (i.e. operating in short development cycles, which makes it possible to better match customer needs) needs to be taught, as does the willingness to learn from mistakes. Students require proper social skills coaching if this is to succeed.
- Most students have no clue of the career opportunities available in retail. As a business sector, retail has an obligation to provide clarity on these opportunities. Providing information on career perspectives is one way to do so; making poster boys and girls of young retail heroes is another tried-and-true method.
- A great many teachers and professors will need additional coaching in a massive operation to bring them up-to-date. By working together with the business world, new practically-minded teachers need to be recruited who are able to bridge the divide between business and education.
- The business world needs to invest in "Just-Do-It projects". Through cross-industry, multi-disciplinary innovation projects, lab research, trend analysis, benchmarks and future studies new retail expertise and skills will be developed. Educational institutions and businesses should be aware of their need to give-and-take with each other.
- Lifelong learning is the future of all retail workers. In the long run, in particular when digital qualifications are agreed upon mutually, this can create a stronger competitive position for a country.

Lifelong learning in retail

A lifelong commitment to learning is, in fact, essential for us all. Many business sectors — healthcare, law, finance — have made learning a requirement by law. Retail, on the other hand, is late in catching on to this important trend. For most traditional retailers, the training of employees is but a balancing item in their budget. Professional retraining or extended training are not even considered, nor are staffers provided with coaching for personal development. Even when there is financial leeway for training, it is rarely adequate.

New generations of onlife retailers hardly manage to do a better job at this. They have generally not even considered or found a way to structurally embed lifelong learning into their organization. Perhaps they assume learning will just take care of itself on the shop floor or in the back-office, according to the 70:20:10 principle often heralded in digital network organizations. This translates into 70 percent of learning happening on the job, 20 percent through informal coaching and feedback and the final 10 percent through formal training.[29] As a matter of fact, even digital network organizations can barely guarantee 10 percent of formal training.

Staffers are the ones that matter in retail, from all-rounders to specialists, the ones that will be making a difference in the future. They need to be (re)trained to work in the new shopping stores, in back offices of online stores, at travel organizations and on platforms and marketplaces. Over the next decades, literally hundreds of new jobs are going to appear, and they will be in dire need of properly qualified experts with e-skills and e-savvy.

Knowledge has always been, and still is, the source of every huge transition in society. Learning is the process of the old order moving forward to a new economic reality.[30] In the end, transition is always accomplished and shaped by people. Innovation is a deeply human endeavor. It will only succeed if people have the right abilities. If we want to keep people working on our own national labor force and stay ahead of the global shopping ecosystems, we need to act now. We can't risk losing our brightest and best talents — we will need them to reach their full potential in the retail industry in the years ahead.

"We are experiencing a radical transformation. The information revolution is changing our mental framework. It is affecting our self-conception and our mutual interactions. It alters our conception of reality and our interactions with reality. We need an update to our conceptual framework. It is the only way for us to grasp our present time."

LUCIANO FLORIDI[1],
PROFESSOR OF PHILOSOPHY AND ETHICS
OF INFORMATION

14

The rise of the network society

Previous chapters have dealt with how new generations of online consumers have become powerful. For the first time in history, retailers need to bow to the demands of the customers instead of the other way around. Onlife consumers are able to reap the benefits of the smart, sharing, circular and platform economy. However, this new economic order does present us with many important social issues. How might we curb the power of large technological companies and shopping ecosystems to leave room for other participants of the retail value chain? Web stores operating in one country and similar suppliers are in danger of being wiped out as the power of huge global operators continues to grow. How can we ensure global neutrality, safety and accessibility for the Internet? Cybercrime, hackers and terrorism already present a huge threat. Last of all, how do we prevent an increased social divide? Even now, billions of people have no Internet access[2], while a mere handful of powerful CEOs and stockholders take advantage of the collection and use of inconceivable amounts of personal data for their own personal wealth, the size of which is virtually beyond comprehension.

In this chapter, I will describe the downsides, the dark side, of the current system of capitalism. It is a system that lacks the ability to equally and fairly distribute the cumulatively acquired wealth amongst the people who help make it happen, nor does it let those who are left out have any real share in that wealth. Luckily, there are counterforces at play, too; governments, retailers and consumers are all involved in top-down and bottom-up initiatives geared at making the world a better place.

Power shift

Every single sizeable shift in society has the establishment — the exponents of the current social and economic order — moving uncomfortably in their chairs as they see their old ways of businesses being dismantled, questioned or simply proving inadequate. Still, plenty of people are under the mistaken impression that the worst is now behind us and that everything will soon get back to normal. Traditional retailers are first among them, as are their representatives, who have immense difficulty accepting and facing the new reality. Diversification, new business models and the appearance of global players means the current economic order is being thoroughly disrupted. Shopping streets and Main Streets in countries the world over are feeling this very pain.

Consumers, on the other hand, have far less trouble bidding adieu to the old and familiar faces: the indistinguishably bland sameness of shopping streets and downtown areas everywhere, stores that refuse to change with the times, dull and unsurprising travel agencies or banks and other financial service providers that refuse to meet the consumers' needs. There is little nostalgia on the part of onlife consumers as they confidently shape the new economic order to their own specifications.

In short, retail has been turned upside down. In the process, there is a hard clash between the old (those who want to keep everything the way it was) and the new (those who want to renew and reinvent everything).

Google paradox
In no time at all, new retail players are jumping into the void to their advantage. The new economic order has only just started to take shape for them. Young startups and fresh, new shopping concepts are popping up everywhere. Consumers have developed a strong preference for globally-minded retail platforms and ecosystems, such as Amazon, Alibaba, Apple, Facebook and Google. At breakneck speed, they have succeeded in creating astonishing added value for their users. Going without the apps and services provided by these tech giants is simply not an option, now that our lives have been immeasurably enriched and simplified through their use. "My kids and I use Google too, simply because it is an

excellent product," the Danish European Commissioner for Competitive Trading, Margrethe Vestager, reluctantly admitted when she announced the charges against Google for abuse of power.[3]

The savvy of these companies is impressive. By harnessing their power in recent years to reap benefits through the whole retail value chain, they've managed to offer many perks to their users. They have shown their true colors as the collectors and keepers of an infinite amount of personal data, which they have increasingly started to use as leverage over other (smaller) businesses. Not playing with the big guys and being invisible, nowhere to be found online, is a surefire way to go out of business.

Empire

Frequent contributor and Internet skeptic Evgeny Morozov has compared the behavior of these global moguls to totalitarian regimes who don't blink at using data from their citizens to shape the world according to their own view.[4] *The Economist* has even stated Mark Zuckerberg resembles a Roman emperor. His goal to provide Internet access to impoverished countries through the use of drones is nothing short of a blatant attempt to spread the Facebook empire beyond its current boundaries.[5] Investing billions in artificial intelligence, chatbots, virtual and augmented reality — all of it is simply aimed at boosting the empire. A scary thought having the presidential aspirations of Zuckerberg in mind.[6]

Google has similar ambitions, with the sky literally being the limit for their battle over consumer data. Using enormous hot air balloons, the company hopes to bring Internet access to people in disadvantaged areas — and access to Google itself, of course. This is a practice that several countries have already outlawed.[7]

Takeovers

Facebook, Google and their compadres are the startups of days gone by. Over the course of 20 years, they've morphed into global shopping ecosystems. In the long run, though, there's a very real danger they will cease to be part of the new economic order. A new generation of startups is likely to push them off their thrones. Several of these large companies love to play down their power by referring to the new startups on their way in. In actual fact, they are determined to prevent that from happening. Tech companies the world over are investing in promising startups. Their hope: acquiring *the next big thing* before it can do any damage to their lofty position. Few startups have the nous to resist the temptation of these tech giants. The immense value of their stock means these companies can afford to spend billions to ensure they get what they want. The table below provides an overview of remarkable takeovers and investments[8] which took place in the last decade or so.

TAKEOVERS AND INVESTMENTS* LEAD TO GLOBAL DOMINANCE

Company	Takeover (year)	Goods/services
Alibaba (Retail)	Intime Retail* (2017)	Department stores
	Ele.me* (2016)	Meal deliveries
	Suning* (2015)	Electronics retailer
	Cainiao* (2013)	Logistics
Amazon (Retail)	Ring (2018)	Smart doorbells
	Whole Foods (2017)	US food chain
	Souq.com (2017)	Arabic online department store
	Zappos (2004)	Online footwear store
Apple (Technology)	Turi (2016)	Machine learning company
	Beats by Dre (2014)	Audio producer
	Siri Inc (2010)	Virtual personal assistant
Expedia (Travel)	Travelocity (2015)	Travel agency
	HomeAway (2015)	Holiday home rentals
	Trivago (2013)	Price comparison site
Facebook (Social media)	Oculus (2014)	Virtual reality hardware creator
	WhatsApp (2014)	Instant Messenger
	Instagram (2012)	Photo-sharing platform
Google (Technology)	Nest (2014)	Smart thermostats
	Motorola (2011)	Technology
	YouTube (2006)	Video-sharing platform
Microsoft (Technology)	LinkedIn (2016)	Social network for professionals
	Nokia (2013)	Telecom producer
	Skype (2011)	Video-calling application
Priceline (Travel)	Kayak (2012)	Travel comparing platform
	Booking.com (2005)	Booking platform

Political reaction

Internationally renowned transition expert Jan Rotmans believes that large-scale social transitions always lead to "changes to the rules, legislation, organizations, concepts and ideas, behavior and human interaction that together define our society." At the same time, power shifts always involve "chaos, turbulence, tension, conflict and uncertainty."[9] We are used to organizing society according to the ideas and concepts of the generation currently in power. This is true of the business world, universities, the media and especially of politics. The power of the ruling tech companies did not grow gradually, as we were accustomed to. It was acquired virtually overnight.[10] However, the bulk of today's politicians came of age prior to the Internet era. We have at least ten to twenty years of waiting ahead of us before we find the new digital generation involved in regulations and legislation.

As a result, governments barely manage to compare their digital initiatives to the pre-digital frame of reference. Regional and local governments tends to base their policies on twentieth century zoning and location plans. Traditional umbrella organizations for business sectors still demand government interference to regulate the new playing field. It was only recently that the taxi business fiercely opposed government attempts to reduce industry regulations. Now, the very same taxi drivers are keen to have government protection against the innovative presence of Uber, with its sharp customer focus.[11]

HANGING ON TO THE OLD

In the 1930s, during the Great Depression, small business owners joined forces to protest the new department stores, discounters, mail order companies and the highly popular uniform-price-stores, where everything was priced from 10 to 100 cents. In Paris, small businesses revolted against the *grand magasins de nouveautés*. The storeowners were afraid of unfair competition and worried that thousands of stores would end up empty. In France, a decree was issued against the expansion of established chain stores, banning the opening of new ones. Germany, too, had its protests. In 1932, a law was passed preventing price discounters from setting up in cities with fewer than 100,000 inhabitants. Belgium went further yet by not only banishing the price discounters, but banning every kind of department store and large-scale retail operation.[12] In the United States, the enormous stores with uniform prices were the bane of the existence of the corner shops, wholesalers and producers of branded goods. Department stores such as Woolworths were charged with underselling. The US government didn't turn a blind eye to the protests and instead established a system of price agreements, the Fair Trade Act (1931).[13] All of these measures would ultimately prove immaterial and pointless.

Europe

Governments all over the world tend to have different responses to the power of international tech giants and shopping platforms. China provides a state-regulated economy, which protects national interests and also boosts the power of corporations like Alibaba, search engine Baidu, Twitter lookalike Weibo and Tencent/WeChat. In the United States, multinationals are regarded with respect by many — though there is more and more criticism of the boundless power and wealth that a small elite garners for themselves. The American economist Irwin Stelzer believes that disruptions of the social status quo are generally seen as a good thing in the United States, whereas Europe sees them as a threat.[14]

A *single market* is still a mainstay of European efforts to stand up to the many technological and social developments. A single digital market is still very much an idyllic dream, though. The 2016 Brexit result made it more elusive than ever. For Europe, it is sink or swim now. Time will tell if that dream of a successful European market is going to come true, with identical terms of guarantee and return, cheaper package delivery rates, one shared cloud amongst all member states, and in-sync sales tax, privacy, cookie consent and online payments.

KA-CHING!

According to the European Commission, a smoothly operating digital market produces over 400 billion euros of annual revenue.[15] That is almost the same amount that the large tech firms have combined: Apple has over 250 billion dollars, Microsoft close to 100 billion, Google over 65 billion and Facebook roughly 10 billion dollars.

Advocates of a single European market have always been vocal in their support of this good idea. It remains to be seen, however, if the individual member states and business world are really holding their breaths for a market where selling products and services throughout Europe becomes mandatory — regardless of whether there's a market for them.[16] What about Chinese and US companies — might they not take even more advantage of the attempts at harmonization within and access to the single market? Precisely those global companies are the ones eager to see every conceivable barrier within the European market wiped out.

The cultural differences and conflicts of interest are what have set Europe back, leaving room for technological titans to gain a foothold. It is not too late, though, to demand *global leadership* for Europe. Harmonization is a means of abolishing the hurdles within the internal market. Technological innovation can be boosted through regulation and government investment. After all, a great many key inventions happened thanks to (indirect) investment by governments: just think of the Internet, Google, the iPhone and self-driving vehicles. The atmosphere for startups and investments in Europe is improving in leaps and bounds.[17] Economist Sir Anthony Atkinson believes governments are able to increase jobs and boost the workforce by investing in startups and new technology.

More important than European harmonization is the drawing up of international agreements and standards for regulating the global arena. It ought to be possible to deal with unfair trade practices internationally so that consumers the world over can be sure they will be protected when things go wrong.

To regulate or not to regulate?

From a global point of view, onlife retail can hugely benefit from supranational regulations, supervision and law enforcement. This is the best way to enforce strict punishment for the abuse of power. However, fresh young startups and midsized businesses prefer to deal with fewer rules on a national scale. They are eager to have plenty of room for conducting business in metropolitan areas with scant regulations, thus avoiding the bind of high administrative costs. Governments would be smart to declare national self-regulatory freedom applicable to all businesses, large and small. This will produce the level playing field businesses are aching for, giving young and innovative retailers the opportunity to succeed.

WORLD TRADE PLATFORM

Founder and CEO of Alibaba, Jack Ma, spoke out in favor of a World Trade Platform in 2015. This would be a digital variation of the familiar World Trade Organization (WTO).[18] As much as possible, international trade barriers ought to be dissolved in order to give small and midsized companies the opportunity to trade their goods and services on a global scale. According to Ma, these entrepreneurs are the very foundation of innovation and, in time, they will emerge as the new global movers and shakers. Ma's idea is for businesses to take the lead, because once they're in agreement with other businesses, there's no need for governments to waste time on complicated multilateral meetings and negotiations.

Network society

More than a few renowned thinkers have come to predict the end of capitalism as the dominant economic model. Jeremy Rifkin is convinced that the tendency towards a more collaborative economy is perfectly obvious and cannot be reversed. Author Don Tapscott believes in a shift to capitalism 2.0. The Internet is bringing people, knowledge and skills together, which can lead to the creation of growth, social development and wealth in the context of a more sustainable world. Tapscott describes how he's noticed a more socially-minded economy where businesses and individuals work together according to their shared worries, efforts and challenges.[19] British author Paul Mason has spoken of post-capitalism. He, too, is confident there will be a transformation towards a more egalitarian society.[20]

It will be decades yet before our current capitalism has been made over. What we do know for sure is that we are seeing the dawn of a *network society*: an onlife society created by governments, digital network businesses and digital citizens working together.

In that very network society, we will see retail transform itself even more profoundly, influenced by unstoppable digitization. I expect to see consumers emerging as the real winners of this battle. They will be pampered to the maximum by all these regulated global shopping platforms and ecosystems. At the same time, local and national retailers will entice and tempt them by reinventing themselves in the next few years. These businesses will be cooperating within deregulated metropolitan areas with one single aim: creating the ultimate customer journey for consumers every single time.

In onlife retail, everything and anything can be purchased, and any information you could ever need about a good and service is at your fingertips. Powerful onlife consumers and retailers are keenly aware of how valuable personal data is. Businesses will make better use of raw materials and will have streamlined their production and delivery procedures to the point of utmost efficiency. This means goods and services can be reproduced and reused far more easily. At the end of the day, new technology and its applications will increase our chances of health, happiness and prosperity.

It's in developing countries that the new network society will have the most impact. New digital infrastructure will provide third world countries in particular with healthcare, education, energy, trade and financial services.

A different scenario

On the other hand, things may well take an altogether different turn. In 2016, the Global Commission on Internet Governance issued a warning that the Internet may well succumb to the abuse of power by governments and businesses.[21] The commission denounced the censorship of countries like China, Iran and Russia by calling for net neutrality. They accused Facebook and Google of making membership of their platforms compulsory for those in developing countries desiring Internet access. According to the commission, this is a typical display of abusing power. On account of encouraging "censorship, digital espionage, manipulation and single-minded pursuit of profit,"[22] the Internet needs a makeover.

Privacy is another sore spot. Apparently, people are more than willing to surrender their privacy if this results in a safer society. Stanford professor Jeffrey Ullman even thinks "the world is a safer place if we know who the good guys are and who the bad guys are. Safety outweighs the need for privacy."[23] Fun fact: Ullman was the faculty adviser for the PhD of Google founder Sergey Brin. He's by no means the only one with this mindset. Besides, a lot of people are willing to relinquish their privacy if they're promised a healthier and longer life in return. In fact, most onlife consumers are prepared to trade chunks of privacy for better performing apps, more enticing offers, price advantages or improved service levels.

In the digital age, the traditional safety nets of individuals and societies are under serious pressure. True, everybody *could* benefit from the digital age, but this doesn't mean that everybody *does*. Automation, globalization and the digital revolution of the future will translate into significant job losses, which will only be balanced out by new jobs over a longer a period of time (see Chapter 13). However, experiments with basic income or job guarantees might provide ways to alter the existing systems from within, using a new mindset.[24]

The complete and utter dependence on and vulnerability of the Internet may well be the greatest price we pay as a society. Virtually every kind of essential infrastructure is based on the Internet, making us more vulnerable. That dependence also increases the divide between people with Internet access and those without. If we do nothing, we'll have to be even more dependent on the global tech giants and shopping ecosystems.

INTERNET IS NOT THE ANSWER

Andrew Keen is a writer, entrepreneur and one of the Internet's biggest critics. I finished his books *The Internet Is Not The Answer*[25] and *How to Fix the Future*[26] in one go. In it, he states that the lofty promises made about the Internet – i.e. how humans and computers would create a beautiful symbiosis and make the world a better place – have not been fulfilled. He makes it clear that the Internet has actually increased the inequality between people and caused job losses, not to mention reducing people to products with no power or identity. According to Keen not even the smartest technology can solve the thorniest problems of our digital world. Only people can. By working together as an Internet of People we are able to build a better world for ourselves. And for our children.

I met with Keen after a lecture he gave in Amsterdam about the crossroads we're facing. Just as was true for the launch of the Internet in 1995, we now have the opportunity to shape its future according to our demands. When I brought up the power of the global shopping ecosystems, he proved to be as gloomy as ever. He believes that consumers are, in fact, all unpaid workers of the tech giants by handing over free personal data, allowing a chosen few superrich to have a field day with it.[27] I'm reminded of the words of philosopher Hans Schnitzler, who believes that "average users have been reduced to cooperative system-slaves working for the technocratic capitalist powers-that-be".[28] Keen pointed out to me the growing income inequality, which is particularly visible and poignant in Silicon Valley. We ought not to settle for a world divided between *haves and have-nots.*

Regaining control

The doomsday scenario need not become reality, though. A decentralized network society, operating in a bottom-up fashion, can prevent it. Power can be returned to civic initiatives through decentralization, and the well-organized collaboration of individuals can produce sufficient fighting power to upend established institutions.[29]

I can see a new consciousness beginning to bud. You might call it a new mindset, a fresh mentality. I've noticed companies eager to take robotization, artificial intelligence and sustainable business to the next level without losing sight of the human limits. There are plenty of developments in the smart, circular, sharing and glocal economy that hint at the very same thing. I believe we will win back — slowly, but surely — control of our own lives, making more responsible and considered decisions as a result. We can already see this starting to happen.

Yes, we *are* at a crossroads, but it's by no means too late to change direction and yank the steering wheel. Back in 1995, on the eve of the Internet revolution, none of us could begin to imagine what was in store for us. Now, we've had the opportunity to learn from its unbridled optimism, as well as its downside, opportunism, of the early years. We can create new economic models for a more equal society. We can invest in business models that truly make a difference to people's lives. We can keep the adage "man is the measure of all things" in mind with everything we do. Together we will — that includes governments, businesses *and* consumers — embrace the possibility of owning digital progress ourselves.

This calls for a transition, a revolution, an altered mindset. After all, we are accustomed to think according to traditional structures and systems, inclined to rate our own interests above everything else. Even in the new Trump era of protectionism and putting one's own interests first, it's not a viable long-term strategy. We must move towards a vision of humanity based on a mutually respectful attitude towards every single person's uniqueness.

If we want to inch towards a network society, it'll be the people who end up making the difference. Whenever people set to work to solve new world problems, they'll make different choices than if this important job is left to businesses. In every single social realm, from CEOs to the teenager stocking shelves, each of us needs to step up to the plate, take responsibility and show we have initiative and entrepreneurial spirit. This means showing courage, bravery and tenacity, all of which we surely have. After all, society has survived the previous industrial and political revolutions. American sociologist W.F. Ogburn coined the phrase *cultural lag* to describe the period in which people are confronted with immense (technological) changes.[30] It always takes time for old values, thought concepts and patterns of behavior to catch up and adapt to the new reality. To quote my eldest son (and possibly his whole generation of millennials with him): "It will all turn out fine."

Thanks

This book took its time to incubate. The first adumbrations of the idea to write a book appeared in May 2013, and I started to do research. In fact, I wrote the first few words in New York, on January 10, 2014. My activities for Thuiswinkel.org and Ecommerce Europe would allow me to travel all over the world, visiting nearly every continent over the past years. As a result, I have been able to speak with many executives, CEOs, directors, reporters, business people, supervisory board members, students, legislators and regulators, scientists and — most importantly — with scores of (former) employees of hundreds of different organizations and companies.

First of all, I would like to thank John Numan, the publisher of Nubiz, for his unequivocal vote of confidence right from the word go, in the production of the English-language edition of my book. He was also my publisher at Business Contact for the Dutch edition and I followed him on his endeavors to start a new business publishing company. I would like to thank his entire team, responsible for the editing, translation, proofreading, photography, cover and interior design and marketing — Martha, Ellen, Sander, and Bart in particular — all of you delivered immaculate work.

This book is the result of hard work by a huge number of people. Some of you referred interesting sources to me, sent me books and articles, and provided me with an endless flow of information. Thank you all. I would, in particular, like to thank everyone who read the book, especially those of you who were ruthlessly critical. The book is the better for it.

Thank you for your constructive criticism and encouraging comments. In alphabetical order, I would like to thank all my associates and colleagues, entrepreneurs, personal friends, scientists, business acquaintances and friends who contributed to one or even several chapters: Jorij Abraham, Martijn Aerts, Christiaan Alberdingk Thijm, Paul Alfing, Dennis van Allemeersch, Prisca Ancion-Kors, Joachim de Boer, Arjan Bol, Arjen Bonsing, Gijs Boudewijn, Bart Combée, Peter Cras, Michel Delissen, Inge Demoed, Hans Dijkzeul, Kees Gabriëls, Henk Gianotten, Pieter van de Glind, Marlene ten Ham, Just Hasselaar, Ank van Heeringen, Michel Hodes, Jouke Hofman, Martijn Hos, Mark van der Horst, Johan Jelsma, Kitty Koelemeijer, Douwe Lyclama, Harmen van der Meulen, Cor Molenaar, Guus Munten, Paul Nijhof, Ed Nijpels, Elaine Oldhoff, Frank Oostdam, Gino van Ossel, Margreeth Pape, Fer van de Plas, Walther Ploos van Amstel, Menno van der Put, Jan-Willem Roest, Joost Romein, Vincent Romviel, Daniel Ropers, Sophie van Rooij, Stefanie Ros, Michel Schuurman, Roy Scheerder, Jerry Stam, Joost Steins Bisschop, Daan Weddepohl, Gert van de Weerthof, and Eelco van Wijk.

I would like to thank the board of Thuiswinkel.org for giving me the opportunity to write this book.

A special thank you is due to my own editors and (critical) readers. First of all, thank you to Mikkie Hogenboom and Richard van Welie, colleagues at Thuiswinkel.org, who edited every single chapter at least twice. A special thank you to Margreeth Pape, Paul Alfing, Elaine Oldhoff and Arjen Bonsing who proved invaluable for the chapters on the circular economy, payment and consumer care. Profound thanks to fellow author Wilbert Schreurs, whom I have been privileged to get to know over the past year. En route to a future joint project of ours, he was ever at my beck and call to edit yet another chapter or offer his comments, regardless of how inconvenient the time of day. Finally, thanks are due to my trusted researcher Niels van Straaten, who was unfailingly meticulous and hard-working in both research and writing. I will cherish happy memories of the many Fridays we spent together, working all hours on producing this book.

Last but not least, I want to thank my beloved wife Gertje, for her never-ending and constant encouragement and support as I wrote this book and prepared for this English edition. I am in awe of her infinite patience with me being preoccupied, my mind clearly elsewhere during very many hours spent with her. I was impatient to spend our first holiday together without my laptop, tablet, books and piles of clippings. It finally happened in the summer of 2017.

I also want to thank all our children, Pelle especially. He was still living at home — last man standing — when his father embraced the idea of realizing his childhood dream.

Wijnand Jongen
Wijk bij Duurstede, September 1, 2017

I am grateful to my publisher John who allowed me to update the book in early spring of 2018. As I reread the book, I was struck by how true a picture the many examples we had added had painted: of the trends, developments and predictions for the retail world, by affirming their veracity, reinforcing their value and even by making them come true.

Wijnand Jongen
Wijk bij Duurstede, April 1, 2018

www.wijnandjongen.com

Wijnand Jongen is a globally recognized author, keynote speaker and futurist on topics in retail and e-commerce. He is co-founder and Chairman of the Executive Committee of Ecommerce Europe and founder and CEO of the Dutch e-commerce association Thuiswinkel.org.

He chairs the Professorship eMarketing & Distance Selling at Erasmus University in Rotterdam and is a member of FIRAE , an alliance of global retail industry leaders with strong ties to the American National Retail Federation (NRF).

In the mid-1990s, Jongen was co-founder and CEO of Macropolis, the first Dutch online shopping portal. Jongen attended the University of Amsterdam in the Netherlands, and Randolph-Macon College and Averett University in the United States.

www.wijnandjongen.com

Notes

Introduction

1   Go to www.wikipedia.org for definitions of retail and ecommerce.

1   The onlification of society

1   Quote Jack Ma in a letter to Alibaba shareholders, October 2016.
2   'The Internet As Mass Medium', Merrill Morris and Christine Ogan, *Journal of Computer-Mediated Communication*, Indiana University, June 2006.
3   www.ec.europa.eu.
4   *The Onlife Manifesto. Being Human in a Hyperconnected World*, Luciano Floridi, Springer, 2015.
5   *The Fourth Revolution*, Luciano Floridi, Oxford University Press, 2014, p. 43.
6   *Networked. The New Social Operating System*, Lee Raine and Barry Wellman, The MIT Press, 2012.
7   '4 Companies That Dominate Your Everyday Life', www.investopedia.com, August 17, 2015.
8   'Online social integration is associated with reduced mortality risk', William Hobbs, Moira Burke, Nicholas Christakis, James Fowler. PNAS, vol. 113, no 46. www.pnas.org, October 31, 2016.
9   'Accepting Facebook friend request may lengthen users' lives, study says', Elizabeth Elizalde, www.nydailynews.com, November 5, 2016.
10   'Why Do People Use Facebook?', Ashwini Nadkarni and Stefan G. Hofmann, *Personality and Individual Differences*, February 2012, vol. 52(3): pp. 243-249.
11   'Networked Individualism: What in the World Is That?', Lee Rainie and Barry Wellman, networked.pewinternet.org, May 12, 2012.
12   Quote of Barry Wellman, *Elsevier*, April 18, 2015.
13   'Gartner Says Competition Is Increasing to Be the IoT Gateway to the Connected Home', August 6, 2015, www.gartner.com.

14 'The Last Medium', Carina Chocano, *California Sunday Magazine*, www.stories.californiasunday.com, October 5, 2014.

15 Based on an adaptation of *The Onlife Manifesto*, www.ec.europa.eu.

16 'A Chip in Your Brain Can Control a Robotic Arm. Welcome to Braingate', Madhumita Venkataramanan, www.wired.co.uk, May 1, 2015.

17 'Social Media and Political Engagement', Lee Raine, Aaron Smith, Kay Lehman Schlozman, Hendry Brady and Sidney Verba, PewResearch-Center, www.pewinternet.org, October 19, 2012.

18 *The Third Industrial Revolution. How Lateral Power Is Transforming Energy, The Economy and the World*, Jeremy Rifkin, Palgrave Macmillan, 2011.

19 *The Third Industrial Revolution. How Lateral Power Is Transforming Energy, The Economy and the World*, Jeremy Rifkin, Palgrave Macmillan, 2011.

20 *The Fourth Industrial Revolution*, Klaus Schwab, World Economic Forum, 2016.

21 www.statista.com.

22 'Why Online2Offline Commerce Is A Trillion Dollar Opportunity', Alex Rampell, https://techcrunch.com, August 7, 2010.

23 Alibaba's Intime Acquisiton Mirrors Amazon's Physical Store Drive, Rachel Gunter, www.marketrealist.com, January 20, 2017.

24 'Alibaba's New Retail Integrates E-commerce, Stores & Logistics: Is This The Next Gen of Retail', Deborah Weinswig, www.forbes.com, April 14, 2017.

25 'Alibaba Makes Another Big Push Into Brick-and-Mortar Retail', www.fortune.com, February 20, 2017.

26 'Here's Why Alibaba Is Investing In A Physical Supermarket', Trefis Team, www.forbes.com, November 23, 2016.

27 'A virtual empire', Suchit Leesa-Nguansuk. Bankok Post, February 6, 2017.

28 *Footprint 2020. Offline Retail in an Online World*, Marco Kesterloo and Marc Hoogenbert, Booz & Company, 2013, www.strategyand.pwc.com.

29 'Getting Physical: Online Retailers Move Offline', Barbara Thau, www.chainstoreage.com, May 7, 2013.

30 'Amazon Plans More Stores, Bulked-Up Prime Services', Greg Bensinger, www.wsj.com, May 17, 2016.

31 'Why Would Amazon Open Physical Stores', Trefis Team, www.forbes.com, February 11, 2016.

32 'Alibaba buys into retail stores strategy', Louise Lucas. Financial Times. www.ft.com, January 23, 2017.

33 'Hema plans 2,000 new stores in China over next five year', Matilda Mereghetti, www.undercurrentnews.com, December 7, 2017.

34 'Zalando buys streetwear retailer Kickz, outlook dents shares', Emma Thomasson, www.in.reuters.com, March 1, 2017.

35 'Zalando denkt über Glitzer-Shops nach – und 3-D-Druck'. Jonas Rest. www.manager-magazin.de, April 29, 2017.

36 'Zalando buys streetwear retailer Kickz, outlook dents shares'. Emma Thomasson. www.in.reuters.com, March 1, 2017.

37 'Amazon is Doubling Down on Retail Stores with Plans to Have Up to 100 Pop-up Stores in US Shopping Malls', Eugene Kim, www.businessinsider.com, September 9, 2016.

38 'Amazon's Treasure Truck rolling up to Whole Foods stores across U.S. starting today', Nat Levy, www.geekwire.com, January 30, 2018.

39 'Here's How Amazon Could Disrupt Health Care (Part 1, 2 and 3)' Chuncka Mui, www.forbes.com, February 7, 2018.

40 'Why Unilever Really Bought Dollar Shave Club', Jing Cao and Melissa Mittelman, www.bloomberg.com, July 20, 2016.

41 www.origami.com

42 'Why Does Kenya Lead the World in Mobile Money?', The Economist, May 27, 2013.

2   Onlife retail in the smart economy

1 *Big Data: A Revolution That Will Transform How We Live, Work, and Think*, Viktor Mayer-Schönberger and Kenneth Cukier, Houghton Mifflin Harcourt, 2013.

2 *Sie Wissen Alles*, Yvonne Hofstetter, C. Bertelsman, 2014.

3 'Gartner 2015 Hype Cycle: Big Data is Out, Machine Learning Is In', Bhavya Geethika, www.kdnuggets.com, August 2015.

4 'Data is giving rise to a new economy', *The Economist*.

5 'Gartner Says Smart Cities Will Use 1.1 Connected Things in 2015', press release, www.gartner.com, March 18, 2015.

6 'The results are in: Retail's 'Holy Grail' is... Beacons', Mike Butler, www.linkedin.com, August 1, 2017.

7 'At Store After Store, a Pitch by Phone', Mark Scott, www.nytimes.com, December 2, 2014.

8 'Five Pieces of Tech That Are Set to Transform the High Street', Jack Torrance, www.managementtoday.co.uk, June 12, 2015.

9 'How Bluetooth Beacons Will Transform Retail in 2016', Kenny Kline, www.huffingtonpost.com, January 15, 2016.

10 '1 in 3 Shoppers Will Never Use Beacons in Stores', Andrew Meola, Business Insider UK, www.uk.businessinsider.com.

11 'Footprint 2020. Offline Retail in an Online World', www.strategyand.pwc.com, p. 14, Booz & Company, 2013.

12 'Timberland Creates Its First Digitally Connected Store', Hilary Milnes, www.digiday.com, January 18, 2016.

13 'New Argos Digital Concept Stores', www.retail-innovation.com, 2015.

14 'Cramming More Components onto Integrated Circuits', Gordon E. Moore, *Electronics Magazine*, p. 4, University of Texas, 1965.

15 Erwin van den Brink, *Het Financieele Dagblad,* January 9, 2016.

16 'The Emerging of "Internet of Things', Mark Fell, www.carré-strauss.com, 2014; figures as interpreted by author, based on Cisco data.

17 'Morgan Stanley: 75 Billion Devices Will Be Connected To The Internet Of Things By 2020', Tony Danova, www.businessinsider.com, October 2, 2013.

18 'Internet of Things Market to Reach $1,7 Trillion by 2020', IDC, Steven Norton, *The Wall Street Journal*, June 2, 2015.

19 'Unlocking the Potential of the Internet of Things', report from McKinsey Global Institute, www.mckinsey.com, June 2015.

20 *The Circle*, Dave Eggers, Hamish Hamilton, 2013.

21 'Teslamania', Arthur van Leeuwen, *Elsevier*, February 1, 2014.

22 'The WHO, WHY and HOW Augmented Reality Will Dominate Retail in 2018', Jeff Tremblay, www.mytotalretail.com, February 11, 2018.

23 'M&S Enters the World of VR with Loft Homeware Tour', Katie Deighton, www.eventmagazine.co.uk, September 15, 2015.

24 'How Oculus and Cardboard Are Going to Rock the Travel Industry', Jennifer Parker, www.bloomberg.com, June 19, 2015.

25 'An Amadeus company, Navitaire, unveils the world's first Virtual Reality travel search and booking experience', Candice Vallantin, www.amadeus.com, April 25, 2017.

26 'Mixed Reality: The Future of Augmented and Virtual Reality, Dennis Williams, www.augment.com, January 24, 2017.

27 'Retail's New Reality: Invisible Shopping Centers and Virtual Assistants', Lance Eliot, CNBC, www.cnbc.com, April 24, 2015.

28 www.shoppingtomorrow.nl, Product visualisation, Thuiswinkel.org, January 2014.

29 Ibid.

30 www.statista.com, February 14, 2018.

31 '12 Things We Can 3d Print in Medicine Right Now', Bertalan Meskó, www.3dprintingindustry.com, February 26, 2015.

32 'Asda Launches 3d Printing Service — Offering Customers a Chance to Clone Themselves As Tiny Figures', Kirstie Mccrum, www.mirror.co.uk, May 28, 2015.

33 '37 Marketplaces to Share, Buy and Sell Designs for 3d Printing', Blog Mathilda, www.makingsociety.com, July 11, 2013.

34 'Amazon Enters 3d Printing Race', tj McCue, www.forbes.com, July 31, 2014.

35 'Amazon Files Patent for Mobile 3d Printing Delivery Trucks', Brian Krassenstein, www.3dprint.com, February 25, 2015.

36 '3D Body Scanning: Fitting the future', Hein Daanen, www.amfi.nl/3d-body-scanning-fitting-future.

37 'Nike ceo Mark Parker Said the Brand Is Working on 3d-Printing Flyknit Sneakers', Riley Jones, www.uk.complex.com, March 30, 2016.

38 '3d printing: Good for Retail? Tesco cio Says So', Colin Neagle, www.networkworld.com, September 27, 2013.

39 'Zalando denkt über Glitzer-Shops nach – und 3-D-Druck', Jonas Rest, www.manager-magazin.de, April 29, 2017.

40 3D printing: a threat to global trade. ING Report, September 2017.

41 'Is this the rise of the retail robots?' Cate Trotter, LinkedIn, April 11, 2017.

42 'Amazon is just beginning to use robots in its warehouses and they're already making a huge difference', Ananya Bhattacharya, June 17, 2016.

43 'Where's the Sugar? Supermarket Robot Creates Product Maps As It Takes Stock', Ben Coxworth, www.gizmag.com, April 18, 2016.

44 'Walmart's new robots are loved by staff – and ignored by customers', Erin Winick, www.technologyreview.com, January 31, 2018.

45 'Mobile Experiments', Katie Evans, *Internet Retailer*, September 2016.

46 Is Artificial Intelligence the Answer to Retail Challenges?, An Internet Retailer Report, sponsored by IBM. www.digitalcommerce360.com, 2017.

47 Quote by Hugh Fletcher, Global Head of Consulting, Salmon Ltd.

48 Interview Werner Vogels. Klaas Broekhuizen and Sandra Olsthoorn, *Het Financieele Dagblad*, February 20, 2017.

49 Franka Rolvink Couzy, *Het Financieele Dagblad*, June 24, 2016.

50 'Are the Robots About to Rise? Google's New Director of Engineering Thinks So', Carole Cadwalladr, www.theguardian.com, February 22, 2014.

51 *The Singularity is Near*, Ray Kurzweil, Viking, February 2013.

52 Nick Kivits, *Het Financieele Dagblad*, September 10, 2016.

53 'Partnership on AI Formed by Google, Facebook, Amazon, IBM and Microsoft', Alex Hern, www.theguardian.com, September 28, 2016.

54 Klaas Broekhuizen, *Het Financieele Dagblad*, September 30, 2016.

55 'CIO Explainer: What is Blockchain?', Steven Norton, *The Wall Street Journal*, www.blogs.wsj.com, February 2, 2016.

56 'Blockchain Technology: 9 Benefits & 7 Challenges. Disrupting Multiple Industries', Jacob Boersma and Jeroen Bulters, www.deloitte.com.

57 *The Blockchain Revolution*, Don and Alex Tapscott, Penguin, 2016.

58 'Here's Why Blockchains Will Change The World', Don and Alex Tapscott, www.fortune.com, May 8, 2016.

59 *The Blockchain Revolution*, Don and Alex Tapscott, Penguin, 2016, page 161.

60 *Reinventing Capatalism in the Age of Big Data*, Victor Mayer-Schönberger and Thomas Range, John Murray, January 2018.

61 'Protection of personal data', www.ec.europe.eu.

62 'WhatsApp, Facebook and Google face tough new privacy rules under EC proposal', Samual Gibbs. www.theguardian.com, January 10, 2017.

63 Interview professor Lokke Moerel, De Brauw Blackstone Westbroek, *Het Financieele Dagblad*, February 15, 2014.

64 Interview with Susan Athey, economist, Michael Persson, *de Volkskrant*, June 13, 2014.

65 'How Target Figured Out A Teenage Girl Was Pregnant Before Her Father Did', Kashir Mill, *Forbes*, February 16, 2012.

66 'How Companies Learn Your Secrets', Charles Duhigg, *The New York Times*, February 16, 2012.

67 *Big Data: A Revolution That Will Transform How We Live, Work, and Think*, Viktor Mayer-Schönberger and Kenneth Cukier, Houghton Mifflin Harcourt, 2013, page 276.

68 'Saving Big Data from Big Mouths', Cesar A. Hildalgo, www.scientificamerican.com, April 29, 2014.

69 'The Eight Most Common Big Data Myths', Joerg Niessing, www.knowledge.insead.edu, March 5, 2015.

70 'The Backlash Against Big Data', www.economist.com, April 20, 2014.

71 *Time Magazine*, December 25, 2006.

72 Richard Smit, *Het Financieele Dagblad*, January 16, 2016.

73 Quote Martijn Hos, public affairs director Thuiswinkel.org, January 14, 2016.

3   Consumers in the sharing economy

1   'Share My Ride', Mark Levine, www.nytimes.com, March 5, 2009.

2   'Free Music, at least while it lasts', David Carr, *The New York Times*, June 8, 2014.

3   *The Age of Access*, Jeremy Rifkin, Tarcher/Putnam, 2000.

4   'When is Ours Better Than Mine? A Framework for Understanding and Altering Participation in Commercial Sharing Systems', C.P. Lamberton and R.L. Rose, *Journal of Marketing*, 76(4), 109-125, 2012.

5   'The Sharing Economy — Seizing the Revenue Opportunity', *Retrieved*, June 16, 2015.

6   'Consumer Intelligent Series. The Sharing Economy', PwC, 2015.

7   *Stuffocation*, James Wallman, Spiegel & Grau, 2016.

8   *What's Mine Is Yours: The Rise of Collaborative Consumption*, Rachel Botsman and Roo Rogers, Harper Business, 2010.

9   '10 Ideas That Will Change The World', Bryan Walsh, *Time*, March 17, 2011.

10   Rachel Botsman on TedxSydney 2010.

11   *What Are the Drivers of the Sharing Economy and How Do They Change Customer Behavior?*, Lea Scholdan and Niels van Straaten, Erasmus University, June 24, 2015.

12   *What's Mine Is Yours: The Rise of Collaborative Consumption*, Rachel Botsman and Roo Rogers, Harper Business, 2010.

13   'A Rough Ride to Profit for CouchSurfing', Kristen Brown, SFGate.com, November 26, 2014.

14   'Seeds of Apple's New Growth In Mobile Payments, 800 Million iTunes Accounts', Nigam Arora, www.forbes.com, April 24, 2014.

15   'Spotify Remains Tops in Music Subscriptions', Matthias Verbergt, www.wsj.com, September 14, 2016.

16   IFPI Global Music Report 2016, www.ifpi.org, April 12, 2016.

17   'Is Uber shortchanging drives? As part of lawsuit, over 9,000 now say yes', Cyrus Farivar, www.arstechnica.com, February 16, 2018.

18   '67 Amazing Airbnb Statistics and Facts', Craig Smith, www.expandedramblings.com, February 11, 2017

19   AlixPartners, www.alixpartners.com, February 4, 2014.

20   'Future of Carsharing Market to 2025', Frost Sullivan, www.frost.com, August 2, 2016.

21   'IKEA Enters "Gig Economy" by Acquiring TaskRabbit', Tiffany Hsu, www.nytimes.com, September 28, 2017.

22 'Why Brands Should Pay Attention to Collaborative Consumption', Ana Andjelic, www.theguardian.com, May 8, 2014.

23 'O2O: Why China Leads the "Online to Offline" Revolution', www.innovationiseverywhere.com, 2015.

24 *The Third Wave: The Classic Study of Tomorrow*, Alvin Toffler, Bantam, 1980.

25 *Makers: The New Industrial Revolution*, Chris Anderson, Crown Business, October 2, 2012.

26 *The Third Industrial Revolution. How Lateral Power Is Transforming Energy, The Economy and the World*, Jeremy Rifkin, Palgrave Macmillan, 2011.

27 *The Zero Marginal Cost Society*, Jeremy Rifkin, Palgrave Macmillan, 2014.

28 'Beyond Uber and Airbnb: The Future of the Sharing Economy', Alex Stephany, *Los Angeles Times*, May 28, 2014.

29 *What's Mine Is Yours: The Rise of Collaborative Consumption*, Rachel Botsman and Roo Rogers, Harper Business, 2010.

30 'Chaos at the world's most valuable venture-backed company is forcing Silicon Valley to question its values', Katy Steinmetz and Matt Vella, *TIME Magazine*, June 26, 2017.

31 'The Sharing Economy Isn't "Collaborative Consumption", It's "Disaster Capitalism"', Alexandra Le Tellier, *Los Angeles Times*, June 5, 2014.

32 'The Case Against Sharing', Susie Cagle, www.medium.com, May 27, 2014.

33 'To Get a Fair Share, Sharing-Economy Workers Must Unionize', Susie Cagle, Aljazeera America, June 27, 2014.

34 'TrustCloud Provides Quality Assurance for the Sharing Economy', Michael Sacca, *Cocktail San Francisco*, October 19, 2014.

35 'The Evolution of Trust', David Brooks, *The New York Times*, June 30, 2014.

36 'An Analysis of the Labor Market for Uber's Driver-Partners in the United States', J.V. Hall and A.B. Krueger, www.nberg.org, 2016.

37 'Uber, Airbnb and Consequences of the Sharing Economy', J. Penn and J. Wihbey, *Research Roundup*, 2015.

38 'The Dark Side of "Sharing Economy" Jobs', Catherine Rampell, *The Washington Post*, January 26, 2015.

39 'In the Sharing Economy, Works Find Both Freedom and Uncertainty', Natasha Singer, *The New York Times*, August 16, 2014.

40 'In the Sharing Economy, a Rift over Worker Classification', Scott Kirsner, *The Boston Globe*, August 17, 2014.

41 'Hiring Independent Contractors: Why Everyone Will Be Doing It By 2020', Jen Cohen Crompton, Business2Community, October 14, 2014.

42 'Working in America', The Aspen Institute, December 2, 2014.

43 'Three Challenges for the Sharing Economy and Collaborative Consumption Initiatives', Michel Bauwens, p2p Foundation, January 1, 2013.

44 'Eerlijk delen. Waarborgen van publieke belangen in de deeleconomie en kluseconomie', Dr. ir. Rinie van Est and Dr. Magda Smink. Rathenau Instituut, May 2017.

45 'Uber Faces Federal Inquiry Over Use of Greyball Tool to Evade Authorities', Mike Isaac, www.nytimes.com, May 4, 2017.

46 'EU Backs Sharing Economy in Boost for Uber and Airbnb', Julia Kollewe & Rob Davies, www.theguardian.com, June 2, 2016.

47 'A European Agenda for the Collaborative Economy', European Commission, June 2, 2016.

48 *Share*, Pieter van de Glind and Harmen van Sprang, Business Contact, 2016.

49 'Sharing Economy Revenues set to Triple, Reaching $20 Billion Globally by 2020', Juniper Research, www.juniperresearch.com, May 23, 2016.

50 'Assessing the Size and Presence of the Collaborative Economy in Europe', Robert Vaughan and Raphael Daverio, PwC UK, April 2016.

51 'How the Millennial Generation and a New "Sharing Economy" Are Transforming the Way Cities Function', Ron Cassie, *Baltimore Magazine*, January 2014.

52 'The Current and Future State of the Sharing Economy', Niam Yaraghi and Shamika Ravi. www.brookings.edu, December 29, 2016.

53 Casper Thomas, *De Groene Amsterdammer*, September 25, 2014.

4 Sustainable shopping in the circular economy

1 'Amazon's No Show on Sustainability', Marc Gunther, www.theguardian.com, December 20, 2012.

2 *Waste to Wealth*, Peter Lacy and Jakob Rutqvist, Palgrave Macmillan, 2015.

3 '"Cars Are Parked 95% of the Time". Let's Check!', Paul Barter, www.reinventingparking.org, February 22, 2013.

4 '2030: A "Perfect Storm" of Global Resource Shortages', Clinton Global Initiative, John W. Schoen, www.cnbc.com, September 23, 2013.

5 'UN Projects World Population to Reach 8.5 Billion by 2030, Driven by Growth in Developing Countries', www.un.org, July 29, 2015.

6 'Has the Earth Run Out of Any Natural Resources', Brian Palmer, www.slate.com, October 20, 2010.

7 'IKEA tests renting out furniture as eco-friendly plan', Tim Wallace, www.telegraph.co.uk, January 24, 2018.

8 *Circulaire Economie: Innovatie meten in de keten*, J. Potting et al., PBL/Universiteit Utrecht, Den Haag, 2016, p. 15.

9 'Manifest circular e-commerce', Margreeth Pape, Thuiswinkel.org, January 2017.

10 'The 2017 Dimensional Weight Pricing Changes You Need To Know', Jillian Hufford, wwwnchannel.com, April 26, 2017.

11 'Amazon Cuts Shipping Fees in Threat to Alibaba's U.S. Business', Spencer Soper, www.bloomberg.com, June 15, 2016.

12 'The Carbon Majors Debate': CDP Carbon Majors Report 2017', CDP, www.cdp.net, July 2017.

13 'Donald Trump doesn't think much of global warming', Chris Cillizza, www.edition.cnn.com, August 8, 2017.

14 'Retailers' Challenge: How to Cut Carbon Emissions as E-Commerce Soars. Aaron Cheris, Casey Taylor, Jennifer Hayes, and Jenny Davis-Peccoud, www.bain.com, April 18, 2017.

15 'What's Really Driving China's $1 Billion Dollar Bike-Sharing Boom?', Paul Armstrong and Yue Wang, www.forbes.com, June 20, 2017.

16 'China's bike-sharing frenzy has turned into a bubble', Michelle Toh, www.money.cnn.com, December 29, 2017.

17 'Project Ara Lives: Google's Modular Phone Is Ready for You Now', David Pierce, www.wired.com, May 20, 2016.

18 MVO Nederland, www.mvonederland.nl, April 2016.

19 'H&M Ups Its Green Game', Joelle Diderich, www.wwd.com, April 4, 2017.

20 'H&M's Latest Conscious Collection Is Their Best Yet For Sustainable Fashion', Susan Devaney, www.huffingtonpost.com, March 24, 2017.

21 'People & Planet Positive. IKEA Sustainability Strategy for 2020', www.ikea.com, June 2014.

22 'Retailers' Challenge: How to Cut Carbon Emissions as E-Commerce Soars. Aaron Cheris, Casey Taylor, Jennifer Hayes, and Jenny Davis-Peccoud, www.bain.com, April 18, 2017.

23 *Waste to Wealth*, Peter Lacy and Jakob Rutqvist, Palgrave Macmillan, 2015.

24 'Remaking the Industrial Economy', Hanh Nguyen, Martin Stuchtey and Markus Zils, McKinsey & Company, February 2014.

25 'Moving Towards a Circular Economy', Markus Zils, McKinsey & Company, February 2014.

26 Waste Conference, Frank Hopstaken and Kees Wielenga, October 30, 2014.

27 'Amazon's No Show on Sustainability', Marc Gunther, www.theguardian.com, December 20, 2012.

28 'Can Amazon's New "Dream Team" Fix the Company's Sustainability Reputation?', Marc Gunther, www.theguardian.com, February 2, 2016.

29 'Environmental Responsibility Report', Apple, 2016.

30 'Apple makes 'closed loop' recycling pledge', Tim Bradshaw, *The Financial Times*, April 20, 2017.

31 'Microsoft Has Been Using 100% Renewable Energy for Its US Operations Since 2014', Laurent Giret, www.winbeta.com, March 22, 2016.

32 'Sustainable Development Goals: 17 goals to transform our world, www.un.org, September 25, 2015.

33 Liza Jansen, *Het Financieele Dagblad*, April 23, 2016.

34 *This Changes Everything, Capitalism vs. the Climate*, Naomi Klein, Simon & Schuster, 2014.

35 Liza Jansen, *Het Financieele Dagblad*, April 23, 2016.

36 'Japan's 2011 Earthquake, Tsunami and Nuclear Disaster. Economic Impact on Japan and the Rest of the World', Kimberly Amadeo, useconomy.about.com.

37 'Ukraine Crisis: Why It Matters to the World Economy. How Ukraine Crises Affects Your Money', Mark Thompson and Gregory Wallace, CNNMoney, March 3, 2014.

38 'Paris climate agreement: World reacts as Trump pulls out of global accord – as it happened', Ellle Hunt. www.theguardian.com, June 2, 2017.

5   Winner takes all in the platform economy

1   *Being Digital*, Nicholas Negroponte, Random House, 1996.
2   www.legatum.com, 2015.
3   'Cisco VNU Global IP Traffic Forecast, 2016-2021.
4   'Saving Globalisation and Technology from Themselves', Rich Lesser, Martin Reeves and Johann Harnoss, www.bcgperspectives.com, July 26, 2016.
5   'Globalization: Made in the USA', Gary Grappo, www.fairobserver.com, July 29, 2016.
6   Caroline de Gruyter, *NRC Handelsblad*, August 4, 2016.
7   'Saving Globalization and Technology from Themselves', Rich Lesser, Martin Reeves and Johann Harnoss, www.bcgperspectives.com, July 26, 2016.
8   'The EU Should Take the Side of the Losers of Globalization', Paul de Grauwe, www.socialeurope.eu, July 4, 2016.
9   'Saving Globalization and Technology from Themselves', Rich Lesser, Martin Reeves and Johann Harnoss, www.bcgperspectives.com, July 26, 2016.
10 '62 People Own the Same As Half the World. Reveals Oxfam Davos Report', www.oxfam, January 18, 2016.
11 www.wikipedia.org and www.dfbonline.nl.
12 www.brainyquote.com.
13 'Google is fined billions: encouragement for (web)stores', Wijnand Jongen, blog on www.wijnandjongen.com, June 28, 2017.
14 'Antitrust: Commission fines Google 2.42 billion euro for abusing dominance as search engine by giving illegal advantage to own comparison shopping service — Factsheet, www.europe.eu/rapid/press-release_MEMO-17-1785_en.htm, June 27, 2017.
15 'Search Engine Marketshare, StatCounter Global stats, www.gs.statcounter.com, August 7, 2017.
16 'As Amazon Meddles in More Markets, What Do Reeling Retailers Have in Store?', Maria Halki, www.dallasnews.com, May 13, 2016.
17 'Amazon Commands Almost Half of All Product Searches, and Marketeers Are Ignoring Omnichannel', Stewart Rogers, www.venturebeat.com, October 6, 2015.
18 'Amazon and the "Profitless Business Model" Fallacy', Eugene Wei, blog on Remains of the Day, October 26, 2013. Eugene Wei was strategist at Amazon from 1997 through 2004.
19 www.statista.com, Q1, 2016.
20 'The Market is Underestimating Amazon', Ken Kam, www.forbes.com, May 27, 2016.
21 www.iresearchchina.com, July 27, 2017.
22 'Top 100 Retailers', Stores, July 2017.

23 'Amazon Reports 28% North American Sales Growth in Q2', Don Davis, www.internetretailer.com, July 28, 2016.

24 'Amazon reports nearly $2 billion in profit, blowing past Wall Street expectations for holiday quarter, Katie Roof, www.techcrunch.com, February 1, 2018.

25 Hanneke Chin-A-Fo and Toef Jaeger, *NRC Handelsblad*, September 19, 2014.

26 '2017 FBA Fee Changes and What They Mean For You', www.channeladvisor.com, January 24, 2017.

27 'Amazon Quietly Launched 7 Fashion Brands While Ramping Up Hiring for Its Own Clothing Line', Eugene Kim, www.uk.businessinsider.com, February 22, 2016.

28 'Third-Party Resellers and Amazon — A Double-Edged Sword in ECommerce', Jennifer Rankin, www.theguardian.com, June 23, 2015.

29 'Has Amazon re-invented High Street Shopping?', Paul Skeldon, www.internetretailing.net, June 21, 2017.

30 *The End of Power*, Moisés Naím, Basic Books, 2013.

31 Interview with Moisés Naím, Wouter van Noort, *NRC Handelsblad*, August 8, 2015.

32 'Amazon Says It Puts Customers First. But Its Pricing Algoritm Doesn't', Julia Angwin and Surya Mattu, September 20, 2016.

33 *Red de winkel!*, Cor Molenaar, Academic Service, 2013.

34 'The Guardian View on the Automated Future: Fewer Shops and Fewer People', www.theguardian.com, February 29, 2016.

35 'Amazon is Doubling Down on Retail Stores with Plans to Have up to 100 Pop-Up Stores in us Shopping Malls', Eugene Kim, www.businessinsider.com, September 9, 2016.

36 'Amazon Opens Checkout-Free 'Amazon Go' Grocery Store to the Public in Seattle', Mitchel Broussard, www.macrumors.com, January 22, 2018.

37 'Trump, a 'blessing in disguise' for retailers?, Wijnand Jongen, blog on www.wijnandjongen.com, November 14, 2016.

38 'Amazon's Monopsony Is Not O.K.', Paul Krugman, www.nyt.com, October 20, 2014.

39 'Amazon to start collecting state sales taxes everywhere', Chris Isidore, www.money.cnn.com, March 29, 2017.

40 'FTC Extends Probe into Google's Android', Jack Nicas and Brent Kendall, www.wsj.com, April 26, 2016.

41 Antitrust: Commission fines Google €2.42 billion for abusing dominance as search engine by giving illegal advantage to own comparison shopping service, www.europe.eu, June 27, 2017.

42 'French economy minister files lawsuit against Amazon', www.chicagotribune.com, December 18, 2017.

43 'E.U. Fines Facebook $122 Million Over Disclosures in WhatsApp Deal', Mark Scott. www.nytimes.com, May 18, 2017.

44 'Mergers: Commission fines Facebook 110 million euro for providing misleading information about WhatsApp takeover', http://europa.eu/rapid/press-release_IP-17-1369_en.htm, May 18, 2017.

45 Action Plan on VAT, http://ec.europa.eu/taxation_customs/business/vat/action-plan-vat_en, April 7, 2016.

46 'Ruling That Apple Led E-Book Pricing Conspiracy Is Upheld', Brian X. Chen, www.nyt.com, June 30, 2015.

47 Interview Jonathan Taplin, *Het Financieele Dagblad*, February 5, 2018.

6 Power to the onlife consumer

1   'The Self(ie) Generation', Charles Blow, *The New York Times*, March 7, 2014.

2   'Gen Z: Get Ready for the Most Self-Conscious, Demanding Consumer Segment', Deborah Weinswig, www.fbicgroup.com, August 29, 2016.

3   'The Digital Native Advance', Ken Hughes, www.kenhughes.info.

4   'Digital Natives, Digital Immigrants Part 1', Marc Prensky, *On the Horizon*, September/October 2001, volume 9, nr. 5.

5   'Amazon promises college students two-minute orders', Jefferson Graham, www.usatoday.com, August 15, 2017.

6   'Digital Natives, Digital Immigrants Part 1', Marc Prensky, *On the Horizon*, September/October 2001, volume 9, nr. 5.

7   Central Bureau of Statistics (CBS) the Netherlands, 2012.

8   'Think older people are technophobes? Think again', Lucas Jackson. www.ampweforum.org, May 23, 2017.

9   'Older Adults and Technology Use', Aaron Smith. www.pewinternet.org, April 3, 2014.

10 'Apple And IBM Are Joining Forces To Help Care For The Eldery — In Japan', Ann Brenoff, *The Huffington Post*, April 30, 2015.

11 'Accessibility', Shawn Lawton Henry and Liam McGee, www.w3c.org.

12 'Internet advertising expenditure to exceed US $200 bn this year', www.zenithmedia.com, March 26, 2017.

13 'Change Consumer Behavior with These Five Levers', Keith Weed, *Harvard Business Review*, www.hbr.org, November 6, 2012.

14 W.L. Tiemeijer, C.A. Thomas and H.M. Prast (red.), Dutch Wetenschappelijke Raad voor het Regeringsbeleid (WRR), page 50 of the digital version.

15 Descriptions and profiles based on research for Shopping2020, Expert group Shopper Behavior, conducted by GfK, December 2013.

16 The Amazon Report, IR Research, August 2017.

17 'Saving, Scrimping and.. Splurging? New Insights into Consumer Behavior', Max Magni, Anne Martines, and Rukhshana Motiwala. McKinsey & Company, March 2016.

18 www.statista.com

19 2017 Adblock Report, www.pagefair.com, February 1, 2017.

20 E-mail exchange with Bart Combée, director Dutch Consumer Association (Consumentenbond), May 25, 2016.
21 'Global Powers of Retailing 2017, Yearly research by Deloitte, Published by Stores Media, January 2017.
22 *Omnichannel in retail: het antwoord op e-commerce*, Gino van Ossel, Uitgeverij Lannoo, 2014.
23 'Marketers Need to Drastically Rethink the Customer Decision Journey', Greg Satell, www.forbes.com, October 12, 2015.
24 http://www.slideshare.net/1000t/ikea-presentation-61846053.
25 Bonsing|Mann Customer Journey Model, www.arjenbonsing.com.

7 Orientation: the N=1 effect

1 Report by Expert Group Orientation, Shopping2020, January 2014.
2 'Chinese Influencers: Internet celebrities (Wang Hong) vs bloggers', www.wgsn.com, February 27, 2017.
3 *Kijken, kijken ... anders kopen*, Cor Molenaar, Academic Service, 2015.
4 'Connected Shoppers Report 2016', www.salesforce.com.
5 'How E-Commerce Brands Can Leverage Influencer Marketing for More Sales', Shane Barker, www.inc.com, September 17, 2017.
6 'When Shoppers Demand a Seamless Experience, What Can Digital Shelves Deliver', Thomas E. Bornemann, ey.com, 2015.
7 'Zero-Moment of Truth: Redefining the Consumer Decision-Making Process', IRI, October 2009.
8 *ZMOT. Winning the Zero Moment of Truth*, Diana Howell, Google/VVook, 2009.
9 'More Than 90% of Consumers Use Smartphones While Shopping in Stores', Glenn Taylor, www.retailtouchpoints.com, August 20, 2015.
10 Research trip to IBM, San Francisco, September 12, 2016.
11 'Macy's Integrates IBM Watson into Its Mobile Site', April Berthene, www.internetretailer.com, July 21, 2016.
12 'Macy's signs up IBM's Watson for AI app to guide shoppers around its stores (and it will even know when you get frustrated)', www.dailymail.co.uk, July 20, 2016
13 Research trip to Big Show National Retail Federation (NRF), New York, January 18, 2016.
14 'Using Oculus Rift to Maximize eCommerce Shopper Engagement and Product Experiencing While Disrupting and Reducing Showrooming', Richard Lee, www.pillarsupport.com.
15 'Can We Use Oculus Rift in E-Commerce in the Near Future?', Szymon Stoczek, www.divante.co, April 13, 2015.
16 'Is E-Commerce in Oculus Rift's Future?', Wendy Parish, www.marketingdive.com, March 30, 2015.

17 'Facebook Mulls Commerce Through Virtual Reality Goggles', Deepa Seetharaman, *The Wall Street Journal*, www.blogs.wsj.com, March 27, 2015.

18 'Alibaba Will Let Consumers Shop the World's Stores via Virtual Reality', Frank Tong, www.internetretailer.com, July 9, 2016.

19 'John Lewis Using Augmented Reality in Flagship Store', Peter Graham, www.vrfocus.com, September 13, 2015.

20 'Amazon's smart mirror patent teases the future of fashion', Kaya Yurieff, www.money.cnn.com, January 3, 2018.

21 'Augmented Reality and Its Possibilities for E-Commerce', Inés Ramírez Nicolás, eMarket Services Spain, March 2012.

22 'Google Glass is back with hardware focused on the enterprise', Darrel Etherington, www.techcrunch.com, July 18, 2017.

23 Product visualization, www.shoppingtomorrow.nl, Thuiswinkel.org, January 2014.

24 'From 'makeover mirrors' to virtual reality and HOLOGRAMS: The clever new retail technologies set to make your shopping experience a breeze', Laura House, www.dailymail.co.uk, July 25, 2017.

25 'Google's "Big Red Button" Could Save The World', Anthony Cuthbertson, www.europe.newsweek.com, June 8, 2016.

8   Selection: new paradigm of choice

1 'When Choice is Demotivating: Can One Desire Too Much of a Good Thing?', S. Iyengar and R. Lepper, *Journal of Personality and Social Psychology*, 2000.

2 *The Paradox of Choice*, Barry Schwartz, Harper Perennial, 2004.

3 Blog www.wijnandjongen.com.

4 'The Future of Online Grocery in Europe', Nicolo Galanta, Enrique Garcia Lopez, and Sarah Moore, McKinsey & Company, 2013.

5 Bida Consulting.

6 'I Tried All the Different Lazy Ways to Get Groceries Without Leaving the House — Here's What's Good About Each One', Jillian D'Onfro, www.businessinsider.com, March 13, 2016.

7 'Subscription Food Boxes: Are They Worth It?', www.news.com.au, June 23, 2015.

8 'Grocery Shopping Might Be Less Painful with This Smart Cart', Stacey Higginbotham, www.gigaom.com, February 11, 2015.

9 'The Age of Grocery "Smart Carts" Creeps Closer', Anna Rose Welch, www.innovativeretailtechnologies.com, March 5, 2014.

10 'Grocery Store Without Checkout Lines', Leena Rao. www.fortune.com, December 6, 2016.

11 'JD.com launches 7Fresh supermarket', www.insideretail.asia.com, January 4, 2018.

12 *Why We Buy. The Science of Shopping*, Paco Underhill, Simon & Schuster,
    New York, 1999 (2009 edition).

13 'Compare.com CEO's Vision for the Future — Right or Wrong', Don Jergler,
    Insurance Journal, April 21, 2015.

14 www.statista.com; data for summer 2014 (South Korea 56%, China 54%,
    United States 37%).

15 'Amazon Patent Would Block Comparison Shopping In Stores', David Z.
    Moss. www.fortune.com, June 17, 2017.

16 'The five big announcements from Google I/O', Dave Lee. www.bbc.com,
    May 18, 2017.

17 'Consumers Have Spoken: 2016 Is the Year of "Webrooming"', Sara Spivey,
    www.marketingland.com, July 29, 2016.

18 'Check Out These Free(!) Fitness Classes at Nike, Lululemon, and More',
    Alison Mango, www.news.health.com, March 2, 2016.

19 'Winning the Shopping Micro-Moments', www.adwords.blogspot.in,
    Google official blog, July 15, 2015.

20 'Google Is Making Shopping on a Smartphone Much Easier',
    Victor Luckerson, *TIME*, www.time.com, July 15, 2015.

21 'Google to Add "Buy Button" to Its Mobile Search Ads', Phil Wahba,
    Fortune, July 15, 2015.

22 'Facebook enhances its online shopping feature', Elias Jahshan,
    www.retailgazette.co.uk, March 24, 2017.

23 'With Buyable Pins, Pinterest Lets You Buy Stuff Right in the App',
    JP Mangalindan, www.mashable.com, June 2, 2015.

24 'Shoppers Flock to Apps, Shaking Up Retail'. Gerg Bensinger, *The Wall
    Street Journal*, www.wsj.com, April 13, 2016.

25 This division is based on the five elementary needs as defined in the
    Customer Relevance Model in: F. Crawford and R. Mathews, *The Myth
    of Excellence*, Three Rivers Press, 2003. I amended this model by using,
    amongst others, the work of Gino van Ossel, *Omnichannel in retail*,
    Uitgeverij Lannoo, 2014, page 53.

26 'Would "the Internet of Smell" Revolutionize Online Food Shopping?',
    www.quora.com, June 9, 2015.

27 'Introducing Google Nose', www.googlenosebeta.com, April 1, 2013.

28 'How To Digest the Omnichannel Elephant', Final Report Expert Group
    Selection, Shopping2020, January 2014.

29 'Amazon Dash Is Here: Push Button, Get Stuff', Samantha Murphy Kelly,
    www.mashable.com, July 30, 2015.

30 'Amazon just launched virtual 'Dash' buttons for one-click buying from the
    homepage'. Jason del Rey. www.recode.net, January 20, 2017.

31 'Amazon Opens Dash Buttons to Developers with Its AWS IoT', Lulu Chang,
    www.yahoo.com, May 14, 2016.

32 'Let's Call The Amazon Echo What It Is', Greg Kumparak,
    www.techcrunch.com, November 6, 2014.

33 'The killer app of the decade: WeChat in China (4)', Wijnand Jongen,
    blog on www.wijnandjongen.com, September 4, 2015.

34 'Target Innovates In-Store Beacon Marketing with Newsfeed-Like Content Stream', Chantal Tode, www.mobilecommercedaily.com, August 7, 2015.

9 How to pay: no-click buying in the blockchain

1 *Blockchain Revolution. How the Technology Behind Bitcoin Is Changing Money, Business and the World*, Don and Alex Tapscott, Penguin, 2016.
2 'How close are we to a cashless society?', Alara Basul, www.bobsguide.com, April 7, 2017.
3 Forrester: Mobile Payments Forecast, 2016 To 2021 (EU-7), www.forrester.com, February 10, 2017.
4 'China Tops in Digital Payment Adoption Worldwide', Meng Jing, *China Daily*, www.english.gov.cn, March 3, 2016.
5 'Global Digital Payments to Reach $3,6 Trillion This Year, Juniper Research Find', www.juniperresearch.com, March 21, 2016.
6 *Powershift*, Alvin Toffler, Bantam Books, 1990.
7 'The Smartphone Becomes The Mobile Wallet', www.nielsen.com, February 23, 2016.
8 'Global Digital Payments to Reach $3,6 Trillion This Year, Juniper Research Find', www.Juneperresearch.com, March 21, 2016.
9 Mark Schenkel, *Het Financieele Dagblad*, April 11, 2015.
10 'Tencent opens first cashierless pop-up store', He Wei, China Daily, Februari 2-8, 2018.
11 'Shanghai Commuters Hail Virtual Supermarket', Malcolm Moore, *The Telegraph*, August 5, 2011.
12 'The curious comeback of the dreaded QR-code', David Pierce, www.wired.com, July 17, 2017
13 'Alibaba to Expand in Hong Kong with Smart Cards', Juro Osawa and Michelle Yuan, February 19, 2014, Digits Tech News & Analysis, *The Wall Street Journal*.
14 'Swedish commuters can use futuristic hand implant microchip as train tickets', Helen Coffey. www.independent.co.uk, June 16, 2017.
15 'The new way to pay: Contactless fingernails', www.finextra.com, July 15, 2016.
16 'The rise of the cashless city: 'There is this real danger of exclusion', Adam Forrest, The Guardian, January 9, 2017.
17 'Ally Financial target shopaholics with 'Splurge Alert', www.finextra.com, April 21, 2016.
18 'WeChat users in China can now gift friends a Starbucks coffee via chat', Jon Russell. www.techcrunch.com, February 10, 2017.
19 In the first position paper on Online Payments, dated March 2002, the Dutch e-commerce organization asked Dutch banks to come up with a single interoperable system for online payments, based on online banking.
20 The latest figures on iDeal: www.currence.nl/producten/ideal/kerncijfers-ideal.

21 'MyBank Pilots Digital Identity Solution', www.pymnts.com, June 6, 2016.

22 'The Big Banks Are Becoming "Dumb Pipes" As Fintech Take Over', www.cbinsights.com, June 9, 2016.

23 *Identity is the New Money*, David Birch, London Publishing Partnership, 2014.

24 'Google waves good-bye to Hands Free payment app.' Dan Graziano. www.cnet.com, February 2, 2017.

25 *Identity is the New Money*, David Birch, London Publishing Partnership, 2014.

26 'The Future of Financial Infrastructure: An Ambitious Look at How Blockchain Can Reshape Financial Services', World Economic Forum, www.weforum.org, August 12, 2016.

27 Rutger Betlem, *Het Financieele Dagblad*, October 11, 2016.

28 'Utility Settlement Coin Aims to Set Industry Standard for Central Banking Digital Cas', Giulio Prisco, www.nasday.com, August 25, 2016.

29 https://99bitcoins.com/who-accepts-bitcoins-payment-companiesstores-take-bitcoins/.

10 Delivery: the last mile's dilemma

1 Margreeth Pape and Ken Zschocke, Thuiswinkel.org, August 2016.

2 Report Expert group Delivery, Shopping2020, January 2014.

3 'Starship Will Test Its Autonomous Delivery Robot in Washington D.C. This Fall', Sean O'Kane, June 28, 2016.

4 'Domino's Will Begin Using Robot's To Deliver Pizza's In Europe', Jeremy Kahn, www.bloomberg.com, March 29, 2017.

5 'Norway's revolutionary initiative for grocery deliveries — Self-driving grocery vehicles', Shilpa Shatterjee. www.newlaunches.com, January 4, 2017.

6 'Amazon to Launch Delivery Service That Would Vie With FedEx, UPS', www.wsj.com, February 9, 2018.

7 'Alibaba's Cainiao Aims for Logistics Efficiency', Meng Jing, Chinadaily.com, June 14, 2016.

8 *Innovation in onlife retail delivery*, Magreeth Pape, study Thuiswinkel.org, August 2016.

9 'Disruption: Is Amazon a Retailer or a Logistics Company?', Carlos Cordon, Pablo Caballero and Teresa Ferreiro, www.imd.org, 2016.

10 'Why Is Google Focusing on Google Express', Trefis Team, www.forbes.com, February 24, 2016.

11 'Google Express expands, now reaches 90 percent of U.S.' Sarah Perez, www.techcruch.com, October 25, 2016.

12 'Your New Life as an UberRUSH Courier', Dan Roe, www.bicycling.com, July 15, 2016.

13 'Uber's Latest Experiment Is Uber Cargo, A Logistics Service in Hong Kong', Jon Russell, www.techcrunch.com, January 8, 2015.

14   *Results Survey Barriers to Growth*, research by Ecommerce Europe,
     www.ecommerce-europe.eu, 2015.
15   www.deliverineurope.eu, launched in September 2016.
16   'The Business Case for the Harmonised Parcel Label', Ecommerce Europe,
     GS1, Thuiswinkel.org, Shopping Tomorrow, www.ecommerce-europe.eu,
     June 2017.
17   'Primary Reason for Digital Shoppers to Abandon Their Carts in the United
     States', www.statista.com, February 2015.
18   Managing purchases and returns for retailers. Thesis by Alec Minnema.
     University of Groningen, January 26, 2017.
19   *Logistics Trend Radar*, DHL Customer Solutions & Innovation, version 2016.
20   *Pulse of the Omni-Channel Retailer. How Retailers Are Adapting to the
     Changing Needs of the Flex Shopper*, UPS, version 2016.
21   'How Big Data and the Internet of Things Will Change the Postal Service',
     Federico Guerrini, www.forbes.com, July 3, 2014.
22   *Internet of Things in Logistics. A Collaborative Report by DHL and Cisco on
     Implications and Use Cases for the Logistics Industry*, DHL Trend Research
     | Cisco Consulting Services, 2015.
23   'First Time in Germany: Car Becomes Mobile Delivery Address for parcels',
     www.dpdhl.com, April 22, 2015.
24   'Ford concept uses drones and self-driving van for deliveries', Stefanie
     Fogel. www.engadget.com, February 28, 2017.
25   'Delivery Service Brings Groceries to Your Fridge When You're Away',
     Matthias Verbergt, www.wsj.com, May 30, 2016.
26   'Perfecting Last Mile Delivery Process in Ecommerce Logistics', Kapil
     Khanna, www.netsolutionsindia.com, November 10, 2015.
27   'How Amazon Is Making Package Delivery Even Cheaper', Reuters,
     www.fortune.com, February 18, 2016.
28   'JD's New On-Demand Delivery Service Opens Up to Anyone with a Bike',
     Josh Horwitz, www.techinasia.com, May 14, 2015.
29   'Big Data in Logistics. A DHL Perspective on How to Move
     Beyond the Hype', DHL Customer Solutions & Innovations,
     www.delivering-tomorrow.com, December 2013.
30   'Will Shipping by Drones Change Ecommerce Industry?', Soumen
     Purkayastha, www.appseconnect.com, 2015.
31   'Domino's delivers world's first ever pizza by drone'. David Reid.
     www.cnbc.com, November 16, 2016.
32   'Amazon makes its first drone delivery in the U.K.'. Matt McFarland.
     www.money.cnn.com, December 14, 2016.
33   'Amazon patents show flying warehouse that sends delivery drones to your
     door', Lora Kolodny, www.techcrunch.com, December 28, 2016.
34   'Reinventing Retail: What Businesses Need to Know for 2015', Walker
     Sands Communications, www.walkersands.com.
35   'Disconnect: Drone Delivery Is Not the Future of Ecommerce', C. Custer,
     www.techinasia.com, November 12, 2015.

36 'Amazon Patent Filing Provides a Peek at Shrouded Delivery Drone Designs', Alan Boyle, www.geekwire.com, August 16, 2016.

37 'The Drone Delivery Race Begins — Google, Amazon, BestBuy and Wal-Mart All Want to Deliver to Your Doorstep via Drone', Charity Johnson. November 5, 2015.

38 www.twinklemagazine.nl, May 24, 2016.

39 Wouter Keuning. *Het Financieele Dagblad*, April 29, 2014.

40 This table is based on the so-called DESTEP model. It links the trends and developments from six viewpoints of society (demographic, economic, socio-cultural, technical, ecological and political).

41 'The Future of Retail Is Fast, Free Delivery', Kathleen Kusek, www.forbes.com, May 14, 2016.

11 Customer care: customer service becomes customer intimacy

1 'A Zappos Employee Had the Company's Longest Customer-Service Call at 10 Hours, 43 Minutes', Richard Feloni, www.uk.businessinsider.com, July 26, 2016.

2 'Zappos' Multimillionaire CEO Explains Why He Lives in a Trailer Park with His Two Pet Llamas', Richard Feloni, www.uk.businessinsider.com, January 31, 2016.

3 'Why Amazon's Anticipatory Shipping Is Pure Genius'. Praveen Kopalle, professor of marketing at Tuck School of Business at Darmouth College, www.forbes.com, January 28, 2014.

4 'Amazon and Anticipatory Shippling: A Dubious Patent? Steve Banker, www.forbes.com, January 24, 2014.

5 *Boo Hoo. $135 million, 18 Months. A Dot.com Story from Concept to Catastrophe*, Ernst Malmsten, Erik Portanger and Charles Drazin, Arrow Books, 2001.

6 As said by Scott Cairns, CTO t-Systems in 'Retail Sets Example for Others', Hugh Wilson, www.raconteur.net, October 21, 2014.

7 'Mobile Messaging and Bots: The Next Frontier of Customer Service', Judith Aquino, www.1to1media.com, July 25, 2016.

8 'The Age of Algorithms', Ilse ZeeMayjer, *Het Financieele Dagblad*, April 25, 2015.

9 'Facebook Launches M, Its Bold Answer to Siri and Cortana', Jessi Hempel, www.wired.com, August 26, 2015.

10 'Get a Peek at Someone Using Facebook's New Assistant, "M"', Cade Metz, www.wired.com, September 6, 2015.

11 'Amazon unveils Echo Look, a selfie camera to help you choose what to wear', Samual Gibbs, www.theguardian.com, April 26, 2017.

12 'Amazon Want the Echo To Be Your Personal Robot Butler', Hayley Tsukayama, *The Washington Post*, June 25, 2015.

13 'How Closely Is Amazon's Echo Listening?', Hayley Tsukayama, *The Washington Post*, November 11, 2014.

14 'Goodbye Privacy, Hello "Alexa": Amazon Echo, the Home Robot Who Hears It All', Rory Carroll, www.theguardian.com, November 21, 2015.
15 'Understanding Financial Consumers in the Digital Era', www.cgi.com, 2015.
16 http://www.web.lark.com.
17 Ilse Zeemeijer, *Het Financieele Dagblad*, April 25, 2015.
18 *Who Cares. Moving Towards a Total Customer Care Experience in 2020*, Shopping2020, Capgemini, January 2014.
19 'Build platforms, not walls. The new platform economy', Wijnand Jongen, blog on www.wijnandjongen.com, April 21, 2017.

12 New business models

1 *Businessmodels of the future*, Shopping2020, www.shoppingtomorrow.nl, January 2014.
2 *Platform Strategy. How to Unlock the Power of Communites and Networks to Grow Your Business*, Laure Claire Reillier and Benoit Reillier, Routledge, 2017.
3 'Ranking 335 marketplaces throughout Europe', www.bvoh.de, February 27, 2016.
4 'How Alibaba Makes Money? 2016 Update', Jitender Miglani, www.revenuesandprofit.com, July 6, 2016.
5 'The Marketplace Race', Thad Rueter, Internet Retailer, www.internetretailer.com, January 2014.
6 See, for example, blog post of Marcel Weiss, www.earlymoves.com, November 19, 2015.
7 'From Transactions to Relationship', IBM Global Business Services, January 2013.
8 'The Future of Shopping in Three Trends', J.J. Colao, *Forbes*, August 4, 2014.
9 *Travel Tomorrow. The Future Customer Journey of Travel*. ANVR, Travel Tomorrow, Cap Gemini, 2015.
10 'Role of Social Media in Online Travel Information', Xiang & Gretzel, *Tourism Management*, 31, 2010, 179-188.
11 'Competing With Your Manufacturers?', Kevin Eichelberger, Blue Acorn, 2008.
12 *Het nieuwe winkelen*, Cor Molenaar, Pearson Education, 2009.
13 'Antitrust: Commission Publishes Initial Findings of E-Commerce Sector Inquiry', press release European Commission, September 15, 2015.
14 'Karl Lagerfeld Lobbies EU on Internet Sales', www.euobserver.com, February 11, 2009.
15 The European Union outlawed price fixing in the 1957 Treaty of Rome.
16 'Manufacturers Find Reasons to Sell Online, Survey Says', Armando Roggio, Practical Ecommerce, June 10, 2014.

17 '2013 Financial Performance Report, Growth Strategies: Unlocking the Power of the Consumer', Grocery Manufacturers Association and PwC US, 2013.

18 'P&G Goes Online to Compete for Sales'. Jonathan Birchall, *Financial Times*, May 19, 2010.

19 'Unilever Looks to Marry In-Store Sampling With E-Commerce', *Adweek*, February 5, 2014.

20 Jeroen Bos and Richard Smit, *Het Financieele Dagblad*, May 1, 2017.

21 Marijke van Moll, Jungle Minds, April 2013.

22 'Strategizing Direct-To-Consumer E-Commerce: When Should Manufacturers Dive In?', Benny Blum, *Marketing Land*, January 17, 2014.

23 'Why Manufacturers Can No Longer Afford to Wait to Sell Direct to Customer', Alex Becker, *Multichannel Merchant*, August 5, 2014.

24 *Het einde van het midden*, Farid Tabarki, Uitgeverij Atlas Contact, 2016.

25 'Looking Forward. What's in store for 2018', Susan Reda, Stores, December 2017.

26 *The Innovator's Dilemma*, Clayton Christensen, Harvard Business School Publishing, May 1997.

27 *Reengineering Retail. The Future of Selling in a Post-Digital World*, Doug Stephens, Figure1 Publishing Inc., 2017.

28 'Disrupt or Destroy Your Own Business to Make It Stronger', Rajesh Srivastava, www.foundingfuel.com, June 1, 2015.

29 'The Future of Retail Is Extreme', Tom Goodwin. www.linkedin.com/pulse/future-retail-extreme-tom-goodwin. February 18, 2017.

13 Work and study in onlife retail

1 'King Ludd is Still Dead', Kenneth Rogoff, www.isole24ore.com, 2012.

2 *The Future of Skills: Employment in 2030*, www.nesta.org.uk, September 9, 2017.

3 'Harnessing automation for a future that works', James Manyika, Michael Chui, Mehdi Miremadi, Jacques Bughin, Katy George, Paul Willmot, and Martin Dewhurst, McKinsey & Company, January 2017.

4 'Robots Will Take Jobs, but Not as Fast as Some Fear, New Report Says', Steve Lohr, www.nytimes.com, January 12, 2017.

5 *The Future of Jobs. Employment, Skills and Workforce Strategy for the Fourth Industrial Revolution*, World Economic Forum, January 2016.

6 *Rise of the Robots: Technology and the Threat of a Jobless Future*, Martin Ford, Basic Books, May 8, 2015.

7 'Where Machines Could Replace Humans — and Where They Can't (Yet)', Michael Chui, James Manyika, and Mehdi Miremadi, McKinsey Quarterly, July 2016.

8 'Robots Are Coming for Your Job: And Faster Than You Think', Szu Ping Cahn, www.telegraph.co.uk, January 21, 2016.

9   '900,000 UK Retail Jobs Could Be Lost by 2025, Warns BRC', Kamal
     Ahmed, www.bbc.com, February 29, 2016.
10   'The robot that takes your job should pay taxes, says Bill Gates'. Kevin J.
     Delaney. Quartz Media, February 17, 2017.
11   Henny van der Pluijm, BoardroomIT, Spring 2017.
12   *The Future of Jobs. Employment, Skills and Workforce Strategy for the
     Fourth Industrial Revolution*, World Economic Forum, January 2016.
13   'Digital economy invents new job fields', Ma Si. China Daily, European
     Weekly, January 20-26, 2017.
14   *Thinking Fast and Slow,* Daniel Kahneman, Penguin Books, 2012.
15   *De Talentafdeling*, Kees Gabriëls, Van Duuren Media B.V., 2016.
16   *Reinventing Organizations. A Guide to Creating Organizations Inspired by
     the Next Stage of Human Consciousness*, Frederique Laloux, Nelson Parker,
     2014.
17   *Freedom, Inc. How Corporate Liberation Unleashes Employee Potential
     and Business Performance*, Brian M. Carney and Isaac Getz, Somme Valley
     House, 2016.
18   'Driving Ecommerce Innovation @WalmartLabs', Jason Bloomberg. Forbes,
     August 5, 2015.
19   Interview Steve Muylle, Professor at Vlerick Business School in Belgium.
     Franka Rolvink Couzy, *Het Financieele Dagblad,* November 12, 2016.
20   Monster Year Report 2015-2016, Monsterboard.
21   'What Millennials Want in the Workplace (And Why You Should Start Giving
     It to Them)', Rob Asghar, www.forbes.com, January 13, 2014.
22   'The Will to Change the World', Krishna Kumar VR, *China Daily, European
     Weekly*, June 12-18, 2015.
23   'Holacracy and Self-Organization', Zapposinsights.com.
24   'California Dreaming. What Makes Silicon Valley's Iconic IT Companies
     Tick?', Jeanne Harris and Russell Hancock, Accenture, 2016.
25   'Alibaba Launches Recruitment Program for International Talent', Tom
     Brennan, www.alizila.com, May 20, 2016.
26   'How Walmart Is Fighting Retail Rivals in the "War of Talent"', Brian Sozzi,
     www.thestreet.com, June 2, 2016.
27   https://www.ted.com/talks/ken_robinson_changing_education_paradigms
28   *The Race Between Education and Technology*, Claudia Goldin and
     Lawrence F. Katz, Harvard University Press, March 2010.
29   '70-20-10: Origin, Research, Purpose', Charles Jennings,
     www.charlesjennings.blogspot.nl, August 13, 2016.
30   'The Learning Economy', Bengt-Åke Lundvall and Björn Johnson, *Journal of
     Industry Studies*, 1994.

14   The rise of the network society

1   *The Onlife Manifesto. Being Human in a Hyperconnected World*, Luciano
     Floridi, Springer, 2015.

2   'Billions of People in Developing World Still Without Internet Access, New UN Report Finds', www.un.org, September 21, 2015.

3   Ulko Jonker, *Het Financieele Dagblad*, April 16, 2016.

4   *The Net Delusion: The Dark Side of Internet Freedom*, Evgeny Morozov, Public Affairs, 2012.

5   'Imperial Ambitions', www.economist.com, April 9, 2016.

6   'Even Mark Zuckerberg can't stop the meme that he is running for president', Abby Ohlheiser, *The Washington Post*, August 3, 2017.

7   'Google kills another mysterious "moonshot"', Maya Kosoff, www.vanityfair.com, January 12, 2017.

8   Alibaba invested $2.6 billon in Intime, bought remaining shares of Ele.me in 2018, invested $4.6 billion in Sunning and owns 48 percent of Cainiao shares.

9   *Verandering van tijdperk. Nederland kantelt*, Jan Rotmans, Aeneas, 2014.

10   *Modernism: The Lure of Heresy*, P. Gay, W.W. Norton & Company, 2007.

11   Yvonne Zonderop, *De Groene Amsterdammer*, May 8, 2014.

12   The *Loi de Cadenas* or *Padlock Law*, 1936.

13   *Fair-Trade Law*, brittanica.com.

14   'American Account: Fear of Change Puts Europe at Odds with US Tech', Irwin Stelzer, www.thesundaytimes.co.uk, December 7, 2014.

15   https://ec.europa.eu/priorities/digital-single-market_en.

16   *Position Paper Ecommerce Europe*, www.ecommerce-europe.eu.

17   'Europe's Startup Economy Is in the Best Shape It's Ever Been and Still Needs Work', Bruce Upbin, www.forbes.com, November 10, 2015.

18   'Jack Ma: Free Trade is a Human Right, Small Firms Need More Help', Eileen Yu, www.zdnet.com, November 18, 2015.

19   *The Digital Economy. Rethinking Promise and Peril in the Age of Networked Intelligence*, Don Tapscott, McGraw Hill Education, 2015.

20   'The End of Capitalism Has Begun', Paul Mason, *The Guardian*, July 17, 2015.

21   'One Internet', Global Commission on Internet Governance, The Centre for International Governance Innovation and The Royal Institute for International Affairs, www.internetsociety.org, June 2016.

22   Huib Modderkolk, *de Volkskrant*, June 22, 2016.

23   Franka Rolvink Couzy, *Het Financieele Dagblad*, February 13, 2016.

24   Interview journalist Ryan Avent, *NRC Handelsblad,* July 4, 2017.

25   *The Internet Is Not the Answer*, Andrew Keen, Atlantic Monhtly Press, 2015.

26   *How to Fix the Future*, Andrew Keen, Atlantic Monthly Press, 2018.

27   'Gerben van der Marel, *Het Financieele Dagblad*, February 20, 2016.

28   Hans Schnitzler, *De Groene Amsterdammer*, March 5, 2015.

29   Rob de Lange, *Het Financieele Dagblad*, April 30, 2016.

30   *Social Change with Respect to Culture and Original Nature*, W.F. Ogburn, B.W. Huebsch, 1922.

Index